M000266262

Jack Ma

Founder and CEO of the Alibaba Group

Chen Wei

Homa & Sekey Books
Paramus, New Jersey

FIRST AMERICAN EDITION

First published in China by Zhejiang People's Publishing House in 2013.
English Translation Copyright © 2014 by Homa & Sekey Books.
Published by arrangement with Zhejiang People's Publishing House.

Library of Congress Cataloging-in-Publication Data

Chen, Wei, 1966 —
　[Zhe hai shi Ma Yun. English]
　Jack Ma : founder and CEO of the Alibaba Group / Chen Wei. —First American edition.
　pages cm
　"Second edition" — Foreword.
　ISBN 978-1-931907-20-0 (hardcover)
　1. Ma, Yun, 1964- 2. Alibaba (Firm) 3. Businesspeople — China — Biography. 4. Electronic commerce — China. 5. Industrial marketing — China. 6. Internet industry — China. I. Title.
　HC426.5.M327W4513 2014
　381'.142092 — dc23
　[B]
　　　　　　　　　　　　2014026805

Homa & Sekey Books
3rd Floor, North Tower
Mack-Cali Center III
140 E. Ridgewood Avenue
Paramus, NJ 07652

Editor: Shawn Ye

Tel: 201-261-8810; 800-870-HOMA
Fax: 201-261-8890
Email: info@homabooks.com
Website: www.homabooks.com

Printed in China
1 3 5 7 9 10 8 6 4 2

Recommendation by Jack Ma

My wife and I were about to go to Maldives on a holiday with some friends. Before our departure, my assistant Chen Wei said he would send me some articles to read at my spare time.

I thought they were some jokes collected as he usually did in the past until after I checked my emails in Maldives.

I was surprised to see that he could remember so clearly about the events and details that had taken place long ago, part of which had nearly escaped from my memories. Now they are put together and are being "replayed" right before my very eyes, making me think about many of the good old days.

Every time I go to the airport I feel a bit uneasy, because from time to time there will be a book that pops-up about me. In truth, none of the books were written by me. At times someone will buy a book at the airport and ask me to sign my name. I feel very awkward because most often it is the first time I have seen the book, just like him or her, and I have no idea what the book is about either.

What Chen Wei sent to me were stories about some of the interesting things that happened in our relationship and life in the past. The most important thing is his relaxed, humorous, and entertaining writing style that keeps you reading on.

CONTENTS

1. Jack Ma and the Ken couple.

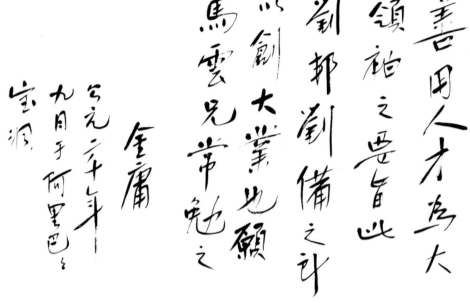

2. Louis Cha's inscription.

3. Group photo of Louis Cha, Jack Ma and Zhang Jizhong in Hangzhou Meijiawu in September 2001.

4. In 2008, Jack Ma making speech at the Y. Elites Group in Hong Kong.

5. Jack Ma and Soros at Lecture Hall of Jiangnan Club.

6. Jack Ma's brushwork in the time of "Jinyu" in Mt. Jinyun in 2008.

7. Jack Ma at the place where Chen Wangting created Taijiquan.

8. Spreading Taiji to India.

9. Attack from a swarm of bees.

10. Jack Ma's punk style at the 10th anniversary celebration of Alibaba.

11. Jack Ma playing the piano.

12. "Handsome (shuai)!" in unison.

13. The day of the end of the world.

14. Poster of Jack Ma at Los Angeles D9 Conference.

15. Group photo at the Hulun Buir Prairie.

16. Front gate of Alibaba's Binjiang new building.

Foreword to the Second Edition

"The first book that I've ever read through from beginning to end is the one I wrote." - It is the truth I kept telling over and over again when the book *Jack Ma: Founder and CEO of the Alibaba Group* was published two years ago. What I was trying to say is that writing a book is not as challenging as we always imagined. But nonetheless, it sounds more like self-bragging.

Others bragged to fake the truth, whereas in my case, I often accidentally made the truth sound fake.

The book was a hit after releasing and the feedback was fairly positive. "Chen Wei, the writing is very entertaining and humorous, but you've missed a few interesting stories of Mr. Ma..." a classmate from the English club so said. "I burst into laughter while reading your embarrassing account in the subway and was despised by people around me..." said another friend. "From you, we get to know that Jack Ma had a happy time when starting his business..." a respected and prestigious entrepreneur told me. "Buddy, it was well written! I finished reading it overnight..." many more friends so claimed. I was really obliged then and thought all those who'd read my book were my loved ones, even though I knew they read it only for the sake of Jack Ma.

Two months after its publication, in the early July 2011, an interactive readers-author book-selling activity was held on Taobao.com. Originally, the activity was scheduled for three days, but in just six hours 8,000 copies were sold, and that was under the condition that each IP address could buy only one copy. The activity was forced to an abrupt halt because of the commitment promising to sell only signed copies. Subsequently, I stayed in the stack room and signed copies of the book for four days.

Thereafter, I was asked by publishing houses to continue the writing. A government leader even created the title of the book, called *More of Jack Ma: Founder and CEO of the Alibaba Group*. But because there wasn't much time for self-reflection, I didn't take the liberty to write.

Days ago I was informed by the publishing house that copies of my book in their warehouse were sold out again. But this time, they hoped it would not be a simple reprint. Instead, they requested an updated version with some supplements. Thus I attempted to put together some of Jack Ma's experiences during the past two years. Chapters 9, 10, 11, and Appendix IV are the newly added contents.

People working in Alibaba all have dreams, but I only have guesses. At the end of every year, I start to guess whether Jack Ma will give me a raise? Will he promote me? Fortunately, I don't expect much from what I've guessed. Therefore, Jack Ma also believes that I am the only one in the company that isn't motivated by his passion.

The key element for bragging is to have good listeners. No matter how profound the thoughts that human beings assume, God will shake his head and smile after hearing them. So bragging isn't about the so-called high or low fashion, as long as it makes you happy. Some people in the company address me as "Chen Ba (Daddy Chen)," have lunch with me, and listen to my bragging. Their highest dream in life is to "publish a book" and the lowest wish is "to appear in a book." In fact, helping them achieve their lowest wish in batches is the real purpose for me to write a book. Helping others without principles is the only principle I adhere to.

Foreword

Look up at the world and you will find there is immense difference between man and man. Look down at the world, and look ahead; you and I are the same brilliant progression of one hundred million years of evolution; look back, you and I are at most a link inevitable in the continuous evolution of living things - nothing more.

Personally, I think the meaning of life is to "brag." The process of a man from being in obscurity to fame is a constant process of "bragging" to different people.

Learn and think to change the content of "bragging." Strive to change the objects of "bragging."

Brag to the employees when you are an employee. Brag to the managers when you are a manager. Brag to the leaders when you are a leader. That's how to make life different.

Sir Francis Bacon once said, "Knowledge is power." Everyone on the earth knows that. But most don't know the latter half. "Much of the knowledge is for ornamentation." That is, for "bragging."

It's easy to understand if you put a thought into it. Do you use Pythagorean Theorem to build a doghouse? Do you calculate the shape of the parabola when you throw a stone? Do you check the molar weight when you add salt in cooking? The answers are all negative. Even the tens of thousands of scientists who have launched satellites used very little part of their professional knowledge.

There are only two kinds of people who are happy in the world: one is those who like to brag and the other is those who like listening to "braggers."

The man who doesn't brag is a miserable man, even if he has a high achievement, such as Michelangelo; the one who can brag, but does not love to brag is miserable too, such as Arthur Schopenhauer. The one who loves and is capable of bragging and loves to listen to others' bragging is the happiest man, such as Jack Ma.

Jack Ma once passed by a work shed and heard the carefree laughter from within. "Listen! How happy the migrant workers are at bragging!" Jack Ma said, full of admiration.

"Maybe what they are bragging about is, if I were Jack Ma, every day I would..." I said.

Milan Kundera said, "Life is elsewhere."

"As a CEO, my job is only to talk, to 'brag.' You'll have to put up with such a CEO. Every time, you think the 'brag' sounds like 'impossible.' But you - Alier have accomplished the 'impossible' impossibly well every time. We always fit in well..." Jack Ma once said at a Taobao annual meeting.

About 2100 years ago, Emperor Wu of Han Dynasty Liu Che said to Sima Qian after reading *The Historical Records*, "Is this official history? You think you really understand me? Those happened and pending to happen..."

I think that the essence of history is a melody of thought. All recorded data is like scattered black and white piano keys. Everyone can only guess the melody according to these keys.

Every year people from famous universities around the world come to the Alibaba Group to do research and write cases. They showed them to Jack Ma and asked him to sign it after they were finished. "Is this about Alibaba? This is not Alibaba!" Jack Ma would question each time.

"You don't understand! This is the Alibaba!" The scholars would say.

"Well then, take it as Alibaba!" I don't know whether Jack Ma wanted to reflect on himself, or he just didn't want to argue with the scholars.

"We didn't work with eBay in the past," Jack Ma said once, "there were a lot of guessing from outsiders. In fact only I myself knew the reason. I just didn't feel comfortable seeing so-and-so on the eBay team. But I admired the female CEO very much." But why Jack Ma would feel uncomfortable somehow or the other, even he himself couldn't give a reasonable explanation!

Just like what Schopenhauer once said, "Man can do what he wills but he cannot will what he wills."

There is a kind of bacteria that wants to fly, but it has no wings, so it invades into frog's eggs. Due to the invasion of the bacteria, the hatched tadpoles and frogs are all disabled and easily eaten by eagles. Thus the bacteria enjoys flying as it wished!

I am not the eagle. I am the flying bacteria.

Being an assistant is a kind of special profession. Different assistants also have a world of difference.

Some of the assistants of the leadership of the state ministries and commissions are cadres at the ministry level, and some assistants of the entertainment stars are life babysitters.

The assistants of entrepreneurs can be secretaries, consultants, or bodyguards...

But I am none. I've known Mr. Zhang Jizhong and Jack Ma for over 10 years, and have been the assistant for the two one after another. Whenever I was asked about my main work, I couldn't come up with an answer, be it either for Mr. Zhang Jizhong or for Jack Ma. To people who are familiar with me, I would say, jokingly: "I am an 'imperial shadow'."

I'll never say that I know them. I've just recorded some of the ordinary things about the extraordinary people. I don't know whether these black and white keys can bring you closer to the melody itself.

In addition, there is a small part of "gossips," which appears to be somewhat irrelevant to Jack Ma, but my life's track is changed to make me who I am today due to Jack Ma's "tampering." So in a way, it has something to do with him. Forgive me if you find that I am "carried away" occasionally with myself.

Chapter 1:
Jack Ma and His English Class

I met Jack Ma in early 1992. Roughly speaking, we've been associated for nearly 20 years. Initially, I was just a student of Jack Ma's English evening school. Years later, we grew familiar with each other and became friends. As for the English I've learned, most of it was "returned' to Jack Ma.

Life in the English evening school brings warmth and joy to me whenever I recall it. Many of the people and events of those days have become the best memories of my life. Some of the classmates became life-long friends till today. What was beyond my expectation was how later my life gradually took on a different track due to the minor decision in that year before I even knew it. At the evening school, I became a good friend with my teacher Jack Ma and his wife Zhang Ying. Later I got to know Fan Xinman, the producer and director of China Central Television (CCTV), who came to do an interview at the evening school, along with her husband Zhang Jizhong. Afterwards, as if by luck, I became Zhang Jizhong and Jack Ma's assistant successively! In retrospect, I could not help but marvel at the miracles in life, in which any incidental move now may become an opportunity that can lead to a positive turn in your life.

English Teacher, Being Late Himself

In the spring of 1992, three years after my college graduation, I lived in a dormitory with nothing in particular to do at night. I heard that there was an evening English class in the Young Men's Christian Association (YMCA) in Jiefang Road offering one class or two a week. Anyway, I was pretty much idling my time back then, so I signed up. I was worried that there might be an interview or something, so I rummaged college English books and reviewed for the whole day. When I got there, there was no examination of sort and just a notice that I could come to classes.

On my first day of school, I came to the classroom early to meet new classmates. Some of them were high school students who wanted to study abroad. Others were college students or factory workers... But most of them were college graduates who just entered services like me.

At the ringing of the bell, all students sat down and got ready for class. But the podium remained empty. The teacher was not yet here. After a few minutes, the classroom became restless. More and more students began to look around. Some even suggested going and asking whether the class was to be held in a different classroom.

Just then, a thin and small man dashed to the podium. "Today's topic is about 'unpunctuality.' I hate unpunctuality most. Because unpunctuality shows disrespect for others, in a sense, unpunctuality is murdering someone for his money..." said he before gaining his foothold. All the students responded with an understanding laughter. The teacher expressed his apologies in a witty self-deprecation way and that teacher was Jack Ma.

Jack Ma was then the English teacher of Hangzhou Institute of Electrical Engineering (now known as Hangzhou Dianzi University). He and his wife Zhang Ying were classmates in the English Department of Hangzhou Normal College (now known as Hangzhou Normal University) and upon graduation both were assigned to the same English Teaching and Researching Office of Hangzhou Institute of Electrical Engineering. Hangzhou Institute of Electrical Engineering ranked far behind other universities and colleges in Hangzhou. Nevertheless, the Ma couple was among the "Top Ten English Teachers" of universities and colleges in Hangzhou.

When it came to the subject of the lesson after the opening remarks, we realized this teacher's English class was nothing we'd imagined. In our past English classes, most teachers would follow the textbooks and do the routine work, teaching us to memorize the words, analyze the text, explain the grammar and so on. Most of the students would get muddleheaded and feel dizzy by the end of the class, as if they had been out to the sea. But Jack Ma had his own way. He didn't stick to the textbook, and much less about the grammar or expressions. He would rather concentrate on the oral communications with the class, and he brought current affair concerns for class discussion, sauced it with humorous language, and exaggerated body gestures, which greatly enhanced the learning enthusiasm of us "Dumb Rookies." Thus we often picked up some spoken language unconsciously amidst the laughter.

In each class, Jack Ma would present a question. The class would take a stand first and leave the "illogical" view to him and continue a debate in between. Some of my classmates were in the medical field and thus once the topic was "commission" on medical kickbacks. We chose the "con" side and in turn Jack Ma alone was left with "pro" side. Unexpectedly, we were utterly beaten in the arguments.

At the end of the debate, Jack Ma commented that in fact he himself was against medical commission too. "If you had brought this and that argument, it would have been tougher for me⋯" he told us.

Some of the students were fairly eloquent, but as far as I can remember, we had never defeated Jack Ma even once. Because Jack Ma's spoken English was far better than ours, and he had a very special perspective as well, the so-called "seeing the world with a different eye."

Ma's Passing Card

In 1995, the F1 Powerboat World Championship was held at the West Lake in Hangzhou. More than 200 Hangzhou beauties signed up for Miss etiquette. Jack Ma had gained some fame for his spoken English in Hangzhou then and was asked by the sponsor to train the group of beauties' oral English and then at the end screen out 50 from the group. During that time, Jack Ma was teaching at his institute and at the evening school as well as training the ladies at the same time. He was always on the run; coming and going like a whirlwind. But not a word of complaint came from his mouth. Instead, he often showed off in high spirit about the "Beauty Class." "⋯ Can you imagine, more than 200 pairs of most beautiful eyes in Hangzhou winked at me all the time, I am even a bit nervous at class..."

"Dear Mr. Ma, if you feel tired, we are very willing to partake in your work⋯" the male students cried out, admiringly.

"Cut it out. I will carry on no matter how tired I am!" Jack Ma replied squarely.

Jack Ma had the power of "yes or no" for whether the girls could success-fully be the Miss etiquette, so we'd tease him, "The difficult pass for a hero is the beauty pass and the difficult pass for the beauty is Jack Ma's pass." This was the so-called Ma's Passing Card of the English class at that time (Need-less to say, it is not the humiliating terms of "Treaty of Shimonoseki" signed in the Qing dynasty, though they bear the same Chinese character).

"What's your standard for choosing Miss etiquette, figure, looks, or the level of spoken English?" we'd ask Jack Ma sometime.

"None! The festival is approaching. In this case, bribing hams talk." Jack Ma jested.

There used to be an "English corner" in the Sixth Park along the West Lake where English fans would go every Sunday morning to practice their spo-ken English. We would join in the fun in groups of three or four. We'd take a stroll at the "English corner" and "chew the fat" in English in the morning and while making planning our afternoon activities, thus killing two birds with one stone.

Jack Ma also went to the "English corner" from time to time. Later he found that the English learning enthusiasm was very high and the weekly "Eng-lish corner" was not enough. So he took us and organized another "English corner" at the square in front of the gate of the Children's Palace every Wednesday evening. Gradually, more and more people joined in, forming a powerful "mental aura" of English speaking. Plus the activity was held in the evening and it was hard to see and distinguish each other, thus encouraging ev-eryone to speak more freely. On Wednesday evenings, the English corner was particularly lively. All kinds of "Chinglish" with speech disorders mingled with Chinese were sounded in the air. English fans tried their best to express their excitement by speaking and gesturing, regardless of how much or how little they were understood.

Seeing this, Jack Ma grinned, "A good idea, isn't it? In speaking English, the less you are seen, the bolder you are!"

After the chat in English, we could go to the Children's Palace to have fun and play with the kids. Everyone was happy as if our childhood came back. The "English corner" at the Children's Palace was very popular for a time be-fore it ended in the winter due to the severe cold.

After Class

Jack Ma and I lived in the same neighborhood, so we often went home together after class. Jack Ma travelled on an electric bicycle, the first generation of its kind in Hangzhou. It produced a sound pretty much like a tractor, not as speedy though, more or less like much cry and little wool. He was late for the first day class simply because his "tractor" broke down half way to class.

Those years were wonderful times. Other than learn English, students would regularly hold activities like drinking tea, playing cards, sharing jokes...

In light of telling jokes, my "performance" was rated "one of the best." Sometimes other classmates' jokes were not that amusing. Jack Ma would cut them off, "Tell your joke 'blank' to Chen Wei and let him 'forge' and retell it, OK?" We came up with many brilliant stories in those days. For instance, the joke of "A butcher and a beauty" is still mentioned at our gatherings.

In the summer of 1992, Wang Dan, a beautiful girl in our class, planned to settle down in Australia with her husband shortly after she joined the class. We all loathed her parting from us. In our eyes, Australia was as remote as the moon. Jack Ma was the only one that had been there and it was the only foreign land that he had set foot on. Jack Ma organized the class to take a trip to the Xinsha Island in Fuyang as a farewell party for Wang Dan.

Jack Ma's son, only one year old then, went with us. At swimming time, Jack Ma put his son under the watch of Ah Xing, the most robust and best swimmer in the class. After everyone got in the water, Ah Xing held the little baby in the shallow water area. The boy wanted to break free from him. "You want to swim?" Ah Xing asked. The child nodded. Ah Xing then put him into the water.

How could a one-year-old child swim? He sank immediately after Ah Xing let go. It so happened that a wave came up and the child was lost to sight! Luckily, the water was not deep and everyone was nearby. With a mad rush, the child was fished up. Although it was only a matter of 10 seconds or so, the boy still coughed a lot of water on shore.

The child has become a young man of 1.82 meters (about 5.97 feet) in height. It is the first thing that comes to his mind when mentioning Uncle Ah Xing.

The relationship between Jack Ma and his students was very close. The students would give their contact information to Jack Ma even after they went abroad. During the Spring Festival in 2007, Zhang Jizhong and I went to Australia. Jack Ma asked us to drop by and see Wang Dan if it suited us and he texted me her address in Brisbane.

However, I didn't go. I preferred to keep the beautiful image of her in my mind, as I know that beautiful girls' biggest "enemy" is time. I think it is acceptable to see beauties often and to watch their pretty faces wither bit by bit. I didn't want to taste the bitterness of crushing my wonderful memories all of a sudden by seeing someone after a dozen years' separation.

Jack Ma was also particularly keen on matchmaking. The most interesting pair was from our class. The man was very sturdy, but had a heavy Shaoxing accent both in his Chinese and English spoken languages. His hobby was playing cards and he had little ambition. The girl, on the other hand, was a seeker of romance and perfection who wished to have her wedding being held in Paris. None of us thought their relation would be promising. But when the man told Jack Ma he had a crush on the girl, Jack Ma immediately promised him his help and became his wingman. Jack Ma's prestige and super power of persuasion eventually convinced the girl. Later they got married and gave birth to a son, whose birthday was on September 3. It so happened that the famous martial arts novelist Louis Cha (Jin Yong) was in Hangzhou that day. Jack Ma thus asked him to give the baby a name. Louis Cha named the child "Sanxu (Chinese characters '三旭' composed of 九, September and 三日, the 3rd day)" based on his birth date. With this name, no one would forget his birthday.

God seems to be tricky and humorous. The pair who was not very promising in everyone's eyes became husband and wife with the help of Jack Ma. The two "model couples" in our English class later quietly broke up. This was much to our surprise.

The wife of one of the couples was our classmate and she was beautiful and generous. She had many rooms in her house and often invited us to play cards or Go (a kind of chess game played with black and white pieces on a board of 361 crosses). When she got pregnant, her expected date to give birth was February 14, the Valentine's Day. Jack Ma said the baby born on that day must be a little heartthrob. The husband's surname was Yang. So he said that if it was a baby girl, it would be called "Yang Yuhuan" or if it was a boy, his name would be "Yang Guozhong."

As expected, on February 14, she had a little boy. I was the first one informed. I went to Jack Ma's place to announce the news. Perhaps I was unusually excited. "Chen Wei is really funny. Someone may think it was him who had a son." Jack Ma's mother-in-law commented.

Jack Ma was also very happy. "Let's go to see 'Guozhong' then," said he.

Later this model couple in everyone's eyes got divorced without rhyme or reason. The woman left the one and a half men behind and settled abroad "smartly." But we still went to her former home to play cards or chess, because by then her ex-husband had become our good friend.

For several years, we would go to his house to play cards, chat on New Year's Eve till dawn. "Every year, we begin and end by playing cards," we so teased each other.

The other girl in our class was a beautiful and graceful lady who got a job through her connection with Jack Ma. Once in a class, she told her love story in English. It sounded much like a fairy tale. She said she hated blind dates. Once her grandmother "lied" to her to dine out, actually it was a blind date again. But right then and there, she met her "Prince Charming." She concluded by expressing her thanks to life and to this "cheating" which envied us all. Later, she also invited us to dine at her home. Her husband was a handsome gentleman. Unexpectedly, they somehow got divorced shortly afterwards.

She didn't show up in the English class again after the divorce. I met her again after 16 years. She was doing fine, still very "gentle" with her reserved and gracious tone.

Hangzhou Hope Translation Agency

One year, all the radio stations in Hangzhou turned to live broadcast. The audience could call in and even possibly win a grand prize. For a time, Walkman became the hot cake and the rate of audience of the radio stations rose continuously. Among them, there was a very popular program called 'Foreign Wind' dedicated to foreign pop songs. Jack Ma was invited to be the guest host. Many Hangzhou people started to slowly understand and appreciate English songs by listening to this program.

Jack Ma also learned Japanese for a while. We asked him how well he did on Japanese and he would recite a long passage to us. It sounded very much like Japanese. But when asked what it meant, Jack Ma said that he made it up all by himself and he had no idea what it meant. Just for fun!

With the deepening of the reform and opening up, foreign language data translation became increasingly in demand. An idea came across Jack Ma's mind when he found many of his colleagues and retired senior teachers were idling at home. "What if I set up a professional translation agency in Hangzhou? In this way, it can reduce my burden and it can offer a chance for those teachers to earn extra money to subsidize households, a double advantage." In January 1994, Jack Ma established "Hangzhou Hope Translation Agency" in the two rooms of YMCA along the street. Its Chinese name "海博" is the transliteration of "hope" in English. "Hope as the boundless sea. Good name, huh!" Jack Ma explained.

When the translation agency was established, only a few students invested and took part in the operation, but the whole class was vigorous about its publicity. I remembered that on the opening day, the class even did a promotion in the Wulin Square with banners.

At that time, the translation agency was staffed only by Jack Ma and a few senior teachers retired from Hangzhou Institute of Electrical Engineering. Jack Ma's main business was still teaching. He could only manage the translation agency in his spare time. Though in those early days, their efforts and return were not balanced. No matter how hard Jack Ma tried, no matter how hard we helped Jack Ma to promote in and out of school, the cheerless fate of the translation agency business remained unchanged. But Jack Ma didn't give up.

Because the translation agency was located at a street front, it also sold flowers and birthday presents. In order to replenish the stock, Jack Ma even took a team to Yiwu Petty Commodities Market to purchase gifts to be sold in the store. By 1995, Hope Translation Agency's business gradually developed. But Jack Ma had turned his center of gravity to the Internet. Thus he gave the translation agency to a share-holding student.

Today the translation agency is still in service in the old place. The storefront remained unexpanded. But now it can do translations of almost all languages, with over 20 languages frequently translated. Today, when we visit the website of Hangzhou Hope Translation Agency, the first thing that comes to our sight is "Never Give Up" written by Jack Ma with his own hand.

Story of Grandma in Ma's English Class

The English Class won its fame day by day and all kinds of students had signed up. Some disabled came in wheelchairs. Some TV hosts came with their mothers. A grandma came along with her granddaughter. Grandma was the Class Star then. No one knew her real name. She was over 80 years old when I met her. Everyone followed the suit of Jack Ma and called her Grandma (hereinafter short for G).

Actually G was my "senior." Jack Ma once had taught English in Yongjin Evening School before he started in YMCA. When dusk fell, G would stroll to Yongjin Evening School to kill time. She would sit in when she found there was an English class. At first, students thought she was "an old leader disguised for investigation."

Others would worry about memorizing words, but G relieved her headaches and insomnia by memorizing words before sleeping.

In the English class in YMCA, G's speaking and listening skills were above average. And she could hear and see well. "Just look at G, can you still find excuses for not learning well?" Jack Ma often made her an example.

G's granddaughter was less than twenty years of age when she also sat in the class. After class she would hang out with us till midnight. We asked her whether her family worried about her going home so late. "Of course if I'm going out with others. But G knows, it's fine to go out with you. She told my family that everyone in our class is good!"

After Hangzhou Hope Translation Agency was established, G offered herself to do promotional work and to make business contact with other companies. We didn't have the heart to let her do this. "It's easy for me to get things done. Who would refuse an 80-year-old granny's request, especially when she can speak English?" she said. Just as G said, the things that could not be done by young people were done by G basically at one time!

G was still riding a bicycle then. Once she lost her way while delivering documents. Later we stopped giving her jobs. Subsequently, she was specifically responsible for promotions in big hotels because they were warm in winter and cool in summer with a good environment.

As the saying goes, old age is a second childhood and that is the truth. G also had her childishness. Once I was discussing Chinese two-part allegorical sayings with some classmates. An old woman drinks gruel — flowing down due to toothless (impudence and dirty—pun); an old woman drinks gruel against the wall — back to the wall and flowing down (mean and dirty—pun). The class burst into laughter. But G came up in a stern face. "Me don't like these!"

During that time, G had three surgeries for intestinal obstruction and even had part of her intestine cut. G was a cheerful granny and soon she got recovered. When she came back to the class again, I said to her: "According to scientific reports, due to the fact that the easterner mainly take vegetarian diet, the 'processes' for digestion and absorption are more complicated. So their intestines are longer than those of the westerners who eat mainly meat. Your intestine was cut short now and I think it must be helpful for you to learn English, because you are now more equal to the foreigners than us." Hearing this, G could not stop laughing.

CCTV learned about the English Class and the producer and director Fan Xinman of "*Oriental Horizon*" was very curious. She took her crew to Hangzhou to shoot a short video of us.

Director Fan lurked in the English Class a couple of times. I found a female student with long hair and big eyes in our class who would sometimes exchange ideas with Jack Ma during breaks. I knew she was from the TV station but I didn't pay much attention, because I was accustomed to all kinds of students coming and going in our class.

G began to walk with difficulty now. Each time for class Jack Ma would assign someone to pick up G. It was my turn that day.

I went to G's home and knocked at the door as usual. The minute the door was opened, a dazzling light was shining directly into my face, and I was utterly startled. It turned out that G's home was "ambushed" by the Station crew. Jack Ma and several classmates had arrived there ahead of me. We were a little nervous in the beginning. "Don't be nervous. Be as natural as you used to. Pretend that we don't exist," Director Fan said.

We sat and chatted at G's home for a while. There was an old photo on the wall and in it there were a lot of people. The middle one was Deng Yingchao and the inscription was "Representatives of Families of Workers and

Staff of National Advanced Workers Representative Meeting."

We could not tell which one was G in the photo. G told us that her husband was a railway engineer. The photo was taken in Beijing in 1956. She was running a nursery and a small canteen with others in the family area then.

We picked up G to go to class. Director Fan shot the whole journey with us.

Shortly afterwards, the story of the English Class appeared in the program of 'Stories of the Common.' It was widely viewed. The second day after it was put on air, I heard many of my acquaintances saying, "Yesterday I saw you on CCTV!"

In the autumn of 1995, G passed away. By that time *Nv You* (*Lady Friend*) magazine had just published an article titled as 'Granny Goes PR' about her. All of us were very grieved. Jack Ma gathered all the students and held a special commemorative activity at the Autumn Moon and Calm Lake Pavilion by the West Lake.

"... G will always be with us in heaven. She wants us to be happy, not sad. Today we'll recall the time we spent together with G at the beautiful West Lake. May she rest in peace..." Jack Ma said. Then we spread G's ashes into the West Lake.

Like Father and Son

When mentioning Jack Ma's past, Ken was a name that should be stroked with heavy ink.

A lot of people know that Jack Ma took the college entrance examination three times before passing it. But few know that he had spent more than 10 years, rain or shine, at the West Lake every day reading English and communicating with foreigners.

Ken was from Australia, and a friend Jack Ma met at the West Lake in his early years. They were like father and son. Ken had invited Jack Ma to Australia.

One thing that impressed Jack Ma deeply in Australia was that there were many people playing Taiji in the park, a fitness exercise Jack Ma loved very much.

Occasionally, Ken would be a guest in the English Class. At that time, he was already over 70 years old, though still hale and hearty. Thus, our class had two elderly, a female and a male, a Chinese and a foreigner.

He spoke a lot of slang words, many of which confused us. Then Jack Ma would explain for us. For example, for the expression "very good," he would say "bloody wonderful."

He had very broad fingers, so he had to use chopsticks to type on the computer otherwise he would hit two keys at the same time.

In 1998, Jack Ma was tied up with business in Beijing, so he asked me to take care of Ken when he arrived at Hangzhou. For a week, I took him everywhere I went and spent all day with him. I thought I did a pretty good job with the reception work. He, however, complained about me to Jack Ma for drunk driving and for not changing after his repeated warnings. I simply shrugged off at the time. But now thinking back, I realize how wrong I was.

Jack Ma is a man who keeps old friends in mind. Ken passed away many years ago, but Jack Ma still kept the group photo of Ken and him both at his home and in his office.

We're All in This Together

Since Jack Ma started his business, the English Class was disbanded. But the students continued to be in contact, drinking tea, playing cards or Go chess, and sharing jokes...

Jack Ma was constantly on business trips and was often away from Hangzhou. When students got together, we would always call Jack Ma, telling him who were at the party and what we were doing.

Some of the students went abroad for further study and delayed their marriages. Each time, when a female student came back alone from abroad and gathered with the class, Jack Ma would tease her from the other end of the phone, "Tell her, find a good man and settle down. Don't wait for me any longer!"

One evening, Jack Ma called me while he was eating at a food stall in Shenzhen. He asked me whether I came up with any new jokes recently. I told him two jokes and he roared with laughter and totally lost control at the other end of the phone. "I was too loud just now, the people next to my table were frightened," Jack Ma said softly on the phone after a while.

A weekend in late autumn, the weather was very good. It was a rare chance to see Jack Ma in Hangzhou. So we decided to go to the Baopu Taoist Temple on Baoshi Hill to drink tea and play cards. Jack Ma was clad in a very smart-looking wind coat. "Crocodile? Famous brand! Same as that of Mr..." said a student after seeing the label of his coat.

"Same as whose? Open your eyes and look closely! Which side does the crocodile head face? Mine is Lacoste!" said Jack Ma.

A happy old couple was playing the military chess game next to us and they happened to lack a judge. We had more than enough players for the cards. Jack Ma thus arranged the one who lost in the card game to be the judge for the old couple. The old couple was having a very good time. When he 'bombed' the Field Marshal of the old woman, the old man grinned from ear to ear. "Deceiving your opponent is a common tactic in the military. But the deceit is 'bombing' (pun in Chinese)" said the old man loudly and proudly.

We were infected by the happy old couple. Actually it is very easy to be happy.

Before long, Jack Ma said he had to leave for the time being for some matters. He didn't come back for lunch. By the time he joined us again, it was nearly five o'clock in the afternoon. "Guess where I went?" he asked us after sitting down.

No one could figure it out. "I took a trip to Guangzhou and just came back! I went there for my exit visa," said Jack Ma.

Everyone was taken by surprise. "Seriously?! You went to Guangzhou and came back again? Even Xiaoshan was beyond our guess."

In 1998, Jack Ma spent most of his time in Beijing and seldom came back to Hangzhou. But each time he came back, he'd call us together for a party. Once after dinner, I drove Jack Ma home. At that time, Jack Ma's son was seven years old, chubby looking. "Hold on for a while. Don't fall asleep, hold on!" All the way, Jack Ma's wife Zhang Ying kept on saying this to her son. "He is just a kid. Let him sleep if he wants!" I said, feeling very strange. "You have no idea how heavy he is now. If he falls asleep, we two have to carry him all the way to the sixth floor," said Zhang Ying.

In 2000, I moved to a new house. On moving day, all the students came to my house to play cards. Jack Ma dropped by to see the students on his way. When he came, we had already had our lunch, but he was hungry with an empty stomach. So he took a bowl of rice soup at my place. Jack Ma was very busy and had to leave in less than half an hour. Before leaving, he made a bet with a student over a small case and lost 200 yuan. "Chen Wei, I was hoping to save some money to eat at your price. God knows that yours is more expensive than that of a fancy restaurant." At that, we all broke into loud laughter.

"Your company is short of money. If your competitors rise, how can you sustain your company? How do you view 'A great man cannot brook a rival' (A mountain can't hold two tigers—a Chinese proverb)?" once a reporter asked Jack Ma at a meeting in Hong Kong.

"That basically depends on gender," replied Jack Ma.

The reporter was at a loss.

"I never think that 'A mountain can't hold two tigers' is correct. If there is a tiger and a tigress on the mountain, that will be harmonious," continued Jack Ma.

The reporter then questioned Jack Ma about the role of electronic commerce. "For a newly born baby, can you tell me what he can do? So it is the same with electronic commerce. Right now it is just a female form (mispronunciation for rudiment)." (Jack Ma spoke in Hangzhou dialect.)

"What is the meaning of 'female form'?" The reporter was puzzled.

"Don't you know female form (rudiment)? It's a chick, a baby," Jack Ma asked in return, feeling surprised.

The reporter finally understood. Jack Ma meant rudiment.

For a time, "female form" hung on Jack Ma's mouth on each occasion. "What a shame! In front of so many people …I've always thought it was pronounced 'female' (rudiment)…"

Jack Ma liked to play the game of Go but his skill was just so-so. During his business startup, Jack Ma often went on business trips to Japan. While waiting at Tokyo Airport, he would play Go with his companions. Go is also quite popular in Japan. Everywhere there is "undiscovered talent," just like the situation of table tennis in China. So while they were playing, from time to time, the Japanese waiting for their flights would come over for a look. "An old man came and watched for a moment, and went away shaking his head; a child came and threw a glance and left, shaking his head too. I think that I can't go on disgracing the Chinese people anymore. What to do? It is impossible to improve my Go playing level in a day. So we began to play Gomoku! I am the invincible hands on this game. Watch as much as they want!" Jack Ma said.

Once I went to Kenya, Africa. I was surprised to see that I actually could communicate with the locals in English. So I texted Jack Ma: "Dear Mr. Ma, the broken English you taught me actually came in handy in Africa."

Jack Ma texted back: "Damned heartless fellow!"

One year, I was shooting a TV play in Hengdian. While eating with the crew, I called Jack Ma and was told he was attending International Leisure & Recreation Expo at the Hangzhou Leisure & Recreation Expo Garden. Unexpectedly, before his speech, he read a text massage I sent him. "The Rich List is out. The top rich one is a woman, 27 billion *yuan*. You won't catch up with her for a while. Better take leisure, drink tea, and play cards."

Indeed as expected, the next day all major Hangzhou newspapers published the news, with the title: Jack Ma at the Leisure & Recreation Expo read a text message before making his speech.

One day after his acquisition of Yahoo China, I paid a visit to Jack Ma's house. "Mr. Ma, you are very rich now. Share some of your wealth with me, your poor student. Andrew Carnegie once said, the man who dies rich, dies disgraced," I said, jokingly.

"And, in turn?" asked Jack Ma.

"What in turn?" I asked.

"The man who dies poor, dies honored?"

Jack Ma always gets the upper hand.

Chapter 2:
Jack Ma into the Net

In 1995, Jack Ma started his first business. Many people are familiar with his start-up stories. But I was impressed with something different during the process. Once, Jack Ma and his wife Zhang Ying even made a desperate decision – to pledge their house for 'China Pages.' I believe there are many similar decisions, and some are even more horrifying, I've learned a few of them but some are well beyond my knowledge. Some could be shared afterwards and some would rather be buried forever for the people involved.

Friedrich Wilhelm Nietzsche once said, "*Every deep thinker is more afraid of being understood than of being misunderstood. The latter perhaps wounds his vanity; but the former wounds his heart, his sympathy···*" I think it goes to entrepreneurs too, who are afraid of being fully understood because their wounds are deep and their past stings.

Lured to the States

In 1995, I lost contact with Jack Ma for a period of time. One day suddenly, I got a call from him asking me to meet him in his house. He told me that he had just returned from the United States and had something important to announce.

Jack Ma's house was fully packed that day. Some were my classmates, and some were strangers to me. Jack Ma, wrapped in a blanket, shrinking in the couch, looked a bit nervous. After we all arrived, Jack Ma started talking about his adventures.

A foreign company came to Zhejiang, claiming to make investment to build highways, and invited Jack Ma to be their translator. Later they took him to the United States and accommodated him with good food and lodging. I remember Jack Ma said that he was put in a room at the top floor of a building in Las Vegas. With a press of a button, the ceiling would be opened, leaving a layer of glass so he could see the stars in the sky while lying on the bed.

Jack Ma later found out that those people were not tally with the facts while negotiating with others. They even asked Jack Ma to "testify" for some fictitious claims. Jack Ma suspected that they might be an international fraud organization and refused to cooperate with them.

Then they threatened Jack Ma that he could never go back to China unless he cooperated with them and they withheld all of his belongings...

Jack Ma had gone through a series of dramatic events, and eventually escaped from their evil hands...

"These people were unbelievably wicked!" Shrinking in the couch with blanket over him, Jack Ma repeated time and again. One could sense that Jack Ma loathed mentioning some of the unbearable details, then and forever.

But I personally think that human potency may well be 'stimulated' by some extreme events. At the critical moment when a gun is pointed at the head, some may fall apart, while others may become strong instantly. You never know!

After escaping from the black den of the gang, Jack Ma did not return to China right away. He remembered that once he had heard about the Internet from a foreign colleague in Hangzhou Institute of Electrical Engineering and his son-in-law happened to work in the only available network company in Seattle.

Jack Ma flew to Seattle and found that company. He was told by the company staff that he could search any information he wanted by typing on the computer. He typed in "beer" and he saw German beer, American beer and Japanese beer, but no Chinese beer. And then he tried "China" and there were only dozens of words introducing the history of China.

Subsequently, I went to Jack Ma's house almost every day to listen to him explaining and demonstrating the Internet. Honestly speaking, I basically did not understand what he was talking about. I just joined the fun and to meet my classmates in passing. Of course, more importantly I was to give face to Jack Ma. Every day, Jack Ma would rattle about the Internet with excitement, gesticulating with hands and feet, and then followed by his business plans. And in the end, he would ask us what we had on our minds.

None of us seemed to buy it.

Some raised a few questions to Jack Ma, largely related to the steps for a startup. Jack Ma couldn't answer them and said that he needed time to think about them. Then we all shook our heads and sighed and poured cold water on to him one after another. "Mr. Ma, how about you run a bar? A restaurant? An evening school? Or continue to be a teacher? Whatever! Just not this. What the hell is this? None of the Chinese knows about it. It's not that it isn't a good thing, or not promising, but simply because it is too advanced... The Chinese people won't buy it."

Jack Ma, however, was not discouraged by everyone's opposition. Before, he had only heard of it, now he could access the Internet in person. This thrilled Jack Ma enough. He decided to start a company in China, specializing in the Internet. Jack Ma went to the United States and registered "China page" with a small amount of money. The computer showed, "You are lucky! This name is not registered."

Jack Ma said on that very day, a young man from Taiwan registered "Taiwan page." Cross straits entered the Internet era on the same day!

This venture was different from establishing the Hangzhou Hope Translation Agency. Jack Ma resigned from his teaching job in the university, which was regarded as a 'golden bowl' by many people, and plunged into the sea of business. He was actually hesitating when he first planned to submit his resignation, so he said. But one day, right before work was through for the day, he met with the chairman of his department on the campus. The chairman was on his bike with two handfuls of vegetables just bought from the market hanging on the handlebar. He stopped Ma and earnestly advised him to devote himself to the very promising work of being an English teacher. Thus, Jack Ma resigned without further hesitation. "Watching him, I suddenly realized, if I continued to stay in school, his current situation could become my 'promising future'!"

In April 1995, Jack Ma rented several rooms at the Jindi Hotel on Wen'er Road, Hangzhou, and started his 'China Pages.' It was said that he pulled out 6,000 or 7,000 *yuan* and even borrowed some money from his mother-in-law.

With the initial funds he raised about 20,000 *yuan*. Jack Ma officially registered his company — Hangzhou DiFe·Hope Computer Service Co., Ltd. This was China's first Internet commercial company, staffed with only three: Jack Ma, his wife Zhang Ying and He Yibing. He Yibing, Jack Ma's colleague at the university, came to engage in the so-called Internet business after being convinced by Jack Ma on the phone.

Although I didn't quite understand Jack Ma's Internet stuff, I would go to help each time he summoned me. One day, the company was hiring and I was called to increase the momentum. After I got there, I found in a quite spacious room that there was only a desk and a chair, somewhat like children's play house. Jack Ma's first secretary, Li Yun, was recruited on that day.

When Jack Ma first started his 'China Pages,' he had no customers. So he laid his hands onto people around him. I worked in a company exporting TV sets then and another female classmate was the lobby manager at the Lakeview Hotel. Jack Ma thus posted the information of my 14 inch color TV sets with a picture of the Lakeview Hotel on the Internet, which was likely to be the earliest product and hotel picture placed on the Internet in China.

Shortly after, the World Conference on Women was held in Beijing. Some of the delegates came to visit Hangzhou after the conference and they picked the Lakeview Hotel, which was not a first-class hotel in Hangzhou. When being asked why they chose to stay at the Lakeview Hotel, they answered that this was the only hotel in China whose information could be found on the Internet.

The lobby manager of the Lakeview Hotel named Zhou Lan, who later became Jack Ma's second secretary and eventually, became the director of the Department of Affairs of Alibaba.

As to what degree does 'good looks' function in life, Jack Ma once discussed with us. "Good looks matter of course. Those who are not so good looking can only be a boss through much effort. Nonetheless, the good looking ones can be a secretary to the boss through much effort, ha-ha!" Jack Ma concluded.

'China Pages' did not attract many customers to the door after going online. Jack Ma had to bear the heavy responsibility of advertising 'China Pages.' Being short of funds for advertisement, Jack Ma had to demonstrate and lobby door-to-door. Upon recollecting that experience, Jack Ma still sighed with emotion. "I was, nominally, the general manager. But in truth, I was just a salesman. No difference from those 'nasty salesmen' who went on the streets selling insurance and health care products. Though their mission was to clinch a deal or two, I, on the other hand, was an out-and-out volunteer." Once I heard from a classmate that he saw Jack Ma babbling excitedly with people sitting next to him at a street food stall. I believe that Jack Ma's entrepreneurial experience at that time was sauced with all flavors in his heart.

Zhang Ying, the Better Half of Jack Ma

"If you get a good wife you'll become happy; if you get a bad one, you'll become a philosopher," Socrates so said. I think that's a way of self-comforting for marrying a shrew. How much can a person get in this life? But "a handful of rice" from the "boundless fertile fields," and "half a bed" from the "numerous buildings." Therefore, "the other half of the bed" is essential in life. "The most important thing when it comes to home is a good bed, with a good wife on it!" Jack Ma has stressed the point repeatedly in his speeches.

Zhang Ying, Jack Ma's wife, used to be his college classmate. Later she worked with him in the same teaching and researching office of Hangzhou Institute of Electrical Engineering.

At the time of English Class, Zhang Ying would substitute for Jack Ma when he couldn't make it, though not many times. From the perspective of the English language teaching, honestly speaking, her lessons were better than those of Jack Ma's. In teaching, Jack Ma imparted more ideological contents and was sometimes easily carried away. Zhang Ying, instead, would induct some English problems, and seriously explain words and expressions and grammar in every class. She was more focused than Jack Ma and seldom went beyond anything other than English.

Jack Ma enjoyed crowds. He often invited students to his house to have fun, and each time there would be a lot of people. Zhang Ying always greeted us with a smiling face, serving tea, even preparing meals at times, and cleaning the mess after we were gone. Their home was in the most western area of Hangzhou, farmland at the farther west. In the evening, one could hear the frogs from their home, and occasionally the barking from the Chinese rural dogs not far away. Zhang Ying had to teach and help Jack Ma with his businesses, so their son was taken care of by a nanny. To save money, she hired a nanny from the countryside. Not for long, their son's accent followed that of the nanny's, with the pronunciation quite distant from standard Mandarin. Zhang Ying had to find a new nanny instead.

Jack Ma had planned to pledge his house when starting 'China Pages.' Once at a class gathering, Jack Ma brought up this idea again. Zhang Ying knew very well that when Jack Ma was determined to do something, it would be impossible to pull him back. "Must we pledge the house? Where shall we live if the house is pledged?" She asked, helplessly.

After the establishment of 'China Pages,' Jack Ma went to the United States on business trips every once in a while. He was quite excited in the beginning. But soon he got tired of it and asked Zhang Ying to go instead of him. "Chen Wei, organize the class to hold activities immediately. From tonight on, we'll have activities every night," Jack Ma told me on the phone one day.

"Mr. Ma, are you free recently?" I asked.

"Zhang Ying has gone to the United States, and she won't be back in 15 days! I feel like a beggar who suddenly has picked up 2 million yuan. I don't know what to do with it!" Jack Ma said.

Zhang Ying was not only a good wife during the startup period, but was more of the "business backbone." The first "huge deal" of RMB 8,000 for "China Pages" was negotiated by Zhang Ying.

In 1998, Jack Ma went to work in Beijing. Zhang Ying went with him too. To make it easy, Zhang Ying learned to drive that year. Not quite skillful, Zhang Ying once hit a Mercedes-Benz while backing up. Zhang Ying shivered from fear. Should anything happen to the Benz, they would lose all the family fortune! She quickly got out of the car and saw the rear bumper of the Jetta Zhang Ying drove was mounted on the Mercedes-Benz. Two others were riding with Zhang Ying that day. They lost no time and lifted the rear of Jetta. Totally to their surprise, the Mercedes-Benz was kept intact, not even a scratch on the paint! Zhang Ying was relieved, feeling even more relaxed than before the crash. She got in the car and took leave at once!

Not everything went on her way after the success of the entrepreneurship. In 2008, Zhang Ying came to the company for a Vice President, whom she fostered with intensive care. But right in the lobby of the company, she was stopped by a girl at the front desk. "Madam, can I help you?"

"I..." words failed Zhang Ying when she saw the reception girl about the same age of her son.

Zhang Ying stopped going to the company after that. "After all the trials and hardships, I can't even get into the company I established. Even if I can, I don't know what to do there."

In recent years, the company has undergone tremendous changes. But Zhang Ying never slacks her management on Jack Ma's health.

Zhang Ying knew Jack Ma enjoyed crowds. He was always in high spirits in discussions and negotiations and only realized how tired he was after they were over. So whenever the meetings were late, Zhang Ying would make timely reminders to ensure Jack Ma to call it off as soon as possible.

Jack Ma's lunch was mostly brought in from home. Zhang Ying would also urge him to eat lunch timely. If you arrived at Jack Ma's office at midday, you would often hear Jack Ma on the phone like this – "...I've eaten, finished two pieces of meat, half of the steamed egg, a lot of vegetables... I am eating fruit right now!"

In order to let Jack Ma and the family have proper meals, Zhang Ying sent two relatives from her parents' side to help the family and to go for cooking lessons. Their culinary skills are good enough to receive 'heads of states' at home now. Celebrities such as Louis Cha (Jin Yong), Wu Xiaoli and others would often be arranged to have family feasts and they were full of praise for the cooking skills of the family chefs.

All the clothes Jack Ma wore were bought by Zhang Ying. Jack Ma would put on whatever bought for him. A couple of times, when they went to Hong Kong, Jack Ma also got personally involved with buying his clothes, but basically was 'body-wise' not 'mental-wise.'

After the company expanded, Jack Ma's every word and deed would be magnified unlimitedly. Be it Alibaba or Huayi Brothers, each time Jack Ma cut his shares, he would be "divorced" once. In my opinion, it's easier to build another Alibaba than to have them divorced.

Crazy Dreams

Once in the English Class the topic was "I have a dream." The dreams of the students were miscellaneous. Some wanted to be scientists; some wanted to roam in the space; some wanted to have many children and grandchildren...

but the most popular dream was to earn enough money and travel around the world wherever they desired to go.

I forgot Jack Ma's comments at the time. But he was a man full of dreams, although the contents of his dreams were constantly changing, he never stopped dreaming.

On a weekend, we went to climb Mt. Tianzhu in Hangzhou. "I've read all of Louis Cha's martial arts novels, more than once. And my dream is to become a martial art master," Jack Ma said, picking up a straw under a big tree. "For example, if I exert my force, this straw will become very hard and strong. With a swing of my arm, it will penetrate into the tree. But when I take back the power, it will become soft as before, with its two ends hanging down from the tree trunk. None of the people passing by can understand how the straw goes through the tree trunk. Hey, if I had outstanding martial arts power, it would be wonderful, like Feng Qingyang."

Jack Ma's martial arts dream never really faded away. After Alibaba was established, Jack Ma once said: "Someday I may suddenly disappear and no one can find me. Everyone is like an ant on a hot pan. A week later I tell my secretary, if anyone asks again, you can tell them, 'Jack Ma went to play Feng Qingyang in a movie.' If someone asks again, 'when will he come back?' You just tell them, 'I don't know. Please keep an eye on the related news. When the movie finishes shooting, Jack Ma will come back.' I think it will be really amusing!"

Once, at a tea party with the students from the English Class, Jack Ma shared with us such a dream: he swaggers in the modern city of Hangzhou. All the others are in suits and ties. But he wears a white silk robe, a pair of sunglasses, with shiny hair − even a fly finds it slippery. His dressing is totally out of tune with the surroundings, with two female bodyguards a head taller than him standing on either side. He stretches out his left hand, a bodyguard immediately hands over a big pancake. He throws it back after taking several bites; he stretches out his right hand, the other bodyguard at once gives him a cigar and lights it for him. When he taps the smoke ash, the bodyguard sticks out her hands to catch it. He takes a few puffs and then twists it out on her hand. A gust of green smoke rises, but the female bodyguard is deadpan. Then, she claps her hands, without leaving any scar. The people around him are impressed and amazed, showing all kinds of expressions...

Later in his entrepreneurial process, Jack Ma went through a lot. So his dreams at this period also changed substantially.

Dream 1: Take all the team members to Paris to celebrate the Spring Festival. While everyone is ravished with joy, he announces that after New Year's Eve dinner, there will be year-end bonuses: each one will get two keys. The people on site again fall in puzzlement. He continues: "I've bought a villa for each of you in Paris, together with a Ferrari sports car." Someone on the spot has tachycardia and is directly taken to the hospital...

Dream 2: Jack Ma walks into a European luxury hotel. The staff turns a cold shoulder to him seeing he is Asian. Jack Ma finds the owner of the hotel and says: "Name a price, I'll buy your hotel!" The boss says, "I won't sell this hotel, unless you pay me USD 300 million." Jack Ma takes out his checkbook. "I thought you'd ask for USD 500 million," he says while signing his name. He quickly completes the procedures and hands the key of the President's office to a tramp playing a guitar at the door front, saying, "From now on, this hotel is yours..."

Jack Ma not only "dreamed" his own dreams, at the most difficult time of his startup process, he also organized everyone to "dream" with him. Once at the end of the year, there were no bonuses, yet they still had to work overtime. One day, Jack Ma organized a meeting. "If each of you has 5 million *yuan* as the year-end bonus, how will you spend it?" All started talking at once, kept on "fantasying" for nearly an hour. "Terrific! What you said will all come true! Now, back to work," Jack Ma cut in suddenly.

"Boss, please don't stop us. I've only spent 3 million *yuan*!" Someone shouted. Everyone laughed and went away for work.

"Happy-go-lucky" could be the most accurate interpretation of the startup stage. Although I wasn't part of the company then, I often went to check on these guys, as the company was next to my house. Jack Ma would always come up with a variety of ways to make everyone happy. For those who performed well, when he could not afford material rewards, Jack Ma would increase their "life span." At summing-up meetings, each time he would increase life spans for his partners, "200" years for one and "300" years for the other. Everyone cherished their own "life span." A partner surnamed Qian got the most increased "life span," totaling 9,000 years. He has now immigrated to Canada. He stayed at Jack Ma's house when he came back in 2010 and even learned Taiji from Jack Ma. He said the most happy thing for him was once he was "Nine Thousand Years (pun — In Chinese, it means Prince, only next to the Emperor who is Ten Thousand Years)."

On New Year's Day in 2011, "Nine Thousand Years" Mr. Qian came back to Hangzhou again. There were two beautiful bronze horses in Jack Ma's sitting room, each the size of a palm. They were bought by Mr. Qian on his way when driving from Chengdu to Jiuzhaigou. Jack Ma was there, and he took a fancy to them at first sight. But seeing they were labeled 4,000 *yuan* each, he decided not to buy them. Later Mr. Qian bought them and gave them to Jack Ma as gifts.

When speaking of this, Jack Ma could not stop laughing. "The price was 4,000 *yuan* each. Chen Wei, do you know what his offer was? 200 *yuan*! And that was for two!" Eyes wide open, Jack Ma stretched out his right hand and made the "V" shape twice. "And he even asked for some small gifts for free!" While speaking, Jack Ma gestured some movements just like the old traditional Chinese medicine physician picking Chinese herbs from different drawers.

"I was so shocked from his bargaining and utterly embarrassed! Likely he would get a good beating by a stick!" Jack Ma kept on.

But Mr. Qian grinned innocently. "Well, this...I've run such small business before. You can make your offer based on the costs of the copper used. Add a little more if the seller refuses," said he with a pleasant Beijing accent. "If you bargain for 2000 *yuan*, bang! He agrees, then it'll be too late for you to regret! Don't you think it makes sense? ..."

Chapter 3:
Jack Ma and Zhang Jizhong

Through Jack Ma, I got to know Fan Xinman, and later her husband Mr. Zhang Jizhong. I often visited his crew and ran some errands when needed while he was making a film in Zhejiang. Before I knew it, my son had become one of his crew members in the TV series *Years of Passion Burning*, and I also became Zhang Sir's assistant. One of the reasons I joined was that I heard the food for Zhang Jizhong's crew was the most delicious across China.

I learned one thing in those days when soaking myself in the entertainment industry that the whole world is made up from the accumulations of innumerable extremely small probability events. Such as Li Yapeng's starring in the TV series *The Smiling, Proud Wanderer*; the West Lake Summit which has been held for 10 years; or the cooperation of TV series *The Return of the Condor Heroes* and Taobao.com... Such news appeared on newspapers, all of which can be traced back to a flash of thought at a certain moment.

First Impression about Zhang Jizhong

After the filming of our English class for the "Stories of the Common" in 1995, Fan Xinman would contact us every time she returned to Hangzhou. She started to pay attention to Jack Ma and keep in touch with me from time to time ever since. On the 1999 New Year's Card, Director Fan wrote to me like this — "Chen Wei, your friend Jack Ma is to fight along your side; your friend, Fan, has to strive on the other side of the Yangtze River, although we're all for the good of whole humanity... It's a comfort for all of us to hear you are still being happy and well, at least the world is not completely annihilated..." That year, Jack Ma came back to Hangzhou with the team he once brought to Beijing from Hangzhou. That year, Alibaba was born.

One Sunday, I got a call from Jack Ma. "Chen Wei, come join us for lunch," he said on the phone, "Fan Xinman and her husband are with me."

I made it to the second floor of the restaurant at Wulinmen on time only to find everyone was there before me. Two students from the English class were present, although I can't remember their names. A man with whiskers all over his face was sitting beside Director Fan. "My husband Zhang Jizhong... This is Chen Wei," Director Fan introduced us.

"Zhang Jizhong is a famous producer from CCTV. The TV series *Three Kingdoms* is his work. He has recently finished another, *All Men Are Brothers*." Jack Ma added.

"What is a producer?" I asked.

"Well, let me put it this way, if the director is the Chief Engineer, the producer is the General Manager who manages the money, the crew — including the director," said Jack Ma.

Zhang Jizhong's hair and beard was still black then and he was not so fat either. He said he had a good appetite for Hangzhou home style dishes, such as braised deep-fried bean curd, soy-sauce duck, and bacon with bamboo shoots... all of them. While we were talking, a dish was served. He took a bite. "This... this is amazingly delicious!" He said, pointing to the dish, eyes wide open.

"There you go again, such a fuss, others would think you bit your tongue," Director Fan commented.

"First time to Hangzhou?" We asked.

"I came to Hangzhou during the 1966 Cultural Revolution mass rallies at the age of 15. Fan Xinman was just born that year, so I missed the chance." With this, everybody laughed.

"People in CCTV address you as Director Zhang (Production Manager). The crew calls you Director Zhang. How shall we address you? How about Zhang Sir (At that time, many Hong Kong gangster movies were very popular, and "Yes, Sir" is very catchy)." Jack Ma said. And "Zhang Sir" was thus called for more than 10 years.

Afterwards, Zhang Sir came to Hangzhou frequently. "Hangzhou is really a good place; a good place to wear down the fighting will," he said. And almost every time we would hear him saying "This is amazingly delicious!" at the dining table.

Zhang Sir was born in 1951. Because of his high class status (His grandfather was a famous capitalist in Beijing) and poor family background, he suffered a lot as a kid. At the age of 17 or 18, he was delegated to receive a "re-education" from the poor and lower-middle peasants in a village of Xiecun Village Commune of Yuanping, Shanxi.

Zhang Sir was quite optimistic. He often told stories about the past, the hard times, in an entertaining way.

"...While I worked in the production brigade in the village in Shanxi, I could not get back to the town due to my family background. Finally I got a job, a ticket taker at a movie theatre. One day, I stopped a leader's wife from getting in as she had no ticket. The next day I was fired... Thanks to that, or I would be still inspecting tickets there...

"A haircut at the village then was five cents. A woman came with her baby in her arms and asked whether the child could have a discount to three cents. Without turning back his head, the barber said, 'Even the core of the wild jujube is five cents.' Meaning the charge for every head is the same.

"A man in the village always hummed bawdy songs while working. One day he told us he had a lover in the neighboring village. She was said to be as pretty as a fairy. I was very curious and went to that village to see his lover. Goodness me, she was extremely ugly!"

Zhang Sir also told me a version of the birth of *Funeral Music*.

In those years, there was only a music band in the neighboring villages. So they were seen in all the wedding parties in the households. Their job was to play gongs and drums and wind instruments to accompany the bride to the bridegroom's house. The music was often very joyful, "ray-doe-me-ray-tea-la-sew-la-tea-doe-me-ray..."

But once on the halfway, due to hyper excitation, the bride had a heart attack and died!

The bridegroom was stricken with grief. He asked the band on the way, can you change the latter half to a sad tune?

The band said that they were capable of only this very tune, but they could slow down the beat. And that's how the *Funeral Music* came into being: "ray – doe – me – ray – tea – la – sew – la – tea – doe – me – ray..."

In truth, each tune, if slowed down to a certain level, could be funeral music!

"Now I really want to have a bunch of poor relatives from a remote village and then I can pull a cart loaded with meat and a cart loaded with flour , take our catering crew and invite the village to eat for three days and three nights..." Zhang Sir would conclude like this each time after his story.

In early 1999, Zhang Sir came to Hangzhou and stayed at the Xihu State Guest Hotel. Jack Ma and I went to see him. Back then, Zhang Sir was making preparations for a TV series *Sun Yat-Sen* and had encountered many difficulties. "Have you ever thought about making TV series of Louis Cha's martial arts plays?" Jack Ma asked on the mentioning of TV plays.

"Of course. But they were already made in Hong Kong."

"That was over 15 years ago. If you come up with a newer version, a version so good that it may even bring about another climax."

I remember the discussion ended up with unanimous decision of the two, that the first Louis Cha's martial arts TV play produced by Zhang Sir should be *The Smiling, Proud Wanderer* if things worked out.

Unexpectedly, later Zhang Jizhong did make Louis Cha's plays and the first one was really *The Smiling, Proud Wanderer*. What's more surprising was, starting from *The Smiling, Proud Wanderer*, Zhang Jizhong's martial arts plays had become a brand and stars, super or common ones, all felt proud to be part of Zhang Sir's martial arts plays.

About *The Smiling, Proud Wanderer*

In the autumn of 1999, while Jack Ma was awfully busy establishing Alibaba, Louis Cha sold the copyright of *The Smiling, Proud Wanderer* to CCTV for the price of one yuan. The signing ceremony was to be held in Hangzhou.

Jack Ma couldn't make himself available, so the activity was taken care of by me.

I arranged the signing ceremony in a relatively quiet hotel at Mt. Santai. The Vice President of CCTV, leaders of China Teleplay Production Center Co., Ltd., Zhang Sir, the director, and screenplay writers all came from Beijing.

At the time, Louis Cha was the Honorary Dean of Faculty of Humanities of Zhejiang University. He stayed in the Zhejiang Narada Grand Hotel and was accommodated with a Red-flag (Hongqi) and an Audi for his transportation. To ensure that Louis Cha could sit in our car, I borrowed a Cadillac Escalade from the wife of the owner of Happiness Hotel, the best hotel in Hangzhou then. The kind of car was facilitated with a refrigerator, a teapoy, and had face-to-face seats. We drove the car to the gate of the Zhejiang Narada Grand Hotel and parked in front of the Hongqi car.

Later, Mr. Louis Cha went to the ceremony in our car. The signing ceremony went very well. After that, Louis Cha even made an inscription for me.

In fact, Zhang Sir had never met Louis Cha, but he had respected Mr. Louis Cha very much. So, in the making of the link of handing over the one *yuan* copyright fee to Mr. Louis Cha, he racked his brain. Of course the final effect was surprisingly good. Until now he kept on self-praising. "You know how I handed the one *yuan* copyright fee to Louis Cha? I made a special trip to the People's Bank of China and chose a brand new one *yuan* paper note with a lucky number and then inlaid it into a crystal cup carved with 'CCTV' and gave it to Louis Cha."

In rounds and rounds of warm applause, the signing ceremony ended smoothly. Thereafter, Louis Cha began to discuss the screenplay of *The Smiling, Proud Wanderer* with the others in the hotel conference room. As a matter of fact, by that time, the leaders of CCTV, the staff of CTPC and even Zhang Sir himself had no concrete ideas about the screenplay and were not fully confident. They asked Louis Cha to raise his requirements as the total programs or basic principles of the adaption of the screenplay. Louis Cha's request was clear and definite – to respect the original work.

"To respect the original work" was easier said than done. At that time, Mr. Louis Cha proposed two ideas for his martial arts plays made in Hong Kong and Taiwan: first, they were overwhelmingly using set constructions rather than real scenes and he thought them unconvincing; second, they were not very true to the original work. In his own words: "Since you are so capable of revising, why don't you write your own instead of buying mine?"

At the end of screenplay discussion, I took Mr. Louis Cha back to his hotel and arranged a dinner party at Happiness Hotel to celebrate the successful signing ceremony. Zhang Sir, still immersed in *The Smiling, Proud Wanderer*, gained special praise from the CCTV leadership, "Looks like you've got yourself quite a good mass base in Hangzhou!"

Jack Ma's favorite swordsman character Feng Qingyang is from *The Smiling, Proud Wanderer*. Intentionally, he wanted to guest star the role of Feng Qingyang in Zhang Sir's play. Pitifully, in the end, he had to give up due to the lack of martial arts foundation. However, Jack Ma still liked to pose as Feng Qingyang. His Taobao ID is "Feng Qingyang." Interestingly, Mr. Louis Cha gave Jack Ma another name – Ma Tianxing, meaning "a heavenly steed soaring across the skies, but always down-to-earth." To this, Jack Ma accepted it with pleasure.

In early 2001, the first run of *The Smiling, Proud Wanderer* profited 75 million yuan for CCTV. Then it snatched the market share in Hong Kong and became a hot cake in Taiwan too. Even many of the original sites in the scenes became famous. The original book of *The Smiling, Proud Wanderer* also became increasingly popular.

Before the shooting of *The Smiling, Proud Wanderer*, Zhang Sir and I went to Xinchang County, Shaoxing, Zhejiang Province to discuss with the leadership of Xinchang Tourism Administration on a few scenes that we planned to shoot there. The secretary of Director General who received us was not quite enthusiastic. "Director General is taking a nap now. Please wait here for an hour." With these words, he went to attend his own matters and left us alone. An hour later, Director General finally appeared. Luckily, our negotiations process about the TV play went very well.

After *The Smiling, Proud Wanderer* was aired, people learned about Xinchang from the TV play and found Xinchang was a good place for tourism. As a result, the tourist income of Xinchang County turned over dozens of times. In the follow-up trips there, Zhang Sir basically could do whatever he wanted to do.

The West Lake Summit

In July 2000, Jack Ma had a meeting in Hong Kong, and afterwards he met with Mr. Louis Cha at the Yung Kee Restaurant. Louis Cha wrote on paper with a pen "Years of spiritually attracted, feeling like old friends at the first meeting" and gave it to Jack Ma.

Before seeing Louis Cha in person, Jack Ma had already worshipped him somewhat like a god. Citing from Wei Xiaobao's (a character in Mr. Louis Cha's novel) frequently used sentence, it would be "like the roaring Yangtze River, running endlessly; also like the flooding Yellow River, totally unstoppable." This, we can see from the offices he named for Alibaba. To outsiders, Alibaba was like a holy land of martial arts. Names such as "Bright Summit," "Dharma Temple," "Peach Blossom Island," "Hall of Arhats," "Mansion of the Virtuous" and so on, all came from Mr. Louis Cha's novels. Even the toilets were renamed "Hall of Raindrops" and "Waterfall Pavilion."

There were many swords on display in Jack Ma's office, and two prop swords of Dragon Spring Sword given by Zhang Sir were among them. Believe it or not, he would carry those swords and move them to each of his working office. Formerly they were placed in his office of Alibaba and later placed in his office of Taobao. Sometimes, he would carry the shining swords and stroll about in the company. In this regard, I often teased Jack Ma as a man from the Jianghu "who never parted with his means of making a living."

One weekend after Jack Ma's return from Hong Kong, my friends and I were drinking tea in a farmhouse in Wengjiashan of Longjing and Jack Ma's name came up during our casual chats. Jack Ma was then already a minor celebrity in Hangzhou. I called him on the phone, "Mr. Ma! We are drinking tea in Longjing, join us for dinner? There are six beauties here..."

Jack Ma had no engagements that day so he did join us. No sooner had he arrived than he began to boast what he had seen and heard during his trip to Hong Kong, including, of course, his meeting with Louis Cha. We talked into the late night with delight. When Jack Ma proposed his idea of holding an Internet Summit in Hangzhou, the girls were also intrigued and came up with random plans. Perhaps the ideas of "the West Lake Summit" and inviting Louis Cha to be the judge had been on his mind before, but I've always stubbornly believed that these ideas all were brewed out that day.

Jack Ma later assigned me with the tasks of selecting the venue for the West Lake Summit and booking the pleasure boat and other things; he even granted me as the supernumerary staff member of Alibaba − "working eight days a week and getting paid on the 32nd of each month."

On September 10, 2000, the West Lake Summit was held, attracting thousands of netizens and hundreds of media across the country. The theme was

"New Century, New Economy, and New Internet Heroes." In addition to the then thriving five Internet heroes of Wang Zhidong, Ding Lei (William Ding), Zhang Chaoyang (Charles Zhang), Wang Juntao and Jack Ma, the spotlight was of course on Louis Cha. It was an Internet economic forum having little to do with martial arts heroes, but with Jack Ma acting as a go-between, the forum was fully seasoned with heroic flavor. What's more surprising though, was that even Louis Cha said he was a layman to the Internet; yet the five entrepreneurs participating in the forum were all his fans. It was said that Wang Juntao came to the summit just to get a close look at his idol Louis Cha and it was also said that Wang Zhidong's twin daughters were named by Louis Cha...

During the West Lake Summit, Louis Cha came to visit Alibaba and wrote a scroll for Jack Ma − "Making the best use of talents is the gist of success for great leaders and also the reason for Liu Bang and Liu Bei's accomplishments of the great course. May Jack Ma always be inspired by it." Mr. Louis Cha's calligraphy was unconstrained and at ease, a wonderful work with the demeanor of a great master.

The two big and small inscriptions of Louis Cha given to Jack Ma are still hanging in Jack Ma's office at the West Lake International Building today.

The West Lake Summit was a great success and later became a tradition. Every autumn, the Internet's elites will hold a summit at the West Lake. It is a changing world. Each year the names of the distinguished participants would change, but all of them were the leading figures of the industry.

On the National Day of 2000, *The Smiling, Proud Wanderer* finished the shooting. Zhang Sir invited the role players.

When I asked why Zhang Sir didn't invite Jack Ma to this holiday in Hangzhou, he replied, "I am still mad with him about the "West Lake Summit"! And I will continue to be so till the end of the year."

Initially, besides inviting Louis Cha to be the judge and to boat on the West Lake eating crabs, Jack Ma also intended to invite the creative list of *The Smiling, Proud Wanderer* including Zhang Sir, Li Yapeng and Xu Qing. But, later because the boat was not big enough, he had to invite Louis Cha only. "I've informed Yapeng and the others," apparently Zhang Sir was still upset, "We all have rescheduled our time to reserve this."

During this vacation, Zhang Sir mentioned the novel *Father Going to the Town* by Shi Zhongshan on more than one occasion. Each time when he spoke of it, he was moved to tears. He was determined to make it into a TV series. Zhang Sir and his wife liked my 5-year-old son very much and decided to let him play a part in the play. "Dad, don't tell anyone about it. I still don't know how to sign my name yet!" My son whispered in my ear.

By the end of the year, the novel *Father Going to the Town* (later renamed as *Years of Burning Passion*) with only 50,000 characters was adapted to a 22-episode TV script by the scriptwriter Chen Ping. Zhang Sir was very satisfied after reading the script. "You're my angel," he would say playfully to Chen Ping from time to time.

At the end of 2000, *Years of Burning Passion* was put into action. Zhang Sir asked my 5-year- old son to play Shi Xiaolin, the grandson of Shi Guangrong.

"Daddy, am I somebody now?" My son asked me.

"Yes, absolutely."

"Better than Uncle Jack Ma?"

Undoubtedly, after the West Lake Summit, Jack Ma has become a known celebrity in Hangzhou.

The Impact of Louis Cha's Plays

In 2001, *The Legend of the Condor Heroes* kicked off. I took Zhang Sir and Li Yapeng to the Longjing Teahouse while on their stop in Hangzhou.

Under the influence of Jack Ma and Zhang Sir, I also became a swordsman-like and even taught a lesson to the owner of the restaurant; changing the menu into the "Secret Recipe." I also especially taught the chef two dishes − Invincible Nine Swords (fried mushrooms with nine tender tips of bamboo shoots) and Eighteen Palms of Subduing a Dragon (steamed eel circled by a round of duck's feet).

It was the time after Zhang Sir's wrath "duration." Jack Ma was with us that day. "Why the Eighteen Palms of Subduing a Dragon has only eight palms? Take mine as the rest 10," Jack Ma said after seeing the dish.

Just like Zhang Sir, Louis Cha was also especially fond of Hangzhou, and he was also keen on farmhouse cuisine.

In the autumn of 2001, the sweet osmanthus were everywhere in Hangzhou City and especially vigorous in the rural areas. It was a sunny day. I accompanied Louis Cha and his wife and Zhang Sir to Meijiawu. I called Jack Ma and he soon came with the first COO of Alibaba, Savio (Guan Mingsheng). Savio was a fan of martial arts too. "You know why I am popular with the company in Hong Kong? Because I have read repeatedly each of the series you wrote in the newspapers and even clipped them out and made them into a book. I share the martial arts stories with my colleagues whenever there was an opportunity," he said respectfully to Louis Cha, who laughed happily.

That day Jack Ma stayed with us for dinner. We still bickered as usual while eating. Louis Cha and Zhang Sir seemed to enjoy listening. Sometimes, I would go too far. And Jack Ma would take out his trump card, "One day as a teacher, a life as a...?"

A Single Word Worthy of a Thousand Ounces of Gold

In 2005, Alibaba acquired Yahoo China. To promote Yahoo Search, Zhang Sir offered a suggestion saying "BMW's global advertising was to choose different companies to complete different plans and to interpret them using the same actors and eventually air them at the same time. You should make reference to this model."

In early 2006, Jack Ma joined hands with Huayi Brothers and invested 30 million *yuan* to make a video commercial with the theme "Yahoo Search." Three Chinese famous directors Chen Kaige, Feng Xiaogang, and Zhang Sir were invited to this program. Hence, the crews began a zealous creation on Yahoo ads. As a major creative person in "Zhang's version," I was assisting Zhang Sir with the shooting of the *Sword Stained with Royal Blood* in Xiangshan. So at each meal, we'd make up stories and raise heated discussions, meanwhile enjoying ourselves.

Though I was part of the creation team for the final version of the story called *Previous and Present Life*, I think the rejected ones tell a better story. Among which, there was *Love in Three Lives* written by me. The synopsis is: first life — in ancient times, a pair of lovers become separated in the warfare. The man later becomes a general. He sends his men to post the woman's portrait everywhere, until his hair turns white... Second life, time in the Republic of China, in a ship travelling far way, the man spots the woman in the crowd. But when their eyes catch each other, the ship is offshore. Later the man posts a search notice in all kinds of newspapers looking for his indescribable lover in his previous life... Third life, modern city, the man and the woman stand back to back on a subway train. The woman gets off from a stop, but when she turns her head and sees the man, the train is already moving...desperately she gets home. Just then her doorbell rings. She opens the door. The man appears at the door with a smiling face and a bunch of flowers. Then comes the voice-over − "No more missing this life - Yahoo Search!"

I went to Jack Ma for his support on my ad planning. "Everyone thinks his plan is the best. It won't be appropriate for me to give comments. Since I leave it to Zhang Sir, then let him decide." Jack Ma so told me.

Eventually, my idea was cut by Zhang Sir. He chose the version *Previous and Present Life* that was later released to the public. The content of the advertisement is: an ancient archaeological worker often dreams of a beautiful woman being pushed off a cliff. One day he is informed that a Tang dynasty mummy was unearthed and hurries to the site to examine it. Finally through a piece of jade pendant, he realizes the mummy is the Tang dynasty beauty that often appears in his dreams. In the previous life, the archaeologist fell in love with this beautiful lady. But her elder sister pushed her off the cliff out of jealousy; in present life, the elder sister is still the wife of the archaeologist. The archaeologist manages to return to ancient times and stops the murder and thus changes the cause and effect. When he goes back to the present, his wife has turned to the younger sister.

The advertising commentary also took a lot of time. The line I came up with was "Our searching idea (sounds the same as "bad idea" in Chinese) will give you the effects (sounds the same as "make you smile" in Chinese)!" Everyone thought it was well versed. Zhang Sir was also very pleased with it. Soon however, an incident occurred. We found a lot of light box ads were using the same pun. This idea had been adopted by others. As a result, we had to come up with new ones.

Eventually, Zhang Sir decided to use the advertisement I wrote − "Just as I wish, with a mere snap of the fingers − Yahoo Search!" After that, I was considered to be a "cultured" man by the crew. To this end, Zhang Sir even paid me a handsome tens of thousands *yuan*. Therefore, I also experienced the luck of "A single word is worth a thousand ounces of gold" in my life.

One day during the commercial shooting, Jack Ma called me and said that he had just been to the Guest Room Sina. Together he was interviewed with an actress named Ma Su, who knew a considerable amount about him. After asking, Jack Ma learned that she gained the knowledge through me. Because Ma Su played "An Xiaohui" in our TV play *Sword Stained with Royal Blood*.

"Hong Ma (promoting Ma) is my duty." I said.

"Hong Ma?"

"Promoting you, CEO Ma!"

"Ha-ha! This is good. Go on promoting, go on." Jack Ma laughed out loud.

Interlaced Rivers

In August 2005, we started the preparation for the TV series *Sword Stained with Royal Blood*. Jack Ma told Zhang Sir that besides Feng Qingyang, Mu Renqing was also a martial arts master that he admired. He asked Zhang Sir to reserve the role for him so he could star in person.

Maybe Jack Ma was just kidding, but Zhang Sir took it seriously and asked me to see to it.

Now and then I would text Jack Ma tempting him with various kinds of funny things during the shooting. I even warned him that this was his "only once in a blue moon" chance. But, in the end, Jack Ma did not come to play the part. "In fact, I am dying to play it, but Zhang Ying does not agree no matter what," he said.

Jack Ma did not get to play "Mu Renqing," but still he visited us in Xiang-shan.

It was the Sea Fishing Festival that day. Jack Ma and several staff members from Alibaba came to visit the crew and then went sea fishing with everyone to "China's easternmost coastal island" via a big speedboat.

We had to have lunch on the isolated island with nothing available. We only brought pans, stoves, and fresh water. We'd eat whatever we caught from the sea or we would suffer from hunger.

Everyone thought it was fun and very challenging.

The one who caught the biggest fish of the day was the Director of the local Tourism Administration while Jack Ma fished the most. Xie Shihuang, the one mostly obsessed with fishing in Alibaba, performed just average. Xie was one of the Alibaba's 18 founders. His dream was to fish all over the world.

Once he went to Australia for a vacation. Instead of travelling around, he just stayed in the same place and fished for five days! Hearing this, I really couldn't wait to give him a good beating. His fishing was too extravagant.

It took over an hour for the trip to the island by speedboat. So on the way coming and going we played "Fight the Landlord," a card game.

A famous entrepreneur went along with us. He was very enthusiastic with card playing claiming himself a very talented card player. Soon after he learned the basic ropes, he was "invincible in his company." Unfortunately for him, after a few rounds, only he lost. He couldn't even win with five rounds of "bombs" (a set of cards gaining the player great advantage in this game) in his hands.

He just couldn't figure it out and became very depressed. He was still wondering after we got off the boat and even after half an hour's car travel to the hotel. He asked, "Jack Ma, in the last game, if I bombed the three '2' of yours, what would've happened?"

Jack Ma patted his shoulder and answered earnestly, "It has nothing to do with the bombing. The key point is that today the players were not your employees. Have you ever heard the story? The next day after the retirement of the director, all his 'strengths' suddenly disappeared, such as bridge, Go chess, table tennis, Chinese chess... That's because no one humors to him anymore, ha-ha!"

For several years during the Spring Festival, Zhang Sir would take Li Yapeng, You Yong and others to visit Hangzhou. One of the essential "highlights" was to inspect real estates with Jack Ma. They never seemed to be bored with it. They would go to any place recommended by people, Peach Blossom Spring, Fuchun Resort...

These real estates were still under construction. At Spring Festivals the construction workers would take leave. We would sneak over the wall to get into the properties and see real samples; by the end of the day we would be covered with dust. Everyone had different opinions. For example, some felt Peach Blossom Spring was good and bought it later. "It's too remote. This place has nothing to do with Hangzhou," You Yong said, disapprovingly.

Jack Ma sometimes would take the backbones of Alibaba to the hotels lodged by the stars and let them take pictures and chat with the celebrities as a bonus for their hard work.

Jack Ma has always been a witty person. He often teased the stars after becoming familiar with them. Once a star said, to build up his body, little by little he could bathe in cold water in winter. "That's nothing fancy. If you keep on warming up, eventually you can bathe in boiling water, and my friend, that is something!"

One year, Jack Ma won the title of "Top Ten Zhejiang Economic Figures." Zhang Sir was invited to issue the award to Jack Ma. Prior to the award ceremony, Zhang Sir was thinking about the prize-giving speech while having dinner with a group of friends. Everyone there gave their opinion vigorously. Eventually Zhang Sir took mine. "(the) Internet industry is crowded. The reason for Jack Ma to stand out is because he has a good body shape..." The next day, the joke was headlined in all major newspapers in Hangzhou.

In 2006, the scenes of Yangzhou for *The Deer and the Cauldron* were all shot at the Tide Resort Yanguan. Since it was so close to Hangzhou, during the shooting we all came to Hangzhou to attend Jack Ma's birthday party. Jack Ma also visited the crew one night and he had to share the same room with Zhang Sir because the hotel was full. The next morning, he even played a round of golf with Zhang Sir.

By then the two had just learned the basics of golf and were very keen on playing, so they made a bet — the loser would cup his hands and bow to the winner, calling out "master" three times. I can remember three of their bets and every time Jack Ma won with a small margin. Zhang Sir was very upset at this!

Jack Ma was not only witty, but would also raise some brainstorming questions for others from time to time at gatherings. When others gave the wrong answers or scratched their heads, he would rock with laughter and kick up his heels. There were plenty of topics, but I just remembered two of them:

One: The soldiers took down the village and held all the villagers captives. Everyone had to walk on the bridge. In the middle of the bridge, each one had to speak a sentence. If they lie, they would be beheaded. If they tell the truth, they would be thrown off the 50-meter-high bridge with no water but rocks below. What would you do if you were in that situation?

Two: There are three lights in a room. There are 3 corresponding switches outside the room. You have to turn on the switches outside (You can't see the lights inside) and then enter the room. How can you determine which switch corresponds to a certain light?

You may think these questions are quite simple today. But when they first appeared, they were not so easy to answer.

If we say Zhang Sir's brushwork was "bad," then Jack Ma's was "worse." Once, a Chinese Chess Championship game was held in Ningbo. Zhang Sir and Jack Ma were invited to attend the opening ceremony. At the entrance, everyone was required to write something with ink and brush. Jack Ma took great care and wrote several terrible characters. He couldn't even bear the horrible sight himself, so he signed "Zhang Jizhong" below. Then he rewrote some more but failed to turn the tide. This time he entered without signing a name. After a while, Zhang Sir cried from behind, "I didn't write this. Why sign my name under such ugly writing! I know, it must be Jack Ma!"

Zhang Sir actually admired Jack Ma very much in his mind. Once, Zhang Sir was invited to have a panel discussion. Cadres there hoped he would create a TV play that could reflect the pioneering spirit of the Hangzhou locals. The script had already been in creation. At that time the head of the Hangzhou Writers' Association was a lady. "In the reform and opening up, Hangzhou marched in with windy speed and with a sunny attitude," she said. "Hangzhou already has the best example, Jack Ma! If the script is written as marvelous as Jack Ma's venture, I definitely will take it," said Zhang Sir.

Chapter 4:
Alibaba, Here I Come!

In March 2008, my 93-year-old grandma passed away. I was raised by my grandmother from childhood. My most distant memory is, when I was five years old, my grandma taught me to guess riddles. At the funeral arrangements, seeing my parents' grey hair fluttering in the breeze, immense pain and helplessness seized my heart. My aging parents reminded me of an old adage – "When your parents are alive, do not travel far."

I didn't return to the casting crew since then.

Later, after I slowly recovered from my grief, I went to Jack Ma's house. To this day, I became an assistant to Jack Ma.

New Assistant, New Start

April 3, 2008 was my first day to work at Alibaba. I donned my suit that had been safely kept for many years and went to Hohhot via a corporate jet arranged by the Chia Tai Group with Jack Ma and the company president Zheng from the Shanghai Branch of the Chia Tai Group. On the plane, president Zheng told me that president Xie from the Chia Tai Group once heard Jack Ma 's speech in English and was full of admiration for him. He insisted that Jack Ma attend the meeting held in Hohhot this time and ordered his two sons to pay a visit to Alibaba as soon as possible.

Our first stop in Hohhot was the Jokhang Temple where there were abundant and numerous Kangxi's stories. Throughout the visit, we deeply felt Kangxi's greatness and wisdom — to lead an alien race, one should respect their culture first. Jack Ma was very interested in history. From time to time he'd ask the guide about some confusing historical events and would sink into deep thought hearing the tour guide's explanation, over and over again.

Subsequently, Jack Ma, president Xie of the Chia Tai Group and the head of the Mengniu Dairy Group held a meeting together and discussed the issue of the construction of a "new socialist countryside."

After dinner, we returned to Hangzhou in the same jet. On our way back, president Zheng told us that Chia Tai was also engaged in the electronic industry in addition to the fodder and breeding industry among many others. He also told us that China's annual pig slaughter was around 650 million head. "Seriously, so many? Fortunately for us, pigs are our food. In opposite situation, Chinese people will be eaten up by pigs in two years," Jack Ma exclaimed in surprise with eyes wide open.

I later made my calculation, taking the size of a pig as only one meter in length, the pigs slaughtered each year in China alone could cover the terrestrial equator in 16 laps if connected from head to toe! It suddenly reminded me of the words said by a Jewish-American writer, Isaac Bashevis Singer (Izaak Zynger), "People often say that humans have always eaten animals, as if this is a justification for continuing the practice. According to this logic, we should not try to prevent people from murdering other people, since this has also been done since the earliest of times." Each livestock farm is a concentration camp of other animals built by humans, as far as I am concerned.

Humans have "no choice," but cannot be "at ease." Humans are the best animal of all animals, as well as the most ferocious beast of the beasts. I don't think "vegetarianism" is solid as stone either. What if in a decade, science proves that plants are more painful than animals when being harmed, what shall we do? This isn't making any sense!

"How am I to compare with you? You are still a young fellow!" I heard this often from Zhang Sir when I was with the casting crew. So for a long time, being young was my capital of pride. But after I joined Alibaba, this pride was gone. With me, Alibaba Group's average age was forcefully pulled up to "Numerous" years. I always felt guilty over this.

In the middle of April, 2008, Jack Ma returned to Beijing from Europe. We took time to see two building projects developed by Guo Guangchang in Beijing. President Guo came out from philosophy profession and his taste was quite distinctive. The balconies of one of the buildings were made of copper and were rusted greenish. Guo said this was the highlight of the building, the longer the time, the greener it would be and the more beautiful it would look as a result.

The rooms inside were not spacious and that the hallways were wide. We thought this was little wasteful. But Guo had a set of theory of his own, that good life is always wasteful. Great minds never think the same as the common mind does.

On April 29, Jack Ma hurried along from Beijing to the Langfang ENN Group. At this meeting, I saw Liu Chuanzhi, Wang Yusuo, and other famous entrepreneurs for the first time. At the buffet lunch, Zhang Ying called to ask about Jack Ma's appetite. I told her that Jack Ma didn't eat much. "That's because Chen Wei brought me the food he loves!" Jack Ma "refuted."

Well then, you can go to fetch on your own, I said to him. As a result, he came back with the same stuff. "Don't you think my fish is prettier than the one you picked for me?" Jack Ma just never yielded.

On May 5, we went to Hong Kong. B2B stocks had been listed for half a year. This was the first general meeting of shareholders. With the drastic drop of the share prices, we were worried that shareholders would complain. But it turned out to be just peaceful, because at that time all stocks were declining. After all, as the old saying goes "Can the eggs remain unbroken when the nest is totally ruined?"

After the general meeting of shareholders, Jack Ma and the leaders of listed companies had a dinner party in a restaurant in Hong Kong. The topic at the casual chat while eating was: What does a middle-aged man want exactly?

Everyone expressed their ideas, and finally it was my turn. "For a middle-aged man, the three things he wants most are promotion, wealth, death of his wife." I quoted a joke I heard long ago. Everybody burst into laughter except the only female executive present frowned to show her hopelessness for all men.

On May 8, I accompanied Jack Ma to Moscow for the ABAC conference (APEC Business Advisory Council). The conference site was set at the location facing Red Square just across the Moscow River.

May 9 was the anniversary of Russia's victory in the Second World War. As if drawn by a magnet, all the people flooded from all directions to the banks of the Moscow River to watch the parade at Red Square. In the evening, we arrived in St. Petersburg, where likewise, everyone went to the streets for celebration. Someone even distributed the replicas ribbons from the Second World War along the way. I also got one which is still in my possession. St. Petersburg is at high latitude, so the whole night was as bright as daylight.

After the victory of our battle against "SARS" in 2003, Jack Ma set May 10 as the company's "Ali Day," which is often scheduled with lots of activities. But there are two key events, the first is that the families of all employees can visit the company and dine there in addition to the "Ali Tour" guided by dedicated personnel; the second is group weddings with all the expenses borne by the company.

On the same day while we were having lunch at St. Petersburg, Jack Ma called back to the company wishing all the group wedding couples to live happily ever after. He also said jokingly, "As a country has its state laws, a family also needs family rules. All those who hold weddings in Ali, you should have the determination to keep your marriage for at least 102 years. This has to be consistent with the company."

This was the agenda for me as the assistant of Jack Ma in the first month. I don't have the habit of keeping a diary, but I do note down the memorabilia. Looking back now, every day is still vivid in my mind. My new life, totally different from the past, began like this.

The Jack Ma Sensation in Bo'ao

On April 11, 2008, a delegate of five people of the company went to Hainan for the Bo'ao Forum for Asia. When we reached Bo'ao, it was already late night. Wang Shuai lost the admission card on the way and we were all kept out. It took nearly an hour to make up a new one. By the time we checked in, it was already after midnight.

Wang Shuai, former senior vice president of Alibaba, Chief Brand Officer (CBO) of Taobao, and General Manager of Yahoo China, now serves as the Chief Marketing Officer of the Alibaba Group. Rumors had it that he was very gallant in the battle field of public relations and was a trusted fellow of Jack Ma. But at the same time, he was also a "model" of defying trivial conventions! In the company, it was known to all that "Wang Shuai not shuai" and "Lao Lu not lao" (in Chinese "Shuai" and "Lao" respectively have the same pronunciations of "handsome" and "old") just like the saying "Long Bridge not long" and "Broken Bridge not broken" known in Hangzhou. Lao Lu referred to the former President of Taobao, Lu Zhaoxi (now CEO of the Alibaba Group). His Taobao ID is Temujin, but we all called him Lao Lu anyway. Of course, as stated above, Lao Lu actually was not at all old. As for Wang Shuai, every time I saw him I would think of the poem Chairman Mao wrote to Ding Ling — "Who can be compared to her slender pen? With Mauser-rifles three thousand picked men!" Was he really handsome (shuai) or not was just a matter of opinion. But no doubt that he is the thinnest tall man I've ever seen.

As a prominent figure of the PR department, Wang Shuai was excellent in literary talent but had terrible eloquence. People not familiar with him might be surprised at the latter. Some often complained to me they had no idea what Wang Shuai was talking about. But one would learn his tenacity after a long association.

I personally think that Wang Shuai's achievements today were mainly built on his worship to Jack Ma. Yes, Jack Ma is worshipped by many, but Wang Shuai topped them all.

Many times when I accompanied Jack Ma on his business trips to Beijing, I would hear Wang Shuai calling Jack Ma late at night. Each time he would call after being drunk with incoherent speeches and no specific contents either. Freud once studied "Interpretation of Dreams." Should he move on and continue the study of "Interpretation of Drunkness," he would undoubtedly conclude like this: The first person that comes to his mind when he gets drunk must be the most important one in his life — the one he worships, the one he loves secretly or the one he hates.

The tasks Jack Ma assigned to Wang Shuai were never "concrete," but were specific principle wise; first of all, be honest and second, do not buy media.

Before I thought it was nothing unusual. But now I've learnt how wise he was! I understand now that a wise man is someone who never plays smart. Think about the milk sellers these few years. This really goes with the saying "time tells no lies," now the dairy makers are not so daring and Ma is the actual smart one.

During the Bo'ao Forum, the center of the "focus" was Jack Ma and Jet Li (Li Lianjie). The passage way of dozens of meters would often take a long time to cover, packed with people who wanted to have signatures and group photos, even at meal times.

Jack Ma's speech was full housed. His talk would be interrupted by applause and laughter every few minutes. After his speech, former US Secretary of State Colin Powell came to him to show his appreciation and to talk with him.

Powell's speech also won Jack Ma's admiration. He later frequently referred to the three points on leadership mentioned in Powell's speech, namely "Train him. Remove him. Fire him."

On April 13, President Hu Jintao came to Bo'ao and granted an interview to Jack Ma and other youth leaders.

Before the meeting, the youth leaders were concentrated together. "I grew up watching your movies." Jet Li whispered to Jack Ma what people would say first to him when they met him.

"Oh my goodness!" Li said, "Many of the people saying this are older than me. To them this is their best way to show admiration, but this is also the one I hate listening to the most. But I'm getting used to it now, ha-ha!"

During the meeting, we also dined with the founder of a famous website. To break the ice, the founder first told us a joke. But we just looked at each other after hearing it because it made no sense.

Then he started to criticize the film *Lust, Caution*. Was it necessary to manifest lust for such a long length of time in a movie? He questioned.

To this, I held a different view. "I'm afraid you didn't get the point of the movie. Ang Lee always tries to explore human nature in his movies. By which, he intended to convey the idea that to invade one's soul, other than faith, religion, or drugs, sex may also be adopted. Women are the animal whose skin directly shoots through to mind."

"I agree with Chen Wei. In truth, I like Ang Lee very much," said Jack Ma.

After I got back to Hangzhou, I posted an article *The Jack Ma Sensation in Bo'ao* on intranet and later was brushed to the home page.

Originally, the home page was for the company's news, such as "such-

and-such leaders came for a visit, accompanied by so-and-so" and so on. But, my articles were different; for instance, the inset photo was the back of Powell with a description like this — Jack Ma is standing facing Powell. We can't see him, but he tells us how to zoom out himself to win more space.

Two days later, Jack Ma and the then CEO of Alibaba Wei Zhe went to Nanjing. Upon returning, I posted another article titled *Nanjing Signal* on the front page. Jack Ma had gone to Europe at this moment. He deliberately reminded me from a phone call that I should not "entertain" the government in the style of entertainment circle.

I am an Internet Idiot

At that time, a project under Koubei.com was under close development at the "Revolutionary Site," the Lakeside Gardens. Speaking of the Lakeside Gardens, many people may only know it as the former residence of Jack Ma. Later it became the office of Alibaba when it was firstly founded. In 2003, when Taobao.com was under secret research and development, a team of a dozen individuals hid there for several months while working on the project. Later, the three-room apartment became the company's "Revolutionary Site." Should there be any new project, the revolutionary kindling would all be ignited from the Lakeside Gardens.

One day, a head of a project team of Koubei.com invited me to "guide" their work at the Lakeside Gardens. I was a little surprised. I'd been in the company for just a few days, how could I possibly guide them? They showed me the product they designed upon my arrival and humbly asked me my views about the product. I was very complacent and made a lot of suggestions I thought was important. Afterwards I got to know it was all arranged by Jack Ma, and the reasons of which wounded me deeply. Because prior to this Jack Ma so told them, "If we want to have more customers, we need to make the webpage extremely simple. It should be easy for any newbie to use it. Chen Wei is the only network idiot in our company. Ask him to see it, if he can understand, then the product is ready."

Later, I learned that this already counted as saving my face. "Take a look at the management personnel in the company, none of them grew by not taking their faces as mops to mop the floor. In so doing, you won't pretend to understand when you actually don't and you will come down to earth," Jack Ma revealed to me.

Since then, I announced to everyone I met that I was an internet idiot. As a result, all my peers vied to help me. Currently, at least I can type a few words.

The one who was responsible for the development project then was Brain Li (Li Junling), who later became the vice president of the Alibaba Group. He was acknowledged as someone in the group who knew best how to study. He had been skipping grades since childhood all the way to a PhD at Stanford University. Now I would introduce him as the classmate of the founder of Yahoo Jerry Yang (Yang Zhiyuan) and that the reason Jerry Yang did not finish his PhD was because he couldn't bear someone who constantly skipped grades and was much younger than him in the same class.

Brain Li served in many different departments. He loved whatever he did. In each of the departments he worked, he would say to me, "Chen Wei, this is the essence of the Internet." So if someone asks you what the essence of the Internet is, remember to answer this, the one that Brain Li is in charge of is the essence of the Internet.

Brain Li was often invited to do sharing. You could name any topic, but he had only one set of content. He had a principle of "three right turns is equal to one left turn." Name any topics you want, but in three sentences he'd shift it to the content he wanted to say.

My Job as Jack Ma's Assistant

As Jack Ma's assistant, the most important job is to accompany Jack Ma to attend various activities.

Apart from accompanying Jack Ma to attend meetings, go for inspections or receive interviews, I have another important job — to handle all Jack Ma's letters and parcels.

In the company, my daily "compulsory course" is to open all the letters to Jack Ma, answer strangers' calls, or "meet uninvited guests."

If I go with Jack Ma on business trips I will find letters piled into a hill when I returned.

I often joke with my colleagues saying that the most ridiculous thing one does in Alibaba is to write letters to Jack Ma complaining about me. Because all the "memorials to the throne" will eventually come to the hands of "Eunuch (me)."

At times, I will get phone calls, asking me excitedly, "Are you Mr. Jack Ma?" Jack Ma cannot remember his phone number, but he can remember mine. If he is ring-fenced outside, he will often hand out his name cards. And if people notice there was no mobile phone number on the card, some may ask for it. At this point, Jack Ma will give out my number which he remembered well.

Such text messages received are common like this, "Jack Ma, I'm the one who took the same flight with you to Hong Kong last week..."

A college student kept on writing letters on a weekly basis, more than 70 by now. His handwriting was pretty good. He kept on writing from college till he went to service. Since there was no contact information in the letters, all I could do was read his "weekly report."

Another letter:

"Jack Ma, I am pretty much like you. First of all, my name is also Jack Ma (Jack Ma)..." The letter was attached with an ID photocopy. Indeed, he has the same family and given name as Jack Ma.

Another letter:

"Jack Ma, I have the same experience with you. I have been teaching for five years, now I decide to be like you..."

More:

"Jack Ma, I have the same frustration with you. I've also taken three college entrance examinations. The different thing is that you were admitted the third year, but I wasn't ..."

More:

"Jack Ma, I have nothing, but I still decided to start a business. I would like to sell one of my kidneys to you. One is enough for me... Please trust me, 'Single renal entrepreneur' will become 'Invincible Swordsman' (Dugu the Invincible) in the future."

Some just directly wrote a receipt with a bank account. I remembered the highest one was written with over 60 million *yuan*.

Not long ago I also received a letter addressed as "asteroid named (Jack Ma)."

No. : 22××××

Diameter: 4 km

The current distance: 450 million kilometers from earth

Of course, there are also a lot of touching and sincere letters.

Such as:

"Hello, Jack Ma! I am Lin from Guangzhou Branch. Although I left Alibaba today and started my own business, I always think I am a member of Ali. The six values of Alibaba have been deeply rooted in my bones and blood and into my current company too... I hope one day my business can also become a company with socially responsibility like you said!... Finally I present you the cartoon bouquet I made with my own hands to express my respect for you..."

For some entrepreneurs' letters, I would give encouragement via text messages or emails. Actually they are all my idols. I sent them the sayings I heard from Jack Ma: "Never give up," "God help those who help themselves," "No excuses for failure, only to find grounds for success," and so on. They are my idols because I know they have far stronger minds than I have. I just passed the messages on. I can never strive to start a business as they did.

I recently received such a text message:

"Hello, Mr. Chen! I'm so and so. A year ago I took the liberty to visit your company. Thank you for your guidance then. I drifted too many places during this year. Now I'm back to Tianjin, and started a software company..."

Such texts delighted me most.

In addition, I, the "imperial idler," also take care of the reception work for a variety of visitors. Once, a woman came to our company. She was a customer of our "TrustPass (Chengxintong)." She "complained" that our "aliwanggwang" (an instant messaging software) could only hold 500 online customers at the same time and said that affected her business development. We had a lot of people talk to her and checked out her information too. She only had a total of more than a dozen customers. But she refused to leave and even spent three nights at the front desk. The guard also regularly bought her food. Eventually, we confirmed that she had a mental problem and had to call 110 (emergency phone number in China) to take her away.

Another time, an old man came to the front desk claiming Jack Ma as his adopted father. I thought his age could well be Jack Ma's adopted father.

Some people claimed to be "Jack Ma's friends." However, they later said that in fact their online stores were suspended because they sold fake goods or hyped their credibility, and they were unhappy. They would often add, "Other vendors' violations were worse than mine."

"You can tell me who they are. If what you said is true after verifying, we'll close their stores too. But, you can't rape someone because others killed someone and were at large, right? I think you understand the logic. What I can do is to review your case. If the punishment is too severe, we will reconsider."

One day, a young man came and said he was Jack Ma's nephew and wanted to see Jack Ma. I told him I knew Jack Ma's nephew. He called in after he had left the company, "I know the lot of you. If one bribes you with money, you'll arrange a meeting with Jack Ma. And for those who don't, you won't give them a chance."

Another young man came to the company and handed a letter for Jack Ma to the front desk. He said he would wait until Jack Ma came to meet him. He would also call Shi Yuzhu, Liu Chuanzhi, and others for a meeting to discuss the world economy. I then went to see him. "I've read your letter. First of all, let me make it clear, the current world's population is not 3 billion, but 6.7 billion. Let's take a look at the wrongly spelled words in your letter... It's good to have the whole world in view, but to come down to earth is more important."

Follies

Chairman Mao once said, "To do one good deed is easy, but to do good deeds and not a bad deed all your life is difficult." From which I extended to three layers of meaning: To do one right thing, not so difficult; always do the right things, not too difficult; never do the wrong things, extremely difficult.

In May 2008, I accompanied Jack Ma to attend ABAC conference in Moscow. I could understand Jack Ma's English. Of course, my English was taught by him after all. But when the foreigners spoke, especially when there was also a lot of jargon, I could not understand them at all. Even if I could hear a word, but by the time I figured out what it meant, the speech had gone two pages away. That morning, I walked out of the meeting hall after five minutes. I crossed the bridge and went to Red Square.

I stepped onto the gravel road of the 15th century and roamed in the haze of Red Square, and saw young men and women from different countries embrace like no one's watching. I walked by the reviewing stand of Battle of Moscow and imagined the stories of the Tsar generation after generation in the Kremlin. The Russian women whose waists were too broad to make an easy turn but still wore a smile on their faces were peddling Russian Nesting Dolls which you could never figure out how many nests...

Wondering in the Red Square condensed of the cost and blood of the changing history of Russia, I totally forgot I had work to do. By the time I went back to the hotel, it was already afternoon. During the intervals, I met Jack Ma. "Chen Wei, I seem to remember there are other arrangements today, yes?" he asked.

I suddenly realized that we have an appointment to meet the CEO and CFO of Russia's famous website Yandex at the hotel at 11 a.m. But I completely forgot all about it! I immediately put through Jack Ma's secretary in China to contact them and was told that they had waited at the scheduled place for an hour and left after we did not show up. I apologized again and again and finally they agreed to meet us again in their company, otherwise I really didn't know how to answer to Jack Ma.

On May 27, 2008, I went to Guangzhou with Jack Ma. After landing, I went to pick up the luggage and pulled out a similar black trunk and left. The security at the exit counter was practically functionless and I got out without trouble. Half way in our car, the airport contacted me after great effort and eventually through the booking record informing me that I might have taken the wrong luggage. How is that possible?! I opened the trunk and found it were all lady's stuff!

"Stupid!" Seeing this, Jack Ma commented with a smile.

"Luckily, the trunk was opened in the car. If it were opened in the airport and if the gossip journalists were present, they would say Jack Ma's luggage was inspected in Guangzhou Airport and it was full of women's supplies. They then would go nuts." Jack Ma said in jest.

Jack Ma mocked me, Wen Jia from the President Office, one of my best female friends who went with us to Guangzhou, also made fun of me for this matter along the way. Her return flight was one night earlier than ours. When I got to the airport with Jack Ma early the next morning, she was still there! She was pale and her hair disheveled. "It stormed all night. The plane didn't take off." I patted her shoulder with sincere sympathy but came up with an English expression in my mind — Justice was done!

When I worked with Zhang Sir in the past, we were "field workers," so we were all loud talkers everywhere. And the culture of the cast crew was the same. Loud speaking meant you were full of passion and loud answering meant you were confident to get the job done.

I didn't pay attention to this when I first got to Alibaba and often talked loudly or spoke on the phone with loud voice even next to Jack Ma. "Chen Wei, are you talking or thundering?! You're so loud! Many times I've turned my train of thought on your phone content," Jack Ma once said to me.

I then began to realize this problem, but it was "forceful and durable" just like the Ali culture.

Once in Guangzhou, Jack Ma was having a meeting with the concerned leadership about the first "Net Products Fair (NPF)" inside. I was waiting outside in another room. Just then, the "child prodigy" of the company Brain Li called me. Due to the bad reception, I had to talk even louder than usual. The leader inside whispered to his secretary, "Go and see who are quarreling outside." The secretary greeted me and reported back inside, "He is from Alibaba. It's not a quarrel. He is on the phone."

The leader said immediately, "Alibaba is really a company of passion. From the volume of the employees on the phone we can feel it!"

After several months, I thought I had overcome that bad habit. "Mr. Ma, am I better on the phone now?" One day, I asked Jack Ma in the car.

"Still very loud," Jack Ma replied.

This was not the end of the embarrassment about the phone. In order not to affect Jack Ma, when I was with him, I always mute my phone. But I sometimes forgot to set it back when we parted.

Once in Beijing, after the activity in the evening, Jack Ma went back to his room. I muted my cell phone and forgot to set it back. Jack Ma called me three times, but I wasn't aware. He called me around 11 o'clock, but I didn't notice it until 12:30. Can you imagine how I suffered at that time? If I don't call back, perhaps Jack Ma has been waiting for me; if I call back, maybe he just fell to sleep and will be woken up by me.

I struggled all night. But this was not the only time such things happened.

Zhang Ying would prepare face cream every time Jack Ma went on business trips. She bought them especially for Jack Ma when she went abroad and they were quite costly. Pity enough, they were all spread across the country by me. Because each time I did the check out for Jack Ma, I would forget to bring back the face cream. I would usually check only three things before we leave: computer, wardrobe, and safe box.

Once I took the initiative to admit my mistakes to Jack Ma: "All in all, I only make one single mistake, and that is keep on making mistakes. Each time I make a mistake I will put a brick on the ground and eventually we have the Great Wall."

Then there was another business trip to Beijing. Since we planned only one day, Jack Ma didn't check in his baggage. But I forgot and checked in my small suitcase which I could have carried with me. I realized I'd made another mistake only when we arrived at the Beijing Airport. While we were waiting for the luggage, Zhang Ying called to ask: "Where are you boys now?"

"Waiting for the luggage," said Jack Ma.

"But you didn't check baggage!" Zhang Ying said.

"Chen Wei did."

I just wanted to look for a hole to crawl into. Jack Ma's schedule in Beijing this time was very tight. We wouldn't probably make it on time even without waiting for the luggage. The 15 minutes waiting then was one of the longest wait in my life.

On September 27, 2008, the day when "Shenzhou VII" was launched, I accompanied Jack Ma to attend the Summer Davos in Tianjin. On the agenda there was a private meeting between Jack Ma and the British Minister at "the meeting room 3," or so I thought. So I took Jack Ma to the "meeting room 3" at the appointed time but only to find there were hundreds of people at the convention. I was sweating all over.

"Are you sure it is here?" Jack Ma asked.

"It's written in meeting room 3." I answered.

Jack Ma turned away and we found the British Minister at the third reception room.

"For such a grand forum, meeting room very likely is the reception room. Why would they arrange for us to meet in the large conference room?" Jack Ma said to me afterwards. "Please don't tell others that you've learned English from me, I can't afford to lose face," he added in jest.

There was a funny mistake. That day we were talking about Taiji with several entrepreneurs. I went to the bathroom in the middle of the conversation. A colleague sent an irrelevant message to Jack Ma using my mobile phone. Jack Ma texted back: "You do the talking."

I came back and saw Jack Ma's message. I thought he was tired and would leave me to do the talking. So I began to "boast" without hesitation.

"Why are you so excited today, Chen Wei?" Jack Ma asked me afterwards.

"Didn't you send me a message to ask me to do the talking?" I was confused.

When Jack Ma found out the reason, he burst into laughter too.

Writing down these follies today made me feel delighted. Because the "devils" hurt me deeply for time finally was "tied up" by me and became the "ingredients" of my "cooking."

In fact, everyone makes mistakes. But when you are not confident enough, you may not dare to disclose them.

Chinese ancients once said, "Sages, however wise, are human and can make mistakes." As recorded in *Life Realization (Shen Yin Yu)* by Lv Kun of the Ming dynasty: "Making a mistake is a mistake; not admitting the mistake is another mistake; admitting the mistake then there is no mistake, but not admitting the mistake makes it two mistakes."

Do you think Jack Ma has never done something foolish? Wrong. In November 2009, Jet Li invited Jack Ma to attend the "Global Philanthropy Forum" at the Marriott Hotel in Beijing. We rushed there from another activity. It was only five minutes before his speech when we reached the hotel and was impossible for him to change in his room. Jack Ma then strode to the washroom. Before he stepped in, I grabbed him from behind — he was pushing open the door of the Ladies' Room.

Two sentences suddenly came across my mind, irrelevant maybe, but I'd like to share them:

"God gives us youth, and pimples too."

"Materials won't die, because they never live."

To expose one's own mistake is actually a good way to improve oneself. For instance, when I am on the phone now, only the one at the other end can hear me. I can't even hear myself clearly. (Kidding)

Chapter 5:
Alier on the Rush

Jack Ma's business trips were highly frequent, far beyond my expectations when I took the job. Once, in a month alone, we went to Beijing four times. Every day the first thought after waking up was to figure out where I was.

Jack Ma was efficient in work. I've lost count of the activities he took part in and the people he met daily, so I can only pick a small part to share with you.

2008, the Hectic Year

On June 2, 2008, Jack Ma and I went to Beijing from Langfang. Previously, four senior executives of the company were informed to come to Beijing to join in Jack Ma's activity during the following two days.

On June 3, Jack Ma was invited to be the judge on the finale of *Win in China* held in Studio 1 of CCTV. Liu Chuanzhi, Niu Gensheng, Michael Yu (Yu Minhong), and Liu Yonghao participated in the program that day. I knew this studio for I took my son there for rehearsals every day for the 2003 Spring Festival Gala.

The entrepreneurs followed Wang Lifen backstage for simple makeup. Though it was not the first time for them to appear on the show, they still seemed reluctant to have makeup. Often you would hear someone say, "All right, come on!" or "So-and-so, you look so white, a bit like a eunuch! Ha-ha!"

"For the sake of the nationwide audience who will be seeing you, just put up with it," Wang Lifen said.

While waiting for the show, they sat together and had a very relaxed and casual chat.

Jack Ma was in his dark jacket with a stand-up collar that day, quite handsome! His comments were marvelous too, which you may find on the Internet. I was most deeply impressed by a comment by Jack Ma regarding the "sea turtles returning overseas." "Entrepreneurs, it's hard for a sea turtle returning overseas to survive without two or three years of freshwater aquaculture." (Domestic training – pun)

On June 5, Jack Ma went to see the then President of Peking University Xu Zhihong. Subsequently, Zhang Weiying showed the table tennis venue for the Beijing Olympic Games in the university. They decided to name the biggest lecture hall of Guanghua School of Management as "Alibaba Hall." "Even if Alibaba can't survive to 102 years, Peking University certainly can. In that case, the name Alibaba lives. Ha-ha!" Jack Ma said jokingly after the event.

That evening, Jack Ma made a speech in Guanghua School of Management.

The next day, Jack Ma made a speech again in the business school in another university in Beijing.

The four senior executives and I sat in the front row at Jack Ma's lecture. Wu Minzhi, the then vice president of 'TrustPass" business (now the CEO of Alibaba International Business Department) sitting next to me bent over to see my notes. She nearly burst into laughter as her notes were Jack Ma's management thoughts and ideas, while I wrote, "A pig, if it grows to 5,000 *jin* (2,500 kg), is no longer a pig..."

After we came back, I published *Classic Quotations of Jack Ma* on the intranet in which I recorded the words from Jack Ma's speech with annotations. Wu Minzhi texted me after reading it, "I get it now. You and I have different division of labor."

"A human's heart beats roughly 2.5 billion times in a lifetime and it never stops. Seemingly, it works very hard. In fact, the heart takes the best 'rest' among all organs, because it works for '0.1 second' and rests for '0.8 second' each time. It works when in contraction and relaxes when in expansion. So work and rest is very important. A man who works from morning till night moves fewer bricks than a man who moves them for half an hour and rests for half an hour," one day in June I said while chatting in Jack Ma's house.

Jack Ma immediately thought of the hard working employees in the company after hearing this. He was most compassionate for the colleagues at "TrustPass" and "Call Center." "We can use the heartbeat form for reference. I will talk to their leadership," Jack Ma said.

On July 30, 2008, I accompanied Jack Ma to attend the Y. Elites Group in Hong Kong.

Jack Ma never prepared written speeches beforehand, but usually he would take a piece of paper to write an outline 10 minutes before his presentation. Jack Ma sat in the front row that day, and I sat in the back of the venue. Less than five minutes before his lecture, Jack Ma suddenly texted me, "What was the quotation by Chairman Mao? About water, two hundred, three thousand?" I didn't know Chairman Mao ever said such a thing, so I rushed out of the venue and called Wang Shuai and was so told, "If I could live for two hundred years, I would swim three thousand *li*." I immediately sent this to Jack Ma.

The next day, this sentence was seen on every newspaper in Hong Kong.

Back in Hangzhou, I reviewed all the poems by Chairman Mao, from *Well* he wrote when he was at private school as a child "*The well is square, and surrounded by high walls. The water is clear and pebbles seen, with the little fish trapped in. Drinking only the well water, it can only grow for inches*" to his criticism of Guo Moruo in 1973 "*Stop blaming Qin Shi Huang, think over about the book-burning,*" but I didn't find the verse in any poems. Despite the fact that this sentence can be found on the Internet, but there was no source. Later I found it in the annotations of a book; In 1958, Chairman Mao made annotations for his poem created before. In making the note for "*Qin Yuan Chun, Changsha,*" Chairman Mao wrote, "I once wrote a poem, but I forgot it, just remember two lines: If I could live for two hundred years, I would swim three thousand *li*."

After I came back, I posted an article titled *Hong Kong Y. Elites Group Sidelights* on the intranet:

Hong Kong Y. Elites Group (Y. Elites Association Limited) was established in May 2007. Many of the backbones are the younger generation of noble families and great clans in Hong Kong. On July 30, Executive Chairman Jack Ma was invited to the Y. Elites Group Forum held in Hong Kong Convention and Exhibition Center and delivered a speech titled "Opportunity and Responsibility of the Youth."

*10 years ago, on the south bank of the Victoria Harbor, the Convention and Exhibi-
tion Center was built on the reclaimed land from the sea. It takes the shape of a "big bird"
facing toward the mainland. With its stretching wings, it implies that Hong Kong will fly
back to the arms of the motherland. Wandering at the edge of the Big Bird, I suddenly came
to a realization; Why should the main court of the Beijing Olympic Games be the "Bird's
Nest"? Why should the torch be an "Auspicious Cloud"? Because when the "Big Bird"
flies in the blue sky, it needs the guidance of the "Auspicious Cloud" and the place it yearns
for is the "Bird's Nest."*

*The forum was held in the "bird's head" and was presided over by the Deputy Man-
ager of Phoenix TV Sally Wu (Wu Xiaoli).Time flew, but her "charm" remained. And
her "size" was 1.2 times more of that which I first imagined. The first thing done when she
came onto the stage was the staff lifted the microphone up 15 cm higher.*

*Chief Executive Donald Tsang, Bo'ao Secretary-general Long Yongtu spoke one af-
ter the other. Experts in economic circles made speeches too and were said to be far-famed figures. Pity, I knew none of them.*

*Sally Wu is from Shaoxing, Zhejiang. So every time when she mentioned Executive
Chairman Ma, she would add a prefix "my fellow villager." Ma made the grand finale
speech, passionate and full of witty words as expected! Ma concluded by a verse from Mao
Zedong's poem - If I could live for two hundred years, I would swim three thousand li!*

*After his speech, Sally Wu said to Ma, "I was guessing what you would say after-
wards. But I guessed it wrong each time. Your thoughts are always beyond my expectations!"*

*One thing needs to be mentioned, from the airport pick up the first day to the end of
the event, there was a friend of Ma who accompanied him all the time. He was the handsome, amiable, Vice Chairman of Hong Kong Y. Elites Association Limited, Kenneth
Fok, the grandson of Henry Fok.*

Without manuscripts, yet full of witty remarks, Jack Ma's speeches had
long aroused the admiration and envy of many entrepreneurs. At the "Yunfeng Capital" conference in Nanjing, the entrepreneurs in the same bus talked
about this matter again. "I once prepped a draft, but I mispronounced six characters in a single page and was out of tune too. It was such an embarrassment.
So I stopped using drafts since," said Jack Ma. Hearing this, all the entrepreneurs burst into laughter.

In early August, in a party of small departments, I imitated the voice of
Lion Li (Li Yang) as a villain to represent the speech of Hitler when attacking
Moscow, in which most of the words were made up by myself. "Soldiers! Mos-

cow is just ahead. Stalin took us for granted. Just this morning, he was still holding the so-called military review in the Red Square. I can't promise he will see the sunrise tomorrow, but I can promise that the sun will be shining on his grave next year... Soldiers! To Moscow! To the Red Square, this will be the battle to end all battles!"

The next day, I accompanied Jack Ma to Shanghai. In the car, I took time to imitate for him. Jack Ma was very amused. "Ma, you can make it after a few tries," I said.

"You mean it?" asked Jack Ma in a very childish way.

"Absolutely!" I said.

"Soldiers…Soldiers..." Jack Ma kept on laughing while imitating, "I can't do this."

Jack Ma's taut nerves needed some "soldiers" to relax, I thought.

During the 2008 National Day long holiday, Jack Ma held a Taobao Executive Meeting in Xi'an. He took us to visit the historical sites during the day and invited local history professors to talk about the rise and fall of the Qin dynasty and the boom and doom of the Tang dynasty at night. Using the past to allude to the present and discussing the strategy of Taobao, we felt it very rewarding. Among which, Jack Ma had his own understanding about the allusion Wang Jian leading 600,000 troops to fight the State of Chu and tactfully releasing Prince of Qin's suspicions. "Prince of Qin was far more resourceful than Wang Jian. He didn't at all believe that Wang Jian wouldn't rebel because Wang Jian was so greedy in asking for rewards. Wang Jian wouldn't have the guts to rebel no matter how he wanted. Prince Qin had too many ways to counter him. The field of vision and level of those who wrote the history could only be up to that of Wang Jian, that's why the history record is such as this."

On October 17, I accompanied Jack Ma to listen to the lectures given by experts in Langfang. At that time, the oil price rose up to USD 147 per barrel and remained high since, exceeding the cost of "coal liquefaction." It is said that in the Second World War, Hitler once practiced "coal liquefaction."

On October 18, Jack Ma attended "The Chinese Lantern on Chang'an Avenue" – the opening ceremony of Beijing Yintai Centre, the tallest building on Chang'an Avenue, rising 249.9 meters high. In the evening, Jackie Chan, Lee Bingbing, and other stars were presented.

A highlight in the evening party was a Russian spider-man climbing the outer wall of the building. Due to the quick flood of the crowd to view this event, the traffic in Chang'an Avenue was paralyzed immediately. Police arrived soon and took the spider-man away.

"Haven't you communicated with the related department beforehand?" the entrepreneurs afterwards asked the man in charge of the activity.

"It's impossible to get permission for activities like this on Chang'an Avenue. So he could climb as high as he could. Take a look at the reports around the world, all the spider-men were taken away by the local police eventually."

Indeed, it made sense!

The next day, I accompanied Jack Ma to the headquarters of the Shanghai Fosun Group for a meeting. In the meeting, only Liu Chuanzhi was in formal wear. "I was informed to put on formal wear. But I am the only one in a suit. I asked them why, they told me that even the formal wear in Zhongnanhai has changed now," he complained at the meeting. All the delegates laughed, because all the attending entrepreneurs were old friends.

Later we went to dine at the City God Temple, and the food was served separately. In less than 10 minutes after I seated myself, a large sea cucumber was served. But before I could have a bite, Jack Ma answered a phone call and said urgent matters in Hangzhou needed his attention. He immediately stood up and said, "Move, back to Hangzhou now."

Later, every time we visited the City God Temple, I'd think of that sea cucumber I hadn't eaten.

On October 24, Jack Ma was invited to Henan. It was the first time for him and me to go to the cradle of the Chinese nation. It was already in the evening when we finished our work in Hangzhou. So we took the last flight and went to Zhengzhou. Jack Ma wanted to immediately check in the hotel and relax, but the local leaders had arranged refreshments and were waiting. It would be ungrateful to turn them down.

Leaders asked where Jack Ma would like to visit best in Henan. "Songshan Shaolin Temple and Chenjiagou (Chen Village, where Taiji started and prospered)." He answered just like any martial arts fan!

Because the next day Jack Ma would be heading to Beijing at the end of the activity, he didn't have time to go to the Shaolin Temple or Chenjiagou. But the organizers were so considerate that they specially invited Shi Yongxin, the abbot of the Shaolin Temple, to have breakfast with Jack Ma the next day.

Before breakfast the next day, Jack Ma and Shi Yongxin met in the hotel conference room. One was a most "swordsman-like" entrepreneur and one a most "business-like" "head" of martial arts sect. I forgot the content of their conversation, but I remembered the abbot saying, "No matter what others think, I'll try every means to promote Shaolin martial arts and culture to the world."

In the morning, Jack Ma made a speech at the Henan Youth Entrepreneurship Lecture Hall. The hot scenes were beyond expectations. The crowd was so huge that half the college students who came to hear him couldn't enter the Lecture Hall. After his speech, Jack Ma fought his way out escorted by dozens of police officers and students of the police school. We then went on our way back to Beijing.

As a result of this speech, I got pretty busy after I went back to Hangzhou. Letters and phone calls from colleges and universities across the country increased considerably and all wished Jack Ma could make speeches in their schools. Representative students in Shandong, Anhui and other places even directly came to the company to present an invitation. Since Jack Ma's agenda was too tight, I could only refuse them nicely and politely and hoped they could understand.

On November 7, I accompanied Jack Ma to Shanghai for the U.S.-China Internet Forum. I only remember the beautiful U.S. Consulate stationed in Shanghai said, "In Hangzhou, not far from Shanghai, Jack and his team have built the world's largest online B2B platform. Taobao has also become Asia's largest C2C website."

In early December, Hangzhou was not quite cold yet. I accompanied Jack Ma to Beijing. It was very cold at night in Beijing. "What's the temperature in Beijing today?" I asked the staff in the airport after landing.

"Three or four degrees Celsius."

"Oh, not too many degrees left." I intended to make a joke.

"Same as our stock, not too many bucks left." Jack Ma joked too. But then Jack Ma said very seriously, "But I won't do anything for investors to create a short-term rescue. I'll take whatever it needs to help the small and medium-sized enterprises to get through the cold winter. Sooner or later, the stock price will come back."

On December 6, the annual meeting of *Entrepreneur* was held in Beijing. I bought a newspaper for Jack Ma in the morning. The newspaper said that a duck was frozen in a lake in Beijing, with a photo illustration.

Jack Ma began his speech from the duck. "A picture of a silly duck appeared on a Beijing newspaper today. It was frozen in the ice on a lake. Apparently, the stupid duck did not expect this year's winter would be so cold. The ducks that were prepared went onshore beforehand and they are safe now... Likewise, the attack of a financial storm was not dreadful. The dreadful thing is we were not prepared... As I said the darkest period of financial turmoil is over now. Being unprepared is like "the silly duck" because we were unaware of the heavy clouds half a year ago, that was the most dreadful thing. The rainstorm is heavy, but everyone is aware of it now, so we will soon get better..."

At the dinner table, I suddenly heard someone calling me "Chen Ba (dad)." It was Zhen, a girl from a periodical office in Hangzhou. For the report of Alifest, she lurked around our company for half a month and even volunteered to do the hard work of "Angel."

Later, I got to know many people from her office. They would also ask me some questions about Jack Ma, such as "Jack Ma is becoming more and more handsome. Does he still claim that 'Appearance is in inverse proportion to IQ'?"

"Advance with the times. Jack Ma has now changed. He says, 'If being handsome is a kind of mistake, I am willing to repeat my mistakes.'" I replied.

"Is Jack Ma well? I always feel that he is getting thinner and thinner."

"Your pronunciation is not correct. The word is not pronounced 'thin (shou)', but 'handsome (shuai).' Listen, shi-wu-ai-shuai (handsome)."

"Jack Ma is more famous than singing stars and movie stars, causing a sensation where ever he goes," someone said.

"Still there is a difference. You won't recognize stars after they remove their makeup. But even though Jack Ma wears makeup, he still can be recognized," I joked.

"At the annual meeting, the entrepreneurs from other companies look older than the previous year, only Jack Ma does not grow old."

"In fact, Jack Ma grows, but not in age," I said.

They all laughed.

Guo Guangchang also helped to "take care of" Jack Ma during the meeting. When people rushed to take pictures with Jack Ma, he would cover him saying, "My company has bought Jack Ma's right of portrait. If you want to take pictures, please line up first and write out an invoice!"

One day, I said to Jack Ma, "Ma, I've summarized several points of your speech skills..."

"Do you think I speak with skills?" Jack Ma cut me off.

"Skills are integrated as part of the speaker; sciolists conclude them and then teach those who never will learn the skills." I explained. "Just like grammar, people become equipped with it during the process of growth, but someone concludes them and then teaches foreigners." Jack Ma smiled, neither shaking nor nodding his head.

On the morning of December 31, Lu Yongxiang, President of the Chinese Academy of Science (now vice chairman of the Standing Committee of the National People's Congress) came to visit with his men. Jack Ma showed them around. I was overwhelmed with a warm feeling seeing President Lu. He was the President of Zhejiang University when I studied there and my diploma also was stamped with his seal.

In the afternoon, the Lecture Hall of Jiangnan Club opened class for the first time. Jack Ma held the first lecture for the attending entrepreneurs.

That day Jack Ma also assigned me another task, hoping I could find him a good Taiji teacher in the coming year. Jack Ma wanted to resume his practice of Taiji. He also wanted to pick up playing Go again, but under the concerted opposition Zhang Ying and everyone else, Jack Ma thought "the opposition was rational" and gave it up.

In the evening, Jack Ma paid a New Year's call to employees of all subsidiaries. The employees were very excited to see Jack Ma himself and lined up to take pictures with him in turn. Many called back home saying, "I just had my picture taken with Jack Ma!"

In the evening, Jack Ma took the company's founders to the Yongfu Temple at Lingyin to ring out the old year and ring in the New Year.

The Yongfu Temple in itself is a peace and quiet place. In the winter night, it looked more ethereal. Listening to Master Yuezhen talking about Zen and Jack Ma about philosophy, we forgot the worldly worries and the fatigue from work. We gained peace in our minds and our souls were sublimed.

Happenings in 2009

On January 20, I accompanied Jack Ma to attend the award ceremony of the "2008 CCTV Chinese Annual Economic Figures" in the Beijing National Indoor Stadium. We had a buffet dinner in the stadium. One man who sat at the same table with me looked very familiar, oh yes — it was the gymnastics prince Li Ning. There was a very beautiful little girl, Lin Miaoke who sang at the opening ceremony of the Olympic Games. The party was put on air later. I was most impressed by an entrepreneur when he received an award, he so said in his speech, "A company should be raised like a son and sold like a pig." Sadly, the "pig" was not sold later.

On February 5, I went with Jack Ma to Qingpu, Shanghai for the Alibaba B2B National Meeting of Regional Managers. "Your dreams are my dreams — to buy a car, to buy a house, marry the one you wish to marry and work out those who don't want to marry... It is the 'old area' that puts me to sleep, but it's the 'new area' that puts me to sound sleep...," Jack Ma said at the meeting, wittily.

On February 17th in the afternoon, Jack Ma made a presentation at Telecom Engineering College of Beijing University of Posts and Telecommunications.

"I heard people say that Alibaba's success is merely based on Jack Ma's ballyhoo. How do you think about it yourself?" A student challenged Jack Ma during question and answer link.

My heartbeat quickened at this question.

"I do hope I have such power of ballyhoo, sadly I don't. Ballyhooing is to tell others things you yourself don't believe, but I have faith for what I am doing. So it is not ballyhoo, but a kind of faith!" Jack Ma responded.

Thundering applause was heard.

On April 25, 26, Jack Ma attended the 12th Huaxia Fellowship Meeting in Beijing.

As there was not much fun in the surrounding area, I sat in the meeting and even made some simple notes.

Some of the views from the attendees:

Liu Chuanzhi:

"PC industry is to twist water from a towel, or we may say, an industry wearing straw sandals."

"The key point is how to make the professional managers dedicate. Enterprise culture is to develop employees to have a sense of responsibility, to motivate them to do better and then encourage them to dedicate."

"Organizational structure decides whether an enterprise is diversified. Are there enough talents? Do the leaders have enough 'energy' resources?"

Liu Yonghao:

"For the 800 million farmers, 140 million of which are migrant workers in the cities, 60 million are engaged in small businesses. Large-scale hoggery owners are losing money because they can never compare with those 200 million farmers who take no account of the cost. As Chairman Mao put it, 'The key point is the education of farmers.'"

Chen Xiao:

"Wong Kwong Yu's (Huang Guanyu) accident will not affect Gome's operation. Gome's business model is 'affordable,' because its settlement cycle with the manufacturers is longer than the goods in the supermarket."

"Gome was driven to this change by Jack Ma, but that's not a revolution, only model improvement."

Feng Lun:

"Foreign companies can cook the dishes according to the recipes but they can't create recipes on their own."

Jack Ma:

"In running a business, one has to be both idealistic and romantic."

Guo Guangchang:

"Jack Ma is an aggregate of super idealism and super realism."

Pony Ma (Ma Huateng):

"I used to think search is the most perfect model for Internet. Now I feel every model has its cons."

A professor:

"In four years, the return of real estate is 8 trillion *yuan*. The loan is 3 trillion *yuan*, which can be paid back in 3 years, not risky at all."

A banking expert:

"In 1998, technically speaking, all banks in China were at the brink of bankruptcy and were sustained only by the strong support from the government resources. In 2004, banks were restructured. In two years after, most banks were successfully listed and then hence embarked in a smooth journey. Concept innovation is deeper-leveled than product innovation and technological innovation."

On May 15, Microsoft CEO Steve Ballmer came to visit with a delegation. Jack Ma and the heads of subsidiaries guided their tour.

In the afternoon, I accompanied Jack Ma to Guangzhou to attend the first "Net Products Fair (NPF)."

Early next morning, before NPF started, we drove past the venue and found there were long queues nearby. "What are these people doing?" Jack Ma asked. I said perhaps they were to participate in the NPF. Ma was surprised. "Really? Wow! So many people!"

The NPF began. Jack Ma, flanked by 20 security guards, struggled his way to the venue amidst cheers. As scheduled, Jack Ma was supposed to take 15 minutes inspection with local leaders. But in no more than five seconds after he came to a booth, it was crushed by the crowds swarming in. So the inspection had to be canceled.

In the afternoon, Jack Ma made a speech in the large conference room of the NPF themed on two aspects: "An important mission of net products is to eliminate profiteering. Do you think it makes any sense for a small leather bag to sell thousands or even tens of thousands of *yuan*? That money can afford a herd of cattle!" There was a round of cheers. "I want to remind internet businessmen to manage with integrity. Don't fraud or infringe, but create network products brand. We make records of all online transactions and we will keep them for 10 years, 20 years. So think it over. Network businessmen should have self-respect and be responsible for yourselves and your customers."

Before ending, Jack Ma had also put on his costume and played Taiji on the stage.

After the meeting I told Jack Ma that the leather bag of thousands of *yuan* was not made of cowhide. "Is that so? But I didn't say it wrong. I didn't say it's made of cowhide. I just said with the few thousand *yuan* we could buy cattle," said Jack Ma with a hearty laugh. His laughter is always very penetrating.

On May 22 in Shanghai, I went with Jack Ma to talk about future cooperation with the newly appointed Chairman Liu Shaoyong of China Eastern Airlines and learned many things about the company. "From now on, we can take the flights of China Eastern Airlines. I feel quite relieved after the talk with Chairman Liu. Ha-ha!" Jack Ma said after the meeting, as we never took their flights before.

At lunch time, Jack Ma and Shi Yuzhu dined together at the former residence of Chin-Jung Huang (Huang Jinrong). It was a very beautiful garden and the houses were full of antique appeal.

Shi Yuzhu is an entrepreneur I admire most. "Every entrepreneur can have a 'drastic rise and fall.' But only two have had a 'drastic fall and rise" in the world and they are Shi Yuzhu and Steve Jobs. The symbol of victory V is the 'drastic fall and rise' graph designed for Shi Yuzhu." I often said this during the internal sharing, which was actually to "brag" when I took out colleagues from different departments to dinners.

Jack Ma and Shi Yuzhu were in the inner room. Shi Yuzhu's assistant and secretaries were in the outer room with me. Shi Yuzhu's secretaries were the most beautiful secretaries and his assistant was the most robust I'd ever seen.

It was very casual as we dined at different tables with our bosses. "Xiao Wang, what's your full name?" I asked one of his secretaries.

"Wang Fei."

"Which 'Fei'?"

"The Fei of Faye Wong."

"How come you are named after a star?"

"Come on! When she was Shirley Wong, my name was already Wang Fei. Who's the copycat here exactly, Chen?"

Although each well-known entrepreneur has the resource to hire beautiful and capable secretaries, not all followed suit. I used to think that's because entrepreneurs being realistic and chose not to judge people by their looks. Now I realize it isn't that case but rather due to "helplessness." Some did not get permission from their wives, some felt embarrassed to say this with the recruiters, or so I guessed.

Most of the entrepreneurs' assistants were very young. I always thought I was the eldest among all. It was not until December 2009 did I realize it was not so. Shi Yuzhu returned to Zhuhai after being away for 12 years and all entrepreneurs went to celebrate. At the party, I met Cai, the assistant to the president of the Juneyao Group who was older than me. I finally felt some relief, because I hated to be the "No. 1." Cai was very eloquent and very sophisticated. He had been the assistant when Wang Junyao died at an early age in 2004.

Several assistants of Jet Li were Taiwanese brought up in the US. His former assistant returned to the United States for his MBA studies. His later assistant was called Xing who practiced martial arts with his Chinese teacher in the United States since childhood. His voices and tones were very much like those of Jaycee Chan (Fang Zuming).

"Your voice is like that of Fang Zuming. Were you told before?" I once asked.

"Fang Zuming? No idea."

"Jackie Chan's son, you know?"

"Oh, you mean Jaycee. I've never heard of his Chinese name," he said "Yeah, yeah, probably because we both speak Taiwanese mandarin."

On May 31, I accompanied Jack Ma for a dental check-up at the best private dentist in Hangzhou. It was the third time we went there. The dentist was a gentle and quiet, beautiful lady. She kept on saying that it was her honor to treat Jack Ma's teeth and the cost never really mattered. Later I texted her, "Doc Zhu, I dreamed of you last night. Is it the time for me to pay you?" She texted back, "No need. Come and pay me when I dream of you."

On June 8, George Soros came to Hangzhou. Jack Ma showed him around the company and then he gave a lecture to the entrepreneurs of Zhejiang Province at the Lecture Hall of Jiangnan Club.

Speaking of Soros, perhaps many Chinese would think of this word – "The Finance Monstrosity." In fact, it was a misconception about him, as that was only one side of him. He just played by rules. To put it in his way, he did nothing but to prick the "pustule" with a "needle" so you could know the defects of the set "rules of the game." He said he had warned another "famous" Jewish person, Alan Greenspan, several times before the financial crisis but he did not listen. Greenspan apologized to him after he had stepped down. In addition, George Soros is also a great philanthropist.

Jack Ma got to know Soros in the 2005 Davos World Economic Forum (WEF). During that time, Jack Ma found himself happened to hold the same views as Soros after hearing his analysis on the world economic situation. They became good friends after further exchange.

Soros' trip to Hangzhou this time was accompanied by his two sons. Jack Ma took them to the West Lake for sightseeing and arranged for them to stay at the Jiangnan Club that night.

On June 20, at the invitation of Professor Zhou Qiren, Jack Ma attended the MBA graduation ceremony of Peking University as the only extramural guest.

Before Jack Ma's presentation, Professor Zhou said, "We've set a topic for Jack Ma beforehand, but don't expect that he will talk accordingly. If sometime you hear Jack Ma make a speech based on the set topic, please believe me it is not Jack Ma, possibly a man who looks very much like him, even though it is rare to find..."

"Congratulations to you all! Congratulations to you for graduating from a great school, a school only second to Hangzhou Normal University..." Jack Ma started his speech like this and all the students guffawed. Graduated from Hangzhou Normal University, Jack Ma claimed it's the best school in each and every circumstance.

Later, I accompanied Jack Ma to New Delhi, India via Hong Kong. New Delhi Airport was livelier than Hangzhou Railway Station. We knew little about India, so we arranged two men from an international security company to pick us up at the airport. They didn't have the pickup card. I greeted them, and prepared to get in the car. Jack Ma was surprised. "Are you sure? How did you get to know them?"

"They have sent their photos to me prior to this. This is my job, boss." I answered.

India was very hot and very dry, 45 degrees Celsius on average. One of the securities was wrapped with a big scarf on his head, which made me hotter. Luckily, Jack Ma was thin and the hot weather didn't bother him much.

Alibaba was India's largest e-commerce site. After doing a series of promotional activities, we flew to another city in India. India's domestic flight was very small, with only one entry at the tail, a few steps from the ground. In the plane we found it was as hot as outside and we were told by the only hostess that the air conditioners would only be turned on after the plane took off. She suggested we use the safety guidelines to fan ourselves.

The plane finally took off. The weather was good but the plane was jolting terribly. As Jack Ma and Wei Zhe were all on board, I felt pretty safe.

At last we arrived at our destination. I saw many cars passing by with many people hanging outside the cars. But the cars just dashed forward.

Unfortunately, in New Delhi or other cities, we didn't find any Roti Prata to eat.

During our trip to India, Jack Ma and I went to a Chinese restaurant only to find all the staff, from waitresses, waiters, and the chefs were foreigners. I was afraid that the food there may not be authentic and suggested we eat elsewhere. The waiter sensed my doubt and said to us warmly in English, "We are not Chinese, but we do cook authentic Chinese food as our boss is a Singaporean Chinese, even though he's not here at this moment."

"Now that it is run by a Chinese, let's give it a try," Jack Ma said in jest. Indeed, the taste was quite authentic.

Before leaving India, Jack Ma bought several bags of local salt to bring home.

Bringing home salt from all over the world was a great hobby to Jack Ma, whether it is from Russia, Japan, or European countries. To Jack Ma, collecting brand watches, pens was far less interesting than collecting salt. When eating at Jack Ma's house while speaking of a country, such as Russia, Ma would cry out happily, "Serve Russian salt!"

When the salt in a saucer was brought on the table, Jack Ma would ask everyone to wash hands again and he would take the lead to dip a little salt with a finger and savor it in his mouth. The salt in each country varies little, but still tastes different by savoring. Tasting the salt of and talking about the country does make you feel different.

And dear readers, collection is actually a kind of temperament and interests which does not need to be proved by "breaking the bank." Even if your collection is ten thousand times the value of Jack Ma's "salt," so what? Why not learn from Jack Ma?

In early July, Jack Ma, Guo Guangchang and other entrepreneurs went to visit the North Pole without me. Jack Ma would tell some jokes to kill the boredom while onboard, though most of which he could remember only half of the jokes. I kept some of the stories for him and he would text me in a few words to find out. Usually I knew what he was talking about and would send back a few keywords to refresh his memory.

"Sometimes it was very boring. For a length of time, we would see nothing but a polar bear," Jack Ma said upon his return from the North Pole.

"Ma, it's worse for the polar bears. For perhaps your ship was the only one they could see in days," I joked back.

"True. They were more bored than us! Ha-ha!"

Jack Ma had his own way of putting it when it came to his poor memories about the stories. "I have a small head. But it comes with two major benefits: first, it racks faster. It racks two rounds while others are in their first. Second, it stores nothing. It's constantly emptied out. So, in the event that I were to be 'double-ruled' (shuanggui — a Chinese term for being detained for investigations), I would come up with nothing." He had so jested in a number of public speeches.

Jack Ma is very interested in history and increasingly so in recent years. Jack Ma often made associations with history in his discussions. Years of events in the history were not something he was good at, but there were exceptions. Once Jack Ma said "In 1069, Wang Anshi made political reform..." I thought he came up with just any year. So I checked it right away, hoping he was wrong so that I would have an opportunity to correct him. To my disappointment, Jack Ma was right.

Therefore, Jack Ma is not forgetful. It's just that sometimes he is good at forgetting.

Yu Dan and Jack Ma are good friends. Jack Ma was full of admiration for Yu Dan's memory and eloquence, saying "She comes up with long passages of prose without hesitation and her text messages are well-versed too."

On October 30, Yu Dan came to the Lecture Hall of Jiangnan Club in Hangzhou to give a lecture upon the invitation of Jack Ma. We went to a bar after the event. She was very forthright and claimed herself, "I the Gongzi (term used to address male in ancient China)." She often invited friends to go out to play. Most of the time, it was very thrilling. For instance, she would invite friends to enjoy the snow at places where it was more than 60 degrees Celsius below zero. Yu Dan equally admired Jack Ma and hoped he would attend every one of her activities. But Jack Ma failed to make it several times. "Gongzi Ma, if you dare to break another promise, in the future I'll say to all the people who break their promises "How can you be so Alibaba?" Yu Dan so said.

"Gongzi Yu, never again." Jack Ma apologized at once, cupping his hands.

Jack Ma also has another female friend, the hostess of *Win in China* Wang Lifen. Jack Ma had invited her to host or attend several large meetings of the company. In September 2008, one day at the Tianjin Davos Meeting (Only then did I learn that there was Klaus Schwab in the world in addition to Arnold Schwarzenegger), I went to pick up Jack Ma but was five minutes delayed. As a result, Jack Ma was surrounded by fans in the hotel lobby and Wang Lifen had to "defend" Ma. "Jack Ma, a lot of people chase you because you appeared on my shows. Look now, you are chased, and I have to act like a bodyguard to help you." Wang Lifen said after they finally made it in the car.

"If this happens again, I'll yell out 'she is the hostess Wang Lifen of *Win in China*' as a way to pay you back," Jack Ma said jokingly.

"Give me a break!" Wang Lifen smiled.

Maybe Jack Ma and Wang Lifen were spotted by "sharp-sighted" "masses" several times together at meetings, so in 2009, when Jack Ma cut down a little bit of the company's stock, he was "divorced" once and Wang Lifen became the "key rumored suspect" of Ma's "divorce."

Jack Ma is quite popular among ladies. Once Jack Ma made a speech at the women entrepreneurs' forum, "Today all of you here are abled. There are two most powerful women in Chinese history, Wu Zetian and Empress Dowager Cixi. Men and women are completely different animals. An abled woman basically can appreciate and make best use of men. The woman who turns men more manly is a woman of the women. From the perspective of management, that is 'to get results through other people'." Ma continued, "Abled women often are not quite successful in marriage. Why? Men are like the home-styled dishes in the canteen, very ordinary, but will be sold out if you are late! Abled women are like the upscale dishes in fancy restaurants, very exquisite, but may not be ordered and are soon replaced by new dishes..." The women all rocked forwards and backwards with laughter.

At the end of November, after Jack Ma finished a series of work in Beijing, he went to Hong Kong accompanied by me.

It was the best season in Hong Kong. I would pick up Jack Ma at 10 o'clock every morning, so I squeezed in some time every early morning to climb Mt. Table. It wasn't crowded with people and I enjoyed the fresh air. I could also have an unobstructed view of Victoria Bay down below. Along my way, I saw many foreigners doing morning exercises with their dogs and I saw some entertainers running from time to time.

There was a circled road on the top of the mountain with about an hour's walking distance.

Jack Ma had invited many entrepreneurs to take a walk on this road, chatting along their way. I was to track the timing. They would cover the lap if they had an hour. If they had only half an hour, I would remind him after 15 minutes saying "Ma, turn back. Come back at the same pace." In this way, we would not hold things up.

Year 2010 and After

At the end of January 2010, the Spring Festival was approaching. Dr. Wang Jian, President of Ali Cloud Computing (now chief architect of the Alibaba Group), came to Jack Ma to ask for some leave after being very busy for a year.

Jack Ma held high regards for Dr. Wang Jian and often praised him "relentlessly" behind his back.

His reason for taking leave was quite unusual – to fly a plane in the United States. He used to be a member of a flying club in the U.S. But he'd never mentioned whether the people who created the September 11 Terror Attacks were his classmates or not.

"It's been long since I flew a plane. I may be quite out of practice," he said that day.

"Same, same," said Jack Ma.

The doctor was startled. "Ma, you've also learned to fly a plane?"

"I mean I haven't flown a plane for more than 40 years, ha-ha!" Jack Ma laughed.

Jack Ma did not spend the 2010 Spring Festival in Hangzhou. Prior to the festival, Jack Ma asked me to pay his regards to the employees on posts on his behalf. I knew who I was. How could I possibly represent Jack Ma? Should I come to a department saying, "Hello, I come to see you on behalf of Jack Ma!" They would probably feel sick for the rest of their lives. But I had my own way. I prepared books with Jack Ma's signature ahead of time and called all the members of each department to draw a lot. Although each department could only get one copy, all the colleagues rushed in and the ones who got a copy were very excited.

Director Fan of CCTV informed me to watch *Moving China* on February 11. To share this touch with more colleagues, I posted an article on the internet, *Moving China, Let's Be Moved Again*.

Fan Xinman, writer, chief director of Moving China of CCTV for a consecutive eight years, informed me by phone yesterday, February 11, at 8 o'clock tomorrow evening, that the 2009 Moving China will be broadcasted on CCTV 1.

For eight years, around each Spring Festival I would receive the same notice and would be asked to prepare tissue... Each year at this time, I would think of many things of the past. Prior to the 2003 Spring Festival, I watched the recording of the first Moving China on scene. The moving figure Wang Xuan was sitting right in front of me. I could almost hear her breathing. Next to Wang Xuan were Liu Shuwei and Zhang Qiandong further next... Throughout the recording, I was touched again and again... the theme song of Moving China was heard over and over again. The singer was Han Hong. It was one of her best songs. The lyric writer was Director Fan's close friend who said the talent in writing lyrics came second. The important thing was to invest your heart and feelings. "···Draw a pair of eyes for the world with the purity of the first ray of light; sing a song for the world with the sound of the first blossoming flower..."

Life is comprised of different elements. But life in the sense of soul is composed of constant touches. I like the word "touching." The other day, I accompanied Jack Ma to Hunan Satellite TV. Director Ouyang was a very talented man. The song 'Little Pannier' made a name for Song Zuying in the past was penned by his own hand. Ouyang was always busy with work, but he never felt tired. "Work does not kill a man. What matters is whether you can experience the touches in your work," he said while communicating with us. Being touched allows us to see that in the world, besides the hard rules, and naked interests, there are a lot of soft things that nurture our hearts. If this touch is not widely known, then it is a kind betrayal of the good. Maybe you are upset with small things — others go home earlier for their Spring Festival, you are on duty and can't go back home for the New Year's celebration, or you worked harder in the year but gained fewer than others...Then go and get touched tomorrow night!

Many things happened after 2010, such as Yahoo and Alibaba, such as what Jack Ma did before and after having charity dinner with Bill Gates and Warren Buffett...

Jack Ma also planned to go abroad to study a few years. "I'd better 'hang' myself first before others decide they've had enough of me!"

"Will you take me to study overseas?" I asked Jack Ma.

"Quite possible! Although you aren't a part of the ones I prefer to take in terms of gender and age," Jack Ma replied.

...

Life goes on and much more will be recorded.

Chapter 6:
Interests and Philosophy

Taobao's martial arts culture is well known to all, mainly because Jack Ma is a fan of martial arts since childhood, but few may know about Taobao's handstand culture. Taobao was isolated due to "SARS" at its early stages. In a small room Jack Ma took the lead to build up their bodies by doing handstands. One could still choose to do a variety of exercises even in a smaller space. Why should Jack Ma choose handstands? That is because Jack Ma had the habit of "seeing the world in a different way" as a child and he thought that "standing on the head could win the world."

Jack Ma never said he was "unhappy." He said he only had the time of "not thinking it through yet." By rubbing elbows with all sorts of miraculous people, and through his understanding of Buddhism, Taoism, and eastern and western philosophies, he came up with his own way of management and life's beliefs.

Master Yuezhen

Jack Ma had long been enthusiastic about philosophy. As early as when he opened the English Class, Jack Ma once said, "Why should Buddha (*fo* (佛), with a left radical of 'man' and 'fu' no, not on the right) be written like that? Because he started as a man and later changed to be no longer a mortal." I also heard him say, "Man is a 'future Buddha.' Buddha is a 'past man.' Buddha was once as naive as you and me."

His grandma often took Jack Ma to burn incense and worship Buddha when he was very young. Like other worshippers, grandma always prayed that Buddha would bless the family to have peace and wealth. And every time Jack Ma would "correct" his grandma by saying we should "bless" Bodhisattva to be in peace and joy. If Bodhisattva also needed money, we should "bless" them to be wealthy. "If Bodhisattva is not happy, how can he make you happy? If he doesn't have enough money to spend, how can he make you rich? Try to think from another perspective. Everybody has something to ask from Bodhisattva, but only you think from Bodhisattva's angle, then whom do you think the Bodhisattva will bless?" Each time speaking of this, Jack Ma would say this lightly. Like right now, Jack Ma takes every small and medium-sized enterprise as the "Bodhisattva" in his mind.

Whenever Jack Ma could not "think something through yet," the first thing that came to his mind was always the Yongfu Temple, which is located at the Shisun Peak west of Mt. Lingyin in Hangzhou with a history of 1600 years. The Yongfu Temple is surrounded by ancient trees and tall bamboos, quiet and tranquil, very much like a land of idyllic beauty.

The abbot of the temple Master Yuezhen is an old friend of Jack Ma. He is adept in brushwork and is capable of copying many of the ancient master hands' calligraphy. In addition, he is an architectural genius. Today's Yongfu Temple covers an area of more than a hundred *mu* (a Chinese area unit, one *mu* is of 614.4 m^2) with five independent courtyards which all were designed by Master Yuezhen alone. The yards were directly built without a blueprint and turned out to be just wonderful.

Whether Master Yuezhen is an "attained eminent monk" or not is not for me to tell. But his preaching of Zen helped me a lot in my bragging. For instance, "Zen is the sum of all wisdom and compassion..." or "Zen is to help remove all artificial disguise..." or "Everyone has a lamp in his heart and Zen is a piece of cloth to wipe the dust on the surface of the lamp..." I think this sentence is very much like Socrates' saying of "In every person there is a sun. Just let them shine."

Master Yuezhen once was an abbot of a temple in Mt. Tiantai. He once took Jack Ma and me there. His photo kept in the Guoqing Temple in Tiantai when he was young looked very much like Jack Ma. "Actually I am you and you are me. I help you do business out there and you cultivate for me in the temple. Thinking of this, I feel much more at ease," Jack Ma often said this to

Master Yuezhen playfully.

"Cultivation is not necessarily done in the temple, it can be done everywhere," Master Yuezhen often said.

"Indeed! Monks are those who thought half way through. Those who thought through fully should return to the world. How can you 'deliver salvation to all' from the temple? Go out to help millions of people and thousands of small and medium-sized enterprises (SMES) and that is delivering salvation to all," Jack Ma said.

The Yongfu Temple is always the top choice when Jack Ma wants to talk about something with others. I guess there are two reasons: firstly, it is a good and quiet place for communication and thinking; secondly, there are many philosophical thoughts in Buddhism. Discussing the dharma with others is much easier than reading books alone and much more fun too.

After animals evolved to primates, they began to have the consciousness of fairness. If you give a bunch of bananas to two monkeys, both of them will be happy. If you give one monkey two bunches and the other three, they will fight. Jack Ma thinks this kind of self-orientation of "the pursuit of fairness" is in fact a kind of regression in the course of evolution. Many of the thoughts in Buddhism and Taoism are to address such kind of regression.

We live in an age with the cheapest access to information but with the most expensive identification of truth from false.

About Li Yi

Jack Ma's association with Master Yuezhen was much more than with Li Yi. In 2010, when there was a report claiming that Li Yi had "30,000 disciples" and even Jack Ma worshipped him as a teacher. Jack Ma burst out laughing. "If Li Yi were my teacher, then Master Yuezhen would be my father. We are no more than chatting friends, and that's all."

So, the reason Jack Ma went to the Taoist Temple in Chongqing to see Li Yi was the same as he went to see Master Yuezhen, nothing but to listen to the difference of Taoism and Buddhism, to "absorb the essence and discard the dross." A few years ago, Jack Ma wrote like this in his recommendation to a book, "More than 2000 years have passed. The Tao is still the Tao and the truth is still the truth." Any man of sense can tell that Jack Ma was not revering to any single man, but the philosophy of Taoism.

Jack Ma has never been superstitious, but he did admire a lot of people: the architecture talent of Master Yuezhen, the eloquence of Yu Dan, the memory of Li Yi, the martial arts skills of Master Wang Xi'an, and the magic of Louis Liu (Liu Qian)...

"I am either superstitious and suspecting or believing and not superstitious," Jack Ma joked privately.

As early as National Day in 2005, Jack Ma took a trip to Mt. Jinyun in Chongqing to see the Taoist Priest Li Yi, which more or less had something to do with me. In September 2005, the pre-production of *Sword Stained with Royal Blood* had begun, with some of the crew at Mt. Wuyi. Due to years of toil, Zhang Sir had high blood pressure and heart problems. Convinced by his wife Fan Xinman, he invited some friends to go to Baiyunguan (the White Cloud Temple) in Mt. Jinyun of Chongqing for rehabilitation.

Some of the elderly from Hong Kong had been in the state of Pigu (refraining from eating grain) by the time we got to the mountain, among which there was a royal police. It usually takes seven days of multiple of seven days to practice Pigu. Zhang Sir was to practice 14 days this time, during which he could only drink water and abstain from eating any food. I was then Zhang Sir's assistant, so it was my duty to safeguard him as precautions.

It was a great time for me on the mountain. Every morning I would practice Xingbugong (Walking Exercise) and Daoyin Shu (Guiding Exercise) and then have breakfast. The elderly from Hong Kong would have porridge to smell without eating.

At day, I would copy down *Dao De Jing (Tao Te Ching, also called The Way and Its Power)* with a brush pen and we would have our bodies scoured by the Taoist priests and revitalized through teleport.

We could also play table tennis. I played better than Zhang Sir. I always struck high balls for him to smash. Once Zhang Sir smashed four times in a row and was as happy as a child.

Zhan Zhuang (Pile standing) and others were also the compulsory course of the day.

There was a health trail in front of the gate paved with tiny pointy pebbles. It hurts when walking barefoot. But after a while of walking, the soles of your feet would feel hot and very comfortable.

Along the health trail, classic quotations from *Tao Te Ching* were written on the wall. Every day when I passed by, I would read and remember in case I might need for boasting after I got down off the mountain later.

The food cooked on the mountain was delicious, specially prepared for those who were not refraining from food. At meal times, Zhang Sir sometimes would come around in the dining room and then snapped out something like, "A bunch of laities!"

Those on rehab would practice a skill at meal times to prevent them from starving. I myself did not try it but I believed it. Zhang Sir was at least 10 *Jin* (5 kg) heavier than me when we first got there. But on the sixth day of practicing, he was the same weight as me and his pants became loose.

We spent our Mid- Autumn Festival on the mountain. With bright full moon in the sky, we talked about the past and present and it was very comfortable. The different thing was that there were moon cakes, fruit, and wine placed before our laities but only water was placed before the "immortals."

During that time, friends from Xiangshan had come to see us with a lot of seafood. Zhang Sir was envious with red eyes… too unworthy for us bunch of "laities."

The two weeks in the mountain was really a pleasant memory. I could not only be together with the idols and stars morning and night and play table tennis with them, but also read *Tao Te Ching* at leisure to appreciate the wisdom of the dust-laden history. At that time I was seen by others as a "bad friend" for two reasons. First, I didn't think the teleport treatment was very magical, because long ago I received the treatment on Mount E'mei. Besides, my friend's brother could also help people to dredge meridians through teleport; second, I knew people generally wouldn't survive seven days without eating or drinking, but scientifically, it was not known whether people could survive 14 days by only drinking water. As for the benefits or harm of Pigu, it was beyond my knowledge, so I decided not to participate in anyway.

The Taoist Priest Li Yi would come to lecture in the evening. Li Yi was an educated man. He could cover a wide range of knowledge from *Tao Te Ching* to quantum mechanics, and was also very insightful on philosophy. I enjoyed listening to his lessons. He once said, "There are only evil women in the world, no evil breasts." I didn't know what Li Yi was before, but I found his philosophical thoughts agreeable, such as "Matter is energy waiting to be released and energy is the released matter." I thought it was a good interpretation to the equation of Einstein's E=mc2.

Later Jack Ma contacted me and jokingly said; "I am coming to see the staved monkey-like Zhang Jizhong." So, he came up to the mountain for a day.

In June 2008, Jack Ma convened a B2B executive meeting at Sandun, Hangzhou, in which he proposed his idea of "cloud computing." Many voiced different or even opposite opinions which I tended to agree with. But Jack Ma had the final say. "I am not sure in the future what cloud computing can do exactly and to what extent, but I know we must do it now. Cloud computing can definitely help small and medium-sized enterprises in the future."

The meeting also covered other matters, but none of them reached consistent agreement. In one key business issue, some argued to focus on a large number of "superior forces" and "to seize" rapidly. But the opposition said it was "to break a fly upon a wheel." "In times of need, we shall not only break a fly upon a wheel, but we will also set off missiles as firecrackers!" Jack Ma concluded after listening to all options.

...

The meeting was consuming and Jack Ma looked very exhausted.

On June 12, at the end of the meeting, Jack Ma and I left for Mt. Jinyun in Chongqing.

Jack Ma seemed delighted soon after we were on the mountain. We took a walk along the path in the bamboo grove. The air was fresh with a sweet scent. Small purple flowers grew all along the path. The travelers on the path were scarce and now and then the crickets chirped from the cracks of the stones at the side of the road.

I found Jack Ma knew a lot about crickets. He could determine the type and size of the crickets by listening to their sounds, which really shocked me. Thus we began to catch crickets along the mountain road. With painstaking effort, we caught two and put them in a bamboo tube. Jack Ma even began to vividly describe his story of "cricket fighting" as a boy.

Cricket fighting left a deep impression from his childhood memories. Later when Jack Ma made the film adaptation of *Yang Luchan*, the first appearance of Yang Luchan in the movie he, as a child, was playing "cricket fighting."

Later while in the mountain Jack Ma practiced "Jinyu (keep silent, no talking)" for three days which was also a tradition in Buddhism. It was helpful for those who were always bustling around at daily life to have some peace of mind and think things through more clearly.

Philosophy, I believe, is interlinked with any domains. A famous director once said in teaching an actor, "When you close your mouth for a long period of time, your eyes will begin to do the talking."

The next day, out of a whim, I wrote a note and showed it to Jack Ma, "I'll try Jinyu for half a day." Ma smiled. But I forgot it in less than an hour and talked a lot.

Jack Ma took walks along the yard every morning. He would read the quotations of *Tao Te Ching* on the wall and sink into quiet meditation.

Jack Ma also worked on Chinese calligraphy. The first day, he was relatively impatient and unstable and his characters looked large and uneven. By the last day, he was writing "teeny regular script," not so well though, yet quite even. His mind was much more peaceful by then.

After three days of "Jinyu," meditation, recuperation, Jack Ma's once tired looking face resumed glowing again.

Jack Ma himself also felt meditation was fruitful, but before leaving, he still bluntly said to the Taoist priest, "It's too wet on the mountain. Even the quilt was humid. Ever thought of placing a dehumidifier in the room? Also, the 'Hall of Taiyi' is too shabby. All these are contrary to Lao Tzu's idea of 'attaining the truth by taking the false form,' right? Ha-ha!"

On August 23, I accompanied Jack Ma to Sanya where he did Jinyu at his own home just to think. Jack Ma had unique insights on many philosophical issues, rarely rigidly adhered to others' ideas, even those of sages.

In July 2009, the company would usher in its 10th anniversary. Jack Ma wanted to find a place to summarize the paths taken in the last 10 years and consider the future direction of the company. So, I went with him to Mt. Jinyun again.

He meditated and rehabbed in the Healthcare Hall. I stayed in the farmhouse nearby. In order not to disturb Jack Ma, we passed massages to each other through the working staff for matters that needed attention. To this matter, I posted an article on the intranet after we got back to Hangzhou. The content was as follows:

Serving as "Dharma Protector" for CEO Ma － Ciphertext "Dried Beef"

CEO Ma works at quick pace at ordinary times and is very thin too. But his annual check-up shows that his blood pressure, blood fat and other indicators are as standard as those of pilots. Occasionally he will go to the hospital just to check whether the small "pet" in his tooth is behaving well or not.

While doing meditation, CEO Ma will find ways to make comprehensive "reinforcement" and "promotion" to his body, which is the so-called "dual cultivation." There is such a saying, "Great mind needs a great body to make it most useful." CEO Ma knows this truth very well.

During the process of meditation, none of us could see CEO Ma. The "Dharma Protectors" of the temple would help pass notes for us to handle urgent matters of the company. They cooked the food and delivered to him too. To fit in healthcare, the food was light and plain. CEO Ma respected others but never blindly followed them. He hardly "kept on the rails" for trivial matters. One day the food was terrible, but CEO Ma wanted to keep the "Dharma Protector" from knowing, so he passed me a message written like this: "oodFay adbay, ingbray 2 agsbay oodgay ydray eefbay, idehay inyay othesclay. atchWay ethay ookcay eachyay ealmay + eatmay." It took me long to figure it out what he wanted to say.

Another time, CEO Ma wanted to go ahead of time. He passed me another cipher: "oTay-orningmay atestlay aneplay otay angHay, atwhay imetay."

"My IQ is lower, when I decoded, they would have decoded too. How about we do like Lurk, you and I each take a book. You find the characters and make the ciphers and send to me," I said jokingly afterwards to CEO Ma.

"No good! What if I can't find the words I want? That will lose time. I've worked out another way..." CEO Ma said, after a second thought.

Have you worked out the two cipher texts? The first one who deciphered will win a prize. No kidding!

(The cipher texts: 1. The food is terrible. Bring two good bags of dried beef and hide them in the clothes. Tell the cooking priest to put some meat for each meal. 2. What time is the latest flight back to Hangzhou tomorrow?)

One evening while he was still in cultivation, Jack Ma suddenly came to me. "Let's go get some midnight snack. I'm hungry."

"Are you not still in cultivation?" I asked in amazement.

"I feel fine now," Jack Ma said. "These days others retreat for cultivation. I just want to be quiet. Our company will soon have its 10th anniversary celebration. I've worked things out regarding the new commercial civilization these few days."

We found a farmhouse. They slaughtered a chicken and braised meat. Jack

Ma ate freely and happily. "Civilization and wisdom are the same. They were not invented, but were awakened. They have always been there as a matter of fact. So the next job for Alibaba is to use the existing capital and information power to awaken a new civilization and bless it to grow," Jack Ma said.

That night, Jack Ma talked a lot during the meal:

Alibaba started from scratch 10 years ago to today's existence. The next 10 years it will go from being to non-being. In non-being, I mean there is nowhere without it.

"E-commerce" will be no commerce without an "electronic" future.

Nothing in the world is difficult for one who sets his mind to it.

The so-called "retire after winning merit" is "body" retires but "heart" stays.

I think the wording of "Best Employer Company" more or less has the sense of class contradictions. We will propose to build "The Happiest Company."

Where does the employees' "happiness" come from? Work today for the future!

...

Later we heard these in Jack Ma's speech at the celebrations of the 10th anniversary of Alibaba. "New Commercial Civilization" put forward by Alibaba also covered this content. And all these ideas came out from the time when Jack Ma practiced Jinyu in the mountain.

After we returned to Hangzhou, the aforementioned story, "*Ciphertext, Dried Beef*" in the Intranet continued. "Ciphertext" was soon deciphered by a colleague. Jack Ma kept his promise and rewarded the colleague who got it all right a book with his autograph. But his inscription became another second ciphertext. The prize this time was a big one — two years of free residency in a small apartment with refined decoration.

Due to limited time, though the answers in the set time were diverse, no one got the right answer. So I announced the answer for Jack Ma. Although no one got the apartment, everyone had fun.

As for whether or not there were any scientific reasons of the regimen of Li Yi or Taoism, Fan Xinman and I argued for years, yet neither convinced the other.

Traditional Chinese medicine originated from Taoist medicine by retaining the essences. The dross was discarded gradually under the validation of modern medicine. Chinese Alchemy which contained a lot of drossy ideas has been "properly" concluded as "the ancients' contribution to the field of chemical industry."

I don't think there is a supernatural power in the world, but there are only the unsolved phenomena.

There is nothing in the world that can't be explained by science, only things yet to be explained by science, because the nature of science is to discover the unknown unceasingly.

Taoists held the healthcare idea that the human body itself is "the law of all" and the best "medicine" is one's body. But modern medicine, on the other hand, thinks the quick recovery of a disease needs the help of "peacekeepers."

Neither is wrong.

As a matter of fact, modern medicine heals faster and is more of "universality."

For instance, "human blood stained bread" might have cured several individual lung diseases and there might be reasons unknown to us. But after modern medicine conquered tuberculosis, ten thousand people with the disease could be healed in a short time.

Taoism stresses the "wholeness" in healthcare and criticizes the modern medicine as "a temporary redress."

Modern medical science pays more attention to "suit the remedy to the case." "If every province gains stability, then the nation naturally will become stable."

I think both arguments are complete in theories.

But it is hard to tell which is more important, "theory" or "practice." Many theories became the milestone in the progress of human civilization. But many other times, practice is more important than theory. Deng Xiaoping took back Hong Kong with the theory of "one country, two systems," a theory many could think of. Even at the food market place, you could hear the people saying "Keep Hong Kong as it is, first take back the sovereignty."

Deng Xiaoping's greatness was not in putting forward the theory of "one country, two systems," but to turn it into a "successful case."

When I accompanied Zhang Sir to the mountain to practice Pigu, I was taken as the "bad friend" for voicing different opinions. But it didn't in any way affect the attraction of Li Yi's lectures.

If I were the one to decide, then I would love Li Yi to be present in each of our chats. The fun about chatting is to hear something rather than to learn something. If during each chat one could "learn" or "absorb" something, then he could, and he should use his judgment. (My personal opinion)

Inspirations from "Jinyu"

After Jack Ma's "Jinyu" in Mt. Jinyun, I realized some philosophical thoughts through his words, which not necessarily were accurate, but l would like to share them with you.

Since 2008, Jack Ma often mentioned, "I object to the thoughts of all professional managers." Could it be Ma ignored the professional managers' skills? Of course not. Actually it is because many professional managers have no sense of ownership, no "root," and they are not confident in their hearts. Also, professional managers need to dedicate their passion while contributing their skills. They will be very happy if they can truly commit themselves. This is one of the reasons why Jack Ma changed his startup slogan of "Seriousness in the work and pleasure in life" to "Pleasure in the work and seriousness in life." Sun Simiao, not Li Shizhen or others, became China's King of Medicine. It was because he had the best medical morals. In his *On the Absolute Sincerity of Great Physicians,* he wrote: *whenever a great physician treats diseases, he has to be mentally calm and his disposition firm. He should not give way to wishes and desires, but has to develop first a marked attitude of compassion. He should commit himself firmly to the willingness to take the effort to save every living creature. If someone seeks help because of illness, or on the ground of another difficulty, a great physician should not be concerned about status, wealth, or age; neither should he question whether the particular person is attractive or unattractive, whether he is an enemy or a friend, whether he is Chinese or a foreigner, or finally, whether he is uneducated or educated. He should meet everyone on equal ground; he should always act as if he were thinking of himself...*" Such a person as this could be called a "great physician for the living," otherwise, they would be a "great thief for those who still have their spirits" regardless of his medical attainment. Don't you think Jack Ma's attitude towards all the small and medium-sized enterprises was the same as Sun Simiao's attitude toward patients? We want to be the "great physicians for the living"!

Ma hoped that all colleagues could sincerely be dedicated to the customers and that was also his requirement for his son. Several times when I visited him at home, I heard Jack Ma talking to his son with the example of the Goose father in the movie *Kung Fu Panda*, "The so-called secret recipe is no secret recipe. When he makes the noodles, he thinks nothing but the joy and satisfaction when the starving customers eating the hot noodles. So he becomes happy in the first place and finally passes the joy to the customers."

"When a pig grows to 5,000 *jin* (2,500 kg), it is no longer a pig," Ma also said.

You might wonder what it meant when you first read it.

Once there was a small manager who had a good employee. So he wrote a letter of appreciation to his parents and thanked them for raising such a wonderful person. All the members of the employee's family were moved by this gesture.

If Jack Ma had 20 thousand of such letters printed and sent to each employee's parents, would the parents also be so moved? Donald Rumsfeld, the former US Secretary of Defense, was reviled by the national public simply because he stamped seals for each of the family letters of the soldiers killed in action, right?

"No?excuses?for?failure,?only to?find?grounds?for?success" was said by Jack Ma repeatedly. Let's set an extreme example. Most people will not make an excuse if they break their own legs. But if his leg is broken by his colleagues, he certainly will make excuses. Jack Ma thinks from the philosophical point of view that, except for your own thoughts and soul, everything is objective existence, even your own physical body. So the two cases are essentially the same as the "leg breaking." That is, you didn't see the objective world clearly.

"We applaud for efforts and pay for results," Jack Ma once said.

At the beginning this statement sounded too practical and too results oriented until after I read another sentence in Jack Ma's book, "The reason the world becomes a hell is simply because someone tries to turn it into heaven."

Therefore, if the result is not good, it is pointless or even a disaster if the starting point is good and the process is painstaking. "For the gambler who lost all the family fortune and made the family fall apart, his starting point was to earn a good small building and to provide his wife and children with a good life," Jack Ma explained it humorously.

"Jinyu" Again on Sanya Vacation

At the end of January 2009, I went with Jack Ma to Sanya on vacation, during which time he practiced "Jinyu" for the first three days and then invited Master Wang Xi'an to teach him Taiji for three days. At the time of "Jinyu," because we couldn't talk, I collected some jokes in my free time and wrote them on the paper for him to read. I also wrote a story about an eagle. Ma wrote "aliway" on the article after reading it. I understood that Jack Ma wanted me to post the article on the Intranet to motivate employees. I was pretty satisfied with the article entitled, "*Eagle, the Model of Metamorphosis*" (see Appendix II). If possible, let it be engraved on the back of my tombstone.

At holiday time, every evening from 6:00 to 8:00, Jack Ma would make the "rapid march," walking along the ring road nearly a kilometer for ten laps. Another colleague and I exercised with Jack Ma. Ma walked faster and faster, we followed him with great effort, as if the sky became dark by our stomps one after another. Later we really could not keep up with his pace, so we decided to follow Jack Ma by turns after each lap.

One evening, it was very dark. Jack Ma took us to take a walk along the beach. Suddenly we found a woman lying alone on the beach, motionless.

We approached slowly, getting nearer and nearer. But the woman was still motionless. We were a bit scared, but luckily there were three of us. We stopped at one meter away. With lights in the distance, we still couldn't tell it was a woman or a sand sculpture. Finally, we confirmed it was a sand sculpture. It was absolutely lifelike and must be a work of professionals. It was so real that you would feel guilty if you touched her legs. The sand sculpture had a good figure, with her bottom warped and head buried in the sand.

After a while, we decided to leave. Jack Ma suggested we stay a bit longer and see how others felt when they passed by.

It was getting very dark and there were fewer passers-by. We waited for a long time before finally witnessing two batches of people. They behaved almost the same as we did. Jack Ma was very happy like a boy.

This time in Sanya, Jack Ma also said something beyond my comprehension. Seeing my puzzled face, he came up with a very childlike and innocent idea. "Chen Wei! If there is a god, what is he doing every day? I guess his daily work is to give souls at day time and receive souls at night," said Ma, laughing and gesturing the movements of god's giving souls "Can he handle it? There should be an automatic transceiver machine for the souls! Ha-ha!" He added.

"Competition is very interesting. It enrages your opponents and they get angry when you are close to your victory," Jack Ma so said in many public occasions. I think this sentence was his realization of the words of "He who in (Tao's) wars has skill assumes no martial port; He who fights with most good will to rage makes no resort" from *Tao Te Ching*.

Jack Ma's learning and applying with full vigor reminds me of Chairman Mao's words, "Dig tunnels deep, store grain everywhere, and never seek hegemony." When Zhu Yuanzhang struggled to seek state power, a Confucian scholar "adviser" Zhu Sheng also said, "Build high walls, stock up rations, and don't be too quick to call yourself a king." I think Chairman Mao must have thought that "building high walls" was no longer safe since the U.S. had already had the atomic bomb, so he changed it to "dig tunnels deep."

Jack Ma had many of such sayings of learning and applying.

Jack Ma believed that Chairman Mao's military thoughts "strategically we should despise all our enemies, but tactically we should take them all seriously" could work equally well if we replaced the "enemies" to be "ourselves" – "strategically we should despise all ourselves, but tactically we should take ourselves all seriously." This is why Ma often said, "We are a team of ordinary people to achieve extraordinary things."

Once, after listening to the work report of a competent leader of the company who had a bit of "individualistic heroism," Jack Ma said, "Well done. But I heard only 'I' just now. I hope in the future I can hear 'we' and 'our team' coming from the bottom of your heart."

One of Jack Ma's sayings also included: "Work truly is meaningless until you give meaning to it." This sentence actually accumulated Ma's deep philosophical thinking.

Philosopher Bertrand Russell once said, "The whole temple of Man's achievement must inevitably be buried beneath the debris of a universe in ruins." Albert Einstein once also said, "Broadly speaking, human survival and development are of no significance." Christians pursue the "eternal life" after the "trial" because without that belief they think life is devoid of all "meaning."

In short, Jack Ma realized that some philosophy thoughts could lead people to extreme passivity. So he believed only by developing "positive desire" one could live a "positive" life. As long as you give a "positive" meaning to life and work, then life and work will be meaningful. I think by speaking "We don't care how much you know, but we want to know how much you care" by Jack Ma was also based on this kind of thinking.

Jack Ma and *Tao Te Ching*

Jack Ma's handbag was always stuffed with a few books with constant replacement except for one, the thinnest *Tao Te Ching*. It is thin because it doesn't have any annotations. Ma wished to have his own understanding rather than being led.

At the lighting ceremony of the 2010 Vancouver Winter Olympics opening, one of the cauldrons of "icicle" failed to rise. Amidst a world of accusations, the Organizing Committee modified the content of the closing ceremony by replacing the "icicle" with a clown. As a result, the whole world forgave the Canadians who had the courage to admit their mistake. After watching the closing ceremony at home, Jack Ma suddenly said, "I understand Lao Tzu's point of 'of greatest fullness, deemed a void.' If there were no accident in the opening ceremony, superficially it looked very perfect but no one would remember the ignition." Ma went on saying, "In fact many things are the same. Each of the classic goals in football matches needs to be 'set off' by the mistakes of the opposite goalkeeper. If everyone is perfect, then nothing is perfect."

Once, Jack Ma suddenly got very excited while reading *Tao Te Ching*. "Alas! It is not I who am reading Lao Tzu. It is Lao Tzu who is reading me! And he has read to the bottom of my heart." This was very much like "Guo Xiang (Kuo Hsiang) making annotation to Zhuang-zi." "2,000 years is too long for a man, but for a species, it is just an instant. With 2,000 years of knowledge explosion, but wisdom is still wisdom. The old sages could completely interpret people's hearts today," Jack Ma said to me once.

Jack Ma is not only a philosophy "lover," but also a philosophy "practitioner," such as Jack Ma's practice of "offense is the best form of defense."

The B2B business of the company went very well those years. But to prevent eBay from overall entering B2B from C2C, Jack Ma founded Taobao. Shortly afterwards eBay was squeezed out of China. Subsequently, to prevent PayPal from mastering Taobao's payment, Ma again founded Alipay, and Alipay's going worldwide is just a matter of time.

Jack Ma has always been stressing that "Taobao needs continuous innovation. Alipay needs even more innovation. Don't make Alipay a model of the bank."

Once I asked Jack Ma in private, "The establishment and development of banks have such a long history. Innovation has already been made by the banks if there is any. Can we really be more innovative?"

"There are only seven music notes, but musicians are numerous. Have you ever had doubt whether they are able to write a new song?" Jack Ma so said instead of answering my question directly.

From the perspective of philosophy, innovation is endless with a difference of difficulty.

"You always say that 'luck is part of the power,' I'm not sure I understand this," I asked Jack Ma once.

"Seriously?" Jack Ma asked. "If one day, the President and vice president and all executives of Taobao leave at the same time, you won't have a chance to be Taobao's CEO. 'Luck' will not fall on your head, because you don't know Taobao. Ha-ha! Also, have you heard of the story of Mark Twain and Alexander Graham Bell?"

Mark Twain was once dedicated to the investment of scientific inventions, but he failed in every investment and lost heart. When another young man who turned up with a strange machine on his back came to him and asked him to invest a fund of 500 dollars, he just refused him. Not to hurt this young man, Mark Twain finally said, "Wish you success, Bell!" And this man was the inventor of the telephone, Alexander Graham Bell.

Superficially, Mark Twain did not have good luck, but essentially, Mark Twain was ill-equipped with the ability to determine the true values of scientific and technological innovations.

Jack Ma held the idea that Alibaba was not a business, but a work of art. "What I am thinking now is, painters create art on paper, and directors solidify their art in films. What we are doing is 'behavior' art. Ours are more unpredictable, but the benefit is that we can change while they can't. Ha-ha!" Ma said after visiting the art exhibition of Wu Guanzhong in Hangzhou.

There is an important principle in Alibaba's culture, to "embrace changes," not only to "embrace" the "changes" from outside, but also "embrace" the "changes" of leadership's in changing their minds. Jack Ma is a man who corrects his mistakes. "I'm not God. I make mistakes, but I correct them too," he said this from time to time.

"CEO Ma, what you said today is contrary to what you said last month," once, a vice president said to Jack Ma.

"Then do as I said today." Jack Ma said it wittily. "You should be happy, because your boss, I, knows more now than last month!" Acknowledge mistakes then correct them, because Jack Ma understood that the direction was more important than efforts.

Jack Ma was very serious in the recruitment work and had invented the post of "Sniffing Officer" who could vote down the appointment made by all the department leaders and leaders of the leadership. The people holding this job are all veteran employees with wealthy experience whose roles are to decide whether the applicants share the same value of the "kindred spirit."

The one who had the sharpest "sense of smell" was Jack Ma himself, of course. At the beginning of 2009, I went with Jack Ma to B2B Shanghai Branch. While we walked past the big office, I found the employees here were as warm and amazed to see Jack Ma as employees from any other branch. But Jack Ma entered the director's office and closed the door. "You've got a situation here. Tell me, what happened?"

"Indeed something happened this morning. CEO Ma, how did you know it?" The director was utterly shocked.

"I think employees have a bit nervous mood behind the enthusiasm," Ma said.

I was very surprised too, because I was totally unaware of anything unusual. Similar things happened later several times. This is something I will never learn. The best I can do is to worship.

Under the influence of Jack Ma's philosophy, I also had some thoughts about the world and wrote an article titled *Adam Hesitated* (see Appendix I) and released it on the Intranet. I think it is by far the best article I've written and can be carved on my gravestone. In the event they think there are too many words, then at least carve the link.

In general, as I've observed, the difference between business owners and entrepreneurs is that, instead of putting their ability first, the latter tend be more grateful. Jack Ma is particularly grateful for the appearance of the Internet in this age. "I would never have the chance if it had come a few years earlier or a few years later." Ma also sincerely thanked the government. "If it were still a 'Cultural Revolution,' 'doing the revolution without reading ABC,' I would have been criticized by students every day with a board hanging on my neck. It would be of no use no matter how creative I can be."

Chapter 7:
Jack Ma's Taiji Dream

Now, practicing Taiji has become Jack Ma's main activity for fitness. He often performs the actions with his hands while walking. He learned many things from Taiji philosophy as well. For example, "the doctrine of the mean" (*zhong yong* literally middle and mediocre) is interpreted in many ways. But Jack Ma argues that *zhong* is a verb which means "hit" and *yong* is the "right point." *Zhong yong* is to "hit at the right point."

Jack Ma thinks Taiji is to express Taiji ideas by boxing. Each stroke (strike) can be both attack and defense. There is a way to break any stroke, that is to say, "there is no desperate situation, only the desperate man to the situation."

Jack Ma is committed to the promotion of Taiji culture recently. Please note, it is not the promotions of a set of fist/fighting techniques, a kind of martial arts, but it promotes a kind of philosophy and lifestyle.

Picking up Taiji at the Age of 40

As mentioned previously, on the last day of 2008, Jack Ma assigned me a task — "Find the best Taiji master."

When Jack Ma was a little boy, he learned Taiji for many years from an old woman named Chen in Hangzhou. Mrs. Chen's style was the "Yang-style Taijiquan" and she was very adept at it. She could easily fight back two or three young fellows at the age of 70. "Mrs. Chen got up early and would quietly stand in the park for a moment with her eyes closed before performing Taiji. I once asked her what she was doing. She said she was listening to the sounds of flowers blossoming." Jack Ma once told me.

On February 4, 2009, I accompanied Jack Ma to Shanghai for a meeting. In the evening, I went to a Taiji Hall alone which I previously found on the Internet. Although I had never learned Taiji before, after two hours of practice, I felt it was somehow different from the Taiji I imagined. Especially the "Aerial Strike" (knock one out without actual physical contact). I'm a materialist and I studied science and was once the champion of the triple jump for two Zhejiang University Games. So I've come to three conclusions. 1. "Aerial Strike" is a fantasy, or the scientists around the world would have been shocked much earlier; 2. The Ching-kung that exists in everybody's imagination is just an illusion. If you can jump 2.46 meters high, you may as well go to the Olympic Games and break the world record, then it is 100 times more effective than your endeavored promotion; 3. Humans can't hold their breath under water for two hours, because the Guinness' record is less than 20 minutes. If you could hold your breath for two hours you would have "won great honors for our country" long ago.

So I decided to take a trip to Taiji's birthplace − Chenjiagou, Henan.

Later, a friend of Jack Ma also wanted to learn Taiji and wished the venue to be in Shanghai for his convenience. I sent Jack Ma the contact information of the Taiji Hall in Shanghai and Jack Ma forwarded to him. I learned that he had been sticking to that place ever since.

As long as you can exercise your body, playing the true or false one, walking the dog or dancing are all conducive to better health, at least I think so.

In mid-February, Jack Ma flew to Japan after a series of work in Beijing. On the same day, I flew to Henan. Before I went there, I had informed my friends in Henan too, "Find the best Taiji master and the best one only."

Led by deputy director Kou from the Wenxian County Sports Bureau, we first visited Chenjiagou, the birthplace of Taijiquan. There, we visited Zhang Fuwang, a disciple of Master Wang Xi'an, one of the "Eight Heavenly Kings" in the local area. Then we went to Wenxian County for lunch, which was not far from Chenjiagou, about 10 minutes' drive.

I originally thought Taijiquan was created by Zhang Sanfeng just like I thought Judge Bao had beheaded Chen Shimei. In fact, the two things...

The Wang Xi'an Taijiquan Research Society was located in the Taiji Hall of Wenxian County. After lunch, we went to visit the 19th generation representative Master Wang Xi'an of the Chen-style Taijiquan. The Taiji Hall was slightly old-fashioned with a small square stretching before it. It was a fine day. Many children were practicing Taiji out there. Some were playing set forms and swords. I even spotted a blond female foreigner.

That day Master Wang was sitting at the gate in a white Taiji costume watching people practicing Taijiquan. He was 67 years old, but looked much younger than his age. Previously, his disciples had reminded me Master Wang didn't like to talk with strangers but he treated me like an old friend. After explaining the history and culture of Taiji, he also demonstrated several techniques of Taijiquan.

Throughout the process, President Yan of the Wang Xi'an Taijiquan Research Society kept at Master Wang's side all the time. She was in poor health before and was a typical "pot of medicine." She had been learning Taijiquan from Master Wang for more than a decade. Now, in the words of Master Wang, she was "an iron ball."

A reporter happened to be there at the time to accompany her daughter playing Taijiquan. She asked me some questions, including the question of "Why should a modern Internet company be interested in Taiji and come all the way to visit a teacher?" "The taller the tree, the more nutrition the root needs. The newer the emerging enterprises, the more traditional wisdom they need..." I said. As a result, all these words appeared in the local newspaper the next day.

On April 3, Jack Ma came to Sanya from Hong Kong. I arrived one day earlier and invited Master Wang and President Yan to Sanya for a four-day holiday, during which time, we could learn some Taiji from Master Wang.

I was a green hand and my main task was to remember the movements and listen to Jack Ma and Master Wang talking about Taiji stories and philosophical thoughts.

Jack Ma had a good foundation and could grip easily. Although he learned less than 20 movements in this first course, he was in a delightful mood and looked very satisfied.

On April 13 to 15, in Hangzhou, the Organization Department had a three-day concentrated meeting. I had just learned a little bit of Taiji and was still in the highest mood. I began to boast about Taiji to my colleagues during break time. Jack Ma asked me to perform on the stage, then he performed after me. Everyone could see a world of difference. "With just three or four days of practice, you began to boast about Taiji. If I don't discourage you, you will soon be the master of the 18th generation disciples and that would harm the young generation! Ha-ha!" Jack Ma said to me afterwards.

Since then, Taiji became Jack Ma's main method of fitness.

After listening to Jack Ma's idea on "*zhong yong*" of Taiji, I had a new understanding of FIFA's debate on the enabling of the "eagle eye." I think it is about an ongoing degree to "justice" and "enthusiasm." If a football match has many timeouts to see the "eagle eye" and the enthusiasm of the audience is interrupted again and again, they will finally lose their enthusiasm; then even the fairest competition means nothing. (My personal opinion)

"Who have higher attainments on Taiji, you or your two sons?" Jack Ma asked Master Wang during his learning course.

Master Wang said although he was very good at skills, due to his low cultural level and incapability of expressing himself, he had gone through many detours on Taiji. He arrived at this stage bit by bit after numerous mistakes. But his two sons didn't take a roundabout course under his instruction, so they had become invincible during their teens.

After a moment of thought, Jack Ma put forward his own views. Jack Ma believed that Master Wang's Taiji had higher attainments. If one day, a rival about the same level came, Master Wang could quickly find a way to win over the enemy, but his sons might not.

"If I am to write a book, I'll write Alibaba's one thousand and one mistakes," Jack Ma often said this before. Now I see, some of the mistakes are inevitable and the sooner made the better. "Sailing with the wind accomplishes our business; sailing against the wind accomplishes ourselves." Jack Ma believed the growth of the two should be inseparable. If by whim or impulse we chose the right direction, our "business" was developed but not the "people." Then sooner or later, we will make a mistake. And the later we make the mistake, the greater it will cost.

Perhaps Lao Tzu's "what is most straight seems crooked" can speak for this.

"Wang Zongyue's theory of Taijiquan and Taiji theory of Chen Xin as well as others contain very profound philosophy, such as the thought of 'lifting your head, relaxing your neck, do not throw your weight any way,' the agility of 'not adding a feather's weight and not dropping a fly's weight.' It is not only conducive to Taijiquan practice, but is also a great guiding role to the management and development of the enterprise," Jack Ma said. "Chen Wei, you have a good memory. I hope you are the first one in the company to learn the Theory of Taijiquan."

For a period of time, Jack Ma took every chance to engage in Taijiquan. Any outdoor flat ground could be his playground, even when he went abroad. A picture was taken when Jack Ma was in India as he was performing Taiji in a temple and the moment attracted monks who wanted to learn Taiji from him. Indian spread yoga to China, and Jack Ma probably was the first person to spread Taiji to India, or so I think, ha-ha!

About Taiji and yoga, there was once a debate between me and the girls of our company.

What they said were a bunch of advertising commentaries like "Yoga is a way of life, building up the body and cultivating the heart."

"At most Yoga is to know oneself, but Taiji is to 'know yourself as well as your enemy'." I said.

"A time of yoga, a time of makeup removal of the mind."

"A time of Taiji, a time of streaking of the soul."

...

Taiji Culture and Alibaba

On the National Day in 2009, when Master Wang came for the third time to teach Taijiquan, Jack Ma decided to do something for the promotion of the quintessence of Chinese culture.

First of all there was a promotion within the company. Jack Ma had invited Master Wang's champion disciples to teach Taiji in Hangzhou. I posted a message for signing up in the Intranet.

Sign up and participate in Taiji with CEO Ma

(Two classes, starting on October 19, 2009)

Chinese traditional culture is extensive and profound and Taiji is one of the representatives.

Master Wang Xi' an, the 19th authentic successor of Taijiquan generation from Chen-jiagou, Henan, is CEO Ma' s Taiji teacher. The Wang Xi' an Taijiquan Research Society will set up a branch in Hangzhou and all the members will be the staff from the Alibaba Group. Master Wang has trained countless national champions and some of his foreign disciples have become champions of their own countries. Under his training, Master Wang' s two sons Wang Zhanhai and Wang Zhanjun are even remarkable in their skills. In the 1980s, Wang Zhanhai became dominant in the martial arts circles. Wang Zhanjun became invincible since he was 16 years old and has been standing out with pride in the martial arts field for years! Learning Taiji can not only "build up the body," the Tao (way) in it can also "inspire the soul." CEO Ma' s achievements today can be accounted for ten thousand and one reasons, but all of them are superficial. There are only two reasons that truly contributed to his success: having learned English for more than a decade at the West Lake and practicing Taiji for nearly 10 years! Alibaba is a company rich in martial arts culture. Now you have the opportunity to practice real Kung Fu! Master Wang will send his outstanding disciples to teach in Hangzhou. He himself and President Yan will also come to instruct on an irregular basis! Many Taiji fans don' t even have the chance to see Master Wang, still less to have him guide a few strokes. What' s more exciting, CEO Ma also will come to watch you practice! All trainees will address CEO Ma as "Shishu (senior apprentice)" according to the seniority in the Taijiquan family. CEO Ma wishes that one day he can be appraised like this: CEO Ma is a Taiji master. He has also started a business, such as Alibaba, Taobao...

In a sense, the Ali Group is the by-product of "Rampant Growth" of Taiji philosophy in the Internet age. When you have accomplished learning Taiji, CEO Ma will take you to join in the Martial Art Assembly! One day, sooner or later, to those dregs of martial arts circle who abused the young and the old, the company will send the worst students carrying medical kits and stretchers to teach them a lesson and cleanse the martial arts circle with a pure heart. Whether this social responsibility is to be regarded as the new commercial civilization or not is not my place to decide. Reply to sign up, the deadline is to be decided according to the application condition. No restrictions to age, gender or foundation (currently the location is set only in Hangzhou, but Binjiang and Chengxi will also make class grouping). Chairman Mao once said that we can draw the freshest and most beautiful picture on a piece of blank paper! From now on, we will be the 21st authentic Taiji generation successors! The history of 10 years of Alibaba tells us one thing: Nothing is impossible for us!

The registration was a total hit and the number soon exceeded 400 people. In order to ensure the quality of teaching, the date for further application was cut-off in advance. The rest of the students would have to wait until the next session.

On the first day of class, I warned the colleagues under the instructions of Jack Ma, "The most important thing about learning Taiji is persistence. We can imagine a scene 50 years from today: A group of healthy people in old age, after playing Taiji, go to see a dying patient in the hospital who is stuck with all kinds of tubes. He speaks with difficulty to the doctor, 'these were my colleagues from Alibaba, we practiced Taiji together but unfortunately I didn't carry on'."

Jack Ma did not break his promise. Busy as he was, he still found time to watch the colleagues practicing Taiji in Chengxi and Binjiang.

Many more colleagues wanted to learn Taiji, so in the spring of 2010, another session of Taiji class was held. Currently, the colleagues from Taiji classes have reached nearly 1,000 people, including many executives, such as Peng Lei.

Peng Lei is the woman I admire most in the Group. She used to be a teacher at Zhejiang University of Finance & Economics and joined in the venture with Jack Ma "in the fog." She's been with Jack Ma for many years. She was a team member when Jack Ma went to Beijing to cooperate with MOFTEC (Ministry of Foreign Trade and Economic Cooperation) in 1997. I always wondered how a young female teacher can spring up in any kind of work she put her hands on. She was the CEO of the Human Recourses Department of the Group for many years. She has made substantial contributions to the construction of Alibaba's corporate culture and values, which is distinctive in the enterprises in China. Fair enough, that was her job. After she was transferred to be the CEO of Alipay for a year (currently the CEO of Alibaba Small and Micro Financial Services Group), Jack Ma praised Alipay every day.

Peng Lei has a tight schedule. So I arranged a Taiji coach to do "door-to-door" teaching, twice a week. Peng Lei would say when I ran into her, "I have a gift in practicing Taiji, the coach praised me." As a matter of fact, the coach says this to everyone.

Jack Ma, Taiji, Movies, Jet Li

In May 2009, I went to Beijing with Jack Ma. "I've worked out a Taiji story while in flight. I think we can ask Huayi to make it into a movie." Jack Ma said this excitedly after landing.

To this end, Jack Ma invited the writer Shen Weifeng for lunch during his working clearance in Beijing. I got to know Shen Weifeng in February 2009. One afternoon after the Spring Festival, Jack Ma called me to his office. "Listen, take Shen Weifeng for dinner tonight. But remember don't take her as those little girls in the company who call you Chen Ba (daddy). She is a famous writer and the author of *Winning on Handstand*, the book about Taobao." But later with our constant association, she finally called me "Chen Ba." But that is another story.

Jack Ma told us the story he came up with while we were on the plane. The story takes place in Cangzhou of Hebei. A couple of children are watching the cricket fighting, and one of them is called Yang Luchan. Not far away, the Four Heavenly Guardians from the Prince Mansion of the capital are making an open challenge to fight and are unbeatable. Yang Luchan can't afford to buy the crickets even if it costs almost nothing. So in a rage, he goes to the ring to challenge. Only 10-year-old though, he wins over two men at the same time and causes a sensation... The story continued with twists and turns, coupled with Jack Ma's vivid description, everyone marveled at it and envisioned the imagery! In our imagination, at the end of movie, a long list will appear on the screen, starting from the Taiji ancestor to N generations... Shen Weifeng said the last name would be, "Jack Ma"!

No sooner had Jack Ma finished than everyone began to add totally unconstrained plots from nowhere. With each highlight, Jack Ma would laugh to tears. "We'll convince several well-known entrepreneurs to be guest performers and each will have a classic line. Li Shufu can take the part of rickshaw puller; Shi Yuzhu will play the fortune-teller; Wang Zhongjun will cross-dress as Cixi... Pop stars shall also take parts. Fan Bingbing can play a servant girl. While the audience is looking forward to her appearance, she makes a turn and goes away, without even a single line..."

Shen Weifeng is a girl, so she contributed to the story with a gentle little girl as the fellow apprentice. I suggested the father of Yang Luchan to tell his son a lot of irrational logic with "sincere words and earnest wishes."

Jack Ma was very serious in making the story of Taiji Master Yang Luchan into a movie. He had started making preparations soon after the plot came up. He had many famous Chinese film directors in his mind, from Ang Lee to Feng Xiaogang and so on.

On April 1, 2010, Jack Ma invited Jet Li, Wang Zhongjun, Shen Guojun, and the screenwriters of Huayi to visit Chenjiagou, the birthplace of Taijiquan. I arrived a day earlier to make preparations.

Jack Ma took the special trip to Chenjiagou of Henan for more than one reason. He wanted to let more heads from the business industry and entertainment circles and stars to know Taiji and to prepare bringing Taiji to a movie. He also wanted to realize his dream – he had long hoped to visit the birthplace of Taijiquan.

Accompanied by Master Wang Xi'an and Wang Zhanjun and others, we visited the Ancestral Hall of Taiji, the China Taijiquan Museum, Donggou, and the place where Yang Luchan learned boxing.

Subsequently, we also watched a Taiji performance presented by a local Taiji school. Each of the performers had special skills. Because of limited time, many national champions didn't have the chance to perform on stage.

Under the vigorous push of Jack Ma, the Taiji film *Yang Luchan* started filming in the first half of 2011.

Spreading Taiji to the World

I came to realize that "If it is national, it is global" through Taiji.

Jack Ma had an entrepreneur friend in Hong Kong. Four or five of his children were studying abroad. "These children are internationalized and can basically fit in with foreign children," the entrepreneur said "proudly."

And there was another boy who became an apprentice of Master Wang at the age of six or seven. Many times he was the champion in the junior team in national competitions. In 2010, he went to study in Canada. His oral English was not very good when he first got there, but all the foreign children called him "Master" and wanted to learn Taijiquan from him. This time, Jack Ma introduced him to Huayi. Very likely, he would play an important role in the movie *Yang Luchan*.

In comparison, who "blended" best in the world? Who was more "internationalized"?

After researching, Jack Ma found that some of the leaders, such as Sun Yat-sen and others all had Taiji masters as their body guards at most critical moments. So Jack Ma began to make up another story.

Jack Ma had many friends from the cultural circles, such as the screenwriter Shi Kang of *Struggle*, and the author of *Plot Against* Mai Jia, etc. Jack Ma would take time to make up stories and discuss with the writers on the phone, which became a habit for relaxation for him after work. Once I heard Jack Ma talking to Mai Jia about a story on the phone. After that, Jack Ma said, "Oh, yes. I've read your novel days ago. Just as I was at a high mood, it ended! What happened?" When he heard that the writer was working on it and it was not yet published, Jack Ma got anxious, "What? Can you tell me the rest of the story? Here and now!"

On the afternoon of January 3, 2011, I went with Jack Ma to the Yongfu Temple to drink tea and chat with Mai Jia, where Jack Ma told a story: Li Kenong, with a Taiji team safeguarding Mao Zedong in Chongqing in the autumn of 1945, had a desperate fight with Dai Li's spies. This team escorted Chairman Mao to Russia at the end of 1949 and compromised the assassination plot of Mao Renfeng's spy organization. Jack Ma told the story with exaggerated facial expressions and various body languages. The story was very dramatic and each character had a name.

"How come I didn't know these stories?" Mai Jia asked after hearing Jack Ma's story.

"Of course you don't know. I just made them up in these two days." Jack Ma grinned. "But things like this must have happened at that time. I was hoping you could enrich and perfect the story..."

"The construction of the story is very complete, with some details it will do." Mai Jia said.

Actually, Jack Ma and I both understood that Mai Jia had known the story was made up. He knew that period very well. We asked him when Dai Li died. Without even thinking, in March 1946, he answered immediately.

When I heard that Mai Jia also majored in electronics at college just like me, I grew more confident to be a man of letters.

The other day I texted Mai Jia, "Sunny day, beautiful girls, old place at Longjing, come for dinner or not?"

Mai Jia replied: "Poor me! Being locked up in the mountains to write *The Message III*. A month from now, I will go to find the organization."

Jack Ma had the fantasy of holding "the West Lake Challenge" at the West Lake, where a ring of martial arts competition would be set up, with lubricate bonus. The challenge would be one on one. Whoever could throw the other players in the West Lake would be the "Taiji King."

With the vigorous promotion by Jack Ma, whatever "situation" comes to Taiji in the future, it won't surprise me.

Chapter 8:
Social Responsibility and Ali Culture

The 2008 Wenchuan earthquake in Sichuan province was a grave disaster for all Chinese. At that time, I was at the side of Jack Ma. He was anxious, grievous and was trying hard to do a lot of things, bearing a lot of criticism at the same time. Alibaba reacted swiftly after the shock. Even today, the company is making every effort to help with the reconstruction at the areas of disaster. The most moving thing is that the company continues to organize monthly volunteers to Sichuan through the Corporate Social Responsibility Department. The employees go there during their annual leave and some even cover the travel expanses all on their own...

After Shock

May 12, 2008 was doomed to be an unusual day. That day Jack Ma and I were attending the ABAC meeting in Moscow. At 10:30 a.m. (four hours' time difference between Moscow and Beijing), Jack Ma, who was at the meeting, received messages from friends in China one after another: Beijing had an earthquake, Shanghai had an earthquake, even Hangzhou had an earthquake... Jet Li confirmed on the phone that the epicenter was in Sichuan.

Jack Ma interrupted the meeting by saying, "Excuse me, ladies and gentlemen. I'm sorry to interrupt you. My motherland was stricken by an earthquake half an hour ago, a grave earthquake..."

"I'm sorry to hear this news... when things get clear, we'll see what can be done," said the rotating chairman from Peru. This was probably the earliest mention in an international conference after the May 12 Earthquake.

Jack Ma decided on that very day to donate one million *yuan* in his own name.

In the following days, Jack Ma kept in close contact with China and paid close attention to the progress of relief work. When hearing that the disaster areas were in urgent needs of tents, Jack Ma immediately called the Social Responsibility Department of Alibaba. "Take one day to buy all the tents possible, regardless of the cost, try all means to deliver them to the stricken areas," ordered Jack Ma.

Jack Ma returned home earlier than he planned to. Without sleeping the whole night, ,he, in high fever, convened a meeting of the executives and deployed work at 8:00 a.m..

Just at this time, some media with ulterior motives made propaganda by garbling a statement Jack Ma said years ago which was "donating one *yuan* in the spotlight" . They distorted the statement by saying that Jack Ma called everyone to donate only one *yuan*. What Jack Ma really meant in the early years was that, donating and charity is the duty and virtue of every citizen, regardless of the amount afforded. Don't affect the public's charitable initiatives due to the announcement of the big numbers donated by the wealthy. Each *yuan* donated by millions of people helps those in need.

Every staff of the company, top and low, all expressed indignation to the release of the distorted facts. We also worried that Jack Ma couldn't stand this because of his high fever. "If every day a bird just thinks how to tidy its feathers, it won't last long, because a basin of dirty water can ruin it. Let them talk! Tide will fall when the time comes. Till then, we will see clearly who weren't wearing underpants (the real fact)," Jack Ma responded.

On May 23, Jet Li came back to Shanghai from the affected areas to resupply relief for the region again. I accompanied Jack Ma to meet him at Jin Mao Tower in Shanghai. Jet Li looked very tired and his lips were dry and parched, a totally different person from Bo'ao a month ago. But his eyes still brimmed with radiating vigor when he talked.

He revealed the conditions of the affected areas and urgent matters needed to be attended: the food was basically sufficient; tents were almost enough.

Body bags were in urgent need now, because the exposed bodies have begun to decay. If disease spreads, the consequence will be unimaginable. In addition, they also needed a lot of sanitary napkins, which can be used as oversized Band-Aids, very functional. Many of the college students who went for "psychological support" could not adapt to such tragic situations from their current experience and knowledge. They fainted, vomited, and cried and it was the victims covered in blood to comfort them instead...

Jet Li was a true warrior! He sounded swift and determined, like a soldier who called to the troops to gather the ammunition and would go back to the frontline again.

Through conversation, Jack Ma became aware of the arduousness and professionalism of the disaster relief work. He immediately found relevant experts, by combining our own advantages and formulated a series of rescue plans without delay. Besides donations from senior executives, the company also set up a special fund of 25 million *yuan*.

The donation window set on the Alipay webpage quickly raised a total of more than 26 million *yuan* from employees and customers.

Group executives were sent again and again to escort goods on trucks to deliver to the disaster areas short of supplies.

Post-disaster Reconstruction

On June 2, 2008, Jack Ma, with private entrepreneurs and experts, held a meeting in Langfang to discuss the post-disaster reconstruction work. Shen Bing, the CCTV host, was also present, as I recalled.

Jack Ma learned from the experts that the post-disaster reconstruction, especially psychological reconstruction, would generally take seven years. So the company designed a seven-year aid plan. Jack Ma said that if seven years was not enough, we would add another seven years. The aid plan included the following: to subsidize 2,000 *yuan* per year to each of the teachers who stayed in their local positions; to help with the local e-commerce development; to sell the agricultural products from the disaster areas to the country with the aid of Taobao; to set up branch offices in the local areas; to recruit local disabled youth to join Alibaba...

Some of the things that happened in those years remain fresh in my memory.

One day, Jack Ma asked the Public Relations Department to write an article calling on Alibaba members to join the relief effort. After reading the first edition, Jack Ma spoke to vice president Wang Shuai, who was in charge of PR, and said; "This article neither expresses my mood now, nor has enough appealing power."

"Well, you... you, please give some directions. I will go back and rewrite it." Wang Shuai often started with "you (ni - you) " to "you (nin - you, honorific language) "when talking to Jack Ma.

"I know you've been utterly exhausted from overwork. Can you find a good journalist friend to help you out? Besides, the principle of our public relations is not to buy in the media, but not to say that we can't recruit a truth-telling reporter with a sense of justice and literary grace in Alibaba, right?"

"I have a journalist friend who meets your requirements. But may I ask, how shall we place him?"

"Uncle Li said (a quote from Feng Xiaogang's movie *A World without Thieves*)..." Jack Ma said, still looking at the souvenirs on the bookshelf without turning back.

"In the 21st century, the most expensive commodity is talents, got it!" Wang Shuai cut in and then left in a hurry.

Jack Ma turned back. "Look at Wang Shuai, he just wouldn't let me finish. Even race the answer!"

Jack Ma had high regards for Wang Shuai, He once told me, "Wang Shuai often did better than I expected!"

With an overnight's work, Wang Shuai brought the second edition the next day early in the morning.

Jack Ma was very satisfied. "Well done! How forceful it is!" He remarked while reading.

At noon, on the day of the mourning for the disaster area, I was at Jack Ma's home. Before the planned time, Jack Ma gathered all people at his home to stand in silent tribute. "I'm not a man of formality. But form has its functions. Just think, such a big event, so many people in the country stand together in silence. On the one hand, it is to mourn the victims; on the other hand, you can experience a kind of power," Jack Ma said at the end of mourning. "Other forms are important too, such as the religious baptism. The holy water is actually no different from tap water. But before the solemn gaze and witness of so many people, this aura will give you power and it will also have constraints on your future behaviors. This is fixing the true by false," he continued.

During that time, a lot of friends called in, "I've heard that Alibaba contributed one *yuan* in total?"

"Not so much. It is a false report, only over a half hundred million." I answered them all like this. "If you are told that 'the deaf heard a mute say the blind saw a ghost, will you believe it? Go and check, whether the people who are the fiercest attackers on the Internet have donated even a penny to others or not?"

Once in the meeting, the Social Responsibility Department suggested many ways to help the disaster areas. After hearing the suggestions, Jack Ma said: "Those are wonderful suggestions. But don't build castles in the air. Better go to the victims and listen to their voices and willingness. That is, before helping an old lady cross the street, first make clear whether she really wants to cross the street." Everyone laughed and understood his points.

Jack Ma also had two principles in supporting the disaster area: do not make a show; do not bother the local government.

In the spring of 2009, Jack Ma, Peng Lei, I and others went to the disaster area. We rented a few SUVs in Chengdu. After more than five hours of driving, we reached Qingchuan. At that time the post-disaster reconstruction was being conducted in an orderly fashion. Our mood was not so heavy then.

The rapeseed flowers were in full blossom along the way. At noon, we found a clearing to eat boxed lunches. After lunch we took a group photo near a field of flowers. Just then, a truck loaded with bees passed by. A swarm of bees came flying head-on. In an instant, everyone's face and body were covered with bees. We were all taken aback with all kinds of expressions and postures and the moment was captured. In the picture, someone quickly took a hat to cover Jack Ma's head, but I pulled far away, really ashamed.

After we arrived at the disaster areas, Jack Ma took us to visit the teachers and students of the funded schools and presented them and the neighboring people with some gifts.

We stayed in the houses built of boards at night. The walls were made of foam material, but the beam at the top was of rectangle metal, hollow inside. Even though, it would hurt people if it fell down. We were afraid to go to bed early. I recommended playing cards and the winner would use the money to take the helpers recruited at the local areas to dinner. With limited options, all agreed.

We took pistachios as chips. At first, Jack Ma won a lot of pistachios. Jack Ma was proud of himself and carelessly ate the pistachios he won as a snack while playing. By the time he realized it, there were not very many left. We were really amused. Jack Ma asked whether he could use two pistachio shells as a pistachio nut. Of course we wouldn't agree.

By 9:30 p.m., the rooms suddenly quaked. We all ran out. A resident next to us spoke in Sichuan dialect; "Don't worry, be easy. Small earthquakes happen every day." It took long for us to get over the shock. But we just got in the room and sat down, the quake came over again forcing us out for the second time.

The next day, Jack Ma took us somewhere else to condole with victims and listen to their needs. On the way back we told stories. I told more. I forgot most of them except for three. The first one was: If there is (has) a car, I drive; Peng Lei sits next to me; Jack Ma sits at the back. Question: Whose car is this?"

No one could give the answer. I then announced the answer; "The car is 'ifs.' As I said, 'If has a car.'" Everyone laughed.

The second one: Once upon a time there was a mouse. A cow was ahead of the mouse and a tiger was ahead of the cow. What was behind the mouse?" Someone vied to answer: "It's a pig. I know the arrangement of Chinese zodiac!" And I answered, "The pig said the same. But sorry, no. The answer was also a worm. As indicated in the topic, once upon a time (cong (there) − chong (worm) homophonic) a mouse is ahead of a worm. Of course a worm was behind the mouse." Everyone burst into laughter again.

The last one: I pointed to a classmate and said, "Wen Jia, if you are a bus driver of No. 11 Bus. At the origin station, 36 people get on the bus. At the second stop, seven people get on. No one gets off. At the third stop, 11 people get on, three people get off... Question: how old is the driver?"

"Jerk! Does the number of passengers getting on and off have anything to do with the age of the driver?" Wen Jia said.

"Did you hear me clearly? I said 'if you are the bus driver,' you don't know your own age?" Everyone laughed again.

That day for the first time, Peng Lei praised me. She said my articles could be described as "meaningful." It was a great honor to me.

On the way, I went to answer the "urgent call" in a farmhouse. A middle-aged woman was sitting in the doorway, leisurely in the sunshine and was cracking a walnut with the back of a chopper. I asked her if we could buy some walnuts, sit down, crack them and relax. "No need to buy. Take them all and eat. I can tell you are the cultured people who came to help people in the disaster area."

Public Welfare

Under the active promotion of Jack Ma, the program for public good developed vigorously in Alibaba.

In July 2009, the Group began to hold "Yuecheng Qingchuan" public welfare activities. Each month employees would sign up, by taking their own annual leave and pay their own expenses to serve in the disaster areas. Many people signed up, and some colleagues signed up for the first phase could only make it in Phase Nine. Among them, two colleagues got to know each other because of the work through Yuecheng Qingchuan and they fell in love and became a loving couple envied by all. By the end of 2010, Yuecheng Qingchuan had carried out 15 phases of activities. Jack Ma encouraged everyone to participate in public welfare. And Ali staff's touching deeds, in turn, moved Jack Ma time and time again.

The Group and each subsidiary had their own public welfare activities. Among them, the Group's recent "Happy Grouping (Xingfu Baotuan)" was as innovative as the "Horse Race" of Taobao business. It was to let the colleagues propose the interesting public welfare activities. Based on the proposed ideas, the company would render corresponding support, such as "The Sound of Love" in which the colleagues recorded good articles and sent them to children at a School for the Blind.

The Company donated 25 million *yuan* to help support victims of the Yushu earthquake in 2010.

"CCTV broadcasted the donation program yesterday," I told Jack Ma.

"I didn't watch it. But many friends have called and told me that the most beautiful and the most well-spoken one was from Alibaba," Jack Ma was very proud.

During the preparations for the Expo, one day, Jack Ma, at the invitation of Guo Guangchang, went to Shanghai to make a mobilization speech to the volunteers of the Private Enterprises Pavilion. It was the time of the worst drought in Yunnan. Jack Ma heard that donating 4,000 *yuan* could help Yunnan to build a small water cellar which would help with future drought. He and Guo promptly decided to draw money from the budget of Private Enterprises Pavilion to do it. "Hurry! Hurry! Yunnan's earth was cracked so badly that with a pour of water it would directly seep to the United States!" Jack Ma urged.

Once again, Wang Bing from the Huaxia Foundation told Jack Ma that an agreement had been reached with the Armed Police Hospital of Guangdong Province on cooperation. With every donation of 10,000 *yuan*, they would provide free heart surgery for a child with congenital heart disease. "Wonderful! Ten thousand *yuan* can save a life. I won't be left behind," Jack Ma said excitedly.

We went to Guangzhou the following day. Jack Ma not only donated some money in his own name, but also visited the children before and after the surgery. He also participated in promotions in the local area.

Jack Ma showed great sincerity when he met the children and their parents. He was clear that the hearts of the poor were fragile and we should never trample on their self-esteem while helping them.

In the recent two years, Jack Ma was most concerned about public welfare and environmental protection in his public speeches. At the 2010 Yabuli meeting, when other entrepreneurs used the meeting as an excellent platform to promote their businesses, Jack Ma talked like this; "The disasters have struck frequently in recent years. I wonder, what has happened to the earth? Trees and forests are like the earth's hair; you cut them down and cover them with cement. Rivers are like blood vessels of the earth, you blocked them one by one and from time to time made a hole in it and buried explosives in it... The earth has a life of its own. If it were me, I would also be angry and I would avenge too..."

In September 1949, Chairman Mao said: "**Let the domestic and foreign reactionaries tremble before us! Let them say we are no good at this and no good at that.**" I would add, "Let them say we've only donated one *yuan*."

Never Give Up

Never give up, this is the core of the Alibaba business culture, and is the common faith for people on their entrepreneurship or about to be on their entrepreneurship.

Jack Ma told me, the only time he wanted to give up was in 1997 when he was thriving in his business of chinapage.com. China Telecom (CT) made a foray in the business and also did a yellow page chinesepage.com, which immediately messed things up. Events followed which forced Jack Ma to cooperate with CT. He, in United States, was at a crossing for a moment.

One Sunday, Jack Ma, depressed and feeling low, as a stranger in a foreign land, stepped into a church.

After prayers, the priest mentioned Winston Churchill and recited Churchill's speech during the Second World War:

You ask, what is our aim? I can answer in one word, it is victory. Victory at all costs-victory in spite of all terrors-victory, however long and hard the road may be, for without victory, there is no survival···

The priest was full of passion while preaching and his eyes fixed on Jack Ma again and again.

"At that time I felt the priest was sent by god to encourage me. I felt he was talking to me only," Jack Ma said.

Jack Ma never think about giving up since that day. His autographs to others were mostly followed by "Never Give Up"!

But personally I have a different opinion. I agree more with Jack Ma's other sentence; "Comparing with what the speakers said, what the listeners heard was more important." Deep in his heart, Jack Ma never really thought of giving up. He just needed some encouragement during difficult times. On the surface, it was the priest's preaching that encouraged Jack Ma, but the truth was that Jack Ma captured what he wanted to hear. (Just like me who captures nothing but jokes every day). I bet no one else in the church remembered exactly what the priest said.

The Power of Culture

Prior to May 2008, the last training classes for newcomers were all held by Jack Ma in person. "...Alibaba won't promise you a high salary and good material wealth. On the contrary, in Ali, you'll have to bear a lot of injustice and pressure..." When I first heard this, I felt this was a blow to the enthusiasm of new colleagues more or less. But thinking back now, these words are really necessary. Although Jack Ma could not find time to teach each group of new colleagues after that, he really hoped that they would know this.

Everyone's life is different, but many share similar spiritual journeys. College students all feel they are capable of everything and are fearless and can ride the whirlwind. **"Now that I dared to come to this world, I wasn't thinking to leave alive!"** After graduation, they fought their way to work at Alibaba only to find that all those "ugly and incompetent" (crooked melons and cracked jujubes) were higher-leveled in the company than they were. Not only were they talented and unrecognized (or so they thought), the ones they hated most were also their "bosses". At this moment, they just wanted to run into the wilderness, hands up high, shouting **"Stop the earth! I want to get off!"** After a few years, with patience and effort, things unconsciously and slowly got better and better. Just then, someone found that the new girl in the other building was appealing in every way possible. He racked his brain for 18 tricks to fawn on her. Mustering all his courage, he came to her, but with only one trick, the girl "yielded," an ecstasy! He took her back to his hometown to show her off at the Spring Festival. Seeing there were not too many places for fun, he just went to a small temple. Randomly he drew a lot. The fortune-teller monk, with abstruse eyes hiding behind sunglasses, told him a universal standard of truth, **"You will live till you die!"** After the Spring Festival, he came back to the company. One day he suddenly realized that he had become the "ugly and incompetent" in the eyes of his new colleagues...

The first time that I strongly felt the Ali culture was on July 1, 2008.

That afternoon, the company held a plenary meeting of the Organization Department at a Best Western Hotel in Hangzhou. One of the contents was to welcome former CCTV host Zhang Wei and other new colleagues to join the Ali Group.

In the evening, a meeting for the B2B middle-level and above was held in the hotel until 3:00 a.m..

At the meeting, everyone called a spade a spade. First the old colleague attacked the "airborne" new leadership and thought the techniques and rules of "professional managers" were not suitable for Alibaba. Alibaba relied on hard work spirit; a kind of "very simple and naive, very strong and durable" spirit. A female colleague also said with tears, "When I was in the front line, I never had the chance to communicate with CEO Ma. One day CEO Ma passed by. He actually mentioned my name and even asked me about my work. I was moved to tears. After that, for three months, I devoted myself to work, did nothing else except to get sleep. I was willing to work hard! Soon I came to the top."

The "airborne" leadership, on the other hand, thought that skill upgrading was a must and the sooner the better.

An old colleague even openly provoked a leader, "You've jumped from many companies before. How long do you think you would work at Alibaba?"

Of course, there were some old colleagues who were supportive to the new leadership. "Alibaba has this value of embracing change. Since everyone keeps saying you love Ali's culture, why not 'embrace' the 'change' of a new leader, and 'embrace' the change of new 'ideas'?"

Someone even challenged Jack Ma at the meeting. "CEO Ma, if you've made an obvious mistake in your decision, who will counterbalance you?"

"First, no one in the company can counterbalance me. Second, if I have made a decision, even if it is wrong, it must be performed. Third, the decision you all think is wrong might not necessarily be wrong at all," Jack Ma calmly replied.

As Jack Ma predicted, shortly after, the financial storm swept across the globe. Jack Ma resolutely implemented the "Tornado Run" which was initially opposed by almost everyone at high-levels. They disagreed with surrendering large amounts of profits to small and medium-sized enterprises in the "severe winter". This was well-received by the small and medium-sized enterprises and the numbers of customers increased rapidly, like a blowout. Although the unit price was lowered, the total revenue increased instead. The "Tornado Run" created great success.

If the meeting that night was a shock to me, then the B2B Sanya Sales

Meeting two days after was overwhelming, because the few regional cadres who "provoked" the leaders had expressed strong support for the decision of the leadership.

Now I know that each of the "Organization Department" meetings was a meeting to speak the truth. Everyone could propose their own ideas and clarify them by debating and no one would take it into heart afterwards. Some colleagues were thoroughly refuted by Jack Ma at the meeting and would appear again in Jack Ma's home in the evening, chatting over a cup of tea, as if nothing had happened.

On the eve of the Olympic Games, an ABAC meeting was held in Hangzhou. The closing party was held at the Jiangnan Club. Jack Ma was very active at the party, singing, dancing and even performing some magic that he had just learned to the representatives from various countries. Everyone had a great time at the party.

On December 15, 2008, after the meeting in Beijing, Jack Ma and I went to the Jingya Restaurant at the second west ring for dinner. It was a Shandong seafood restaurant with more than one branch in Beijing. They were all Jack Ma's "fans", from the boss to the staff. After dinner, the staff said they had prepared a surprise for us. Just then background music *On the Road* came from the TV and the PPT showed photos and quotes of Jack Ma's speeches in different places as well as our value "Six Pulses Magic Sword" etc. The fruit served was an orange, engraved with 102, standing for the 102 years that Alibaba would grow.

Back to the company, I published *A Moving Dinner* on the Intranet.

On December 23, Professor Zhou Qiren from Peking University visited Alibaba. Professor Zhou showed great interest for the "Trust Store" of the Ali culture in the company. There are many "Trust Stores" in the company which have no assistant. Everyone pays the price as labeled and takes the goods consciously. Over the years, "Trust Store" is always in operation and not a penny has ever been missed.

The 10th Anniversary Celebration

In 2009, with the company's 10th anniversary drawing near, all branches were busy preparing their own programs in their spare time.

The "executives show" highly expected had no landing, since it was too hard to gather all nine senior executives together.

Jack Ma decided to sing an English song from *The Lion King* in the show.

There was also another episode of the story. A few months ago, Jack Ma attended a project discussion of Taobao, called "Simba's Plan". Simba is the name of the small lion in *The Lion King*. During the meeting break, someone sang two lines of the theme song of *The Lion King*, to which Jack Ma thought it was good and thus sowed the seed.

I put the disc with the theme song of *The Lion King* in Jack Ma's car and played it for him whenever there was time. But he was too busy to calm down and concentrate on listening.

The evening of September 6 was the only time for the nine executives to get together for rehearsal. Jack Ma still couldn't sing it at the rehearsal and part of it was sung by me. All program groups felt tension over this single program.

On September 7, Jack Ma had a full schedule as usual. I reserved a KTV room nearby and forcibly dragged Jack Ma to sing. Jack Ma sang several times. "The lyrics are very difficult to remember. Shall I try another song that I can sing," said Jack Ma. Then Ma sang another song named *You Are So Beautiful to Me* for several times.

The next day when I informed the band that Jack Ma decided to sing a different song, it was met with strong oppositions from the Director Group and several executives. It was a song from an American movie, which talked about the story of the head gangster who fell in love with a woman but was incapable of doing anything due to his position. But Jack Ma thought it in a different way. "I am singing to all employees. All employees are so beautiful to me."

On the performance day, Jack Ma decided to sing both songs. In case he might forget the lyrics, I printed several copies for him.

In the evening, the whole show was very successful. Nearly 30,000 employees and their families came to the show. Many entrepreneur friends also came to enjoy the show. The "Executives Show" brought the party to a climax. The executives of the company, in very cool punk outfits, stepped on the stage in the form of a band. The whole stadium bubbled up. When Jack Ma appeared with feathers in his head, heavy make-up, singing *"Can you feel the love to-*

night," the stadium quaked with screaming. Yu Dan was late that night. When she passed by the front of the stage, Jack Ma happened to rise from the stage in punk outfit. The audience erupted. "Is that Jack Ma? Oh, my goodness! He's crazy!" Yu Dan was stunned.

Everyone on the site thought Jack Ma's singing was amazing. But at the end of the song, he said with a smile, "I was a lead singer who could not remember the lyrics and wearing sunglasses I could hardly see the lyrics in my hand." But this did not affect his dazzling light.

After the "Executives Show," Jack Ma came onto the stage again after changing his costumes and made a speech. "...in the next 10 years, we'll help 10 million enterprises survive, grow and develop, create 100 million jobs, provide a really cheap and fine platform for 1 billion people..." This was a very classic speech, known as "*I Have a Dream*" speech. It pointed out the direction for the development of Alibaba for the next 10 years in a very stimulating way.

Jerry Yang was present that night too. He was also a very humorous man. At the end of the party, someone asked him how he felt about it. "Nice programs. I just fell asleep twice in the whole process. Ha-ha!" He said.

After the party, some well-known enterprises in Hangzhou also came to the company to exchange ideas. Their leadership also "valued" enterprise culture, but the participation and employee enthusiasm was not high.

"What is 'valuing'? It's only valued when the big boss took the lead in person. The power of example is endless. Any language spoken loud without action is pale," said I.

They thought that made sense.

Pain Yes, But Integrity First

On the afternoon of February 21, 2011, the company held a plenary meeting of all Organization Departments; a meeting that no one knew what it was about.

Before the meeting, I saw Wei Zhe, CEO of B2B leaving Jack Ma's office with an unprecedented expression of fatigue.

The meeting started by Jack Ma's announcement of "approving Wei Zhe's resignation from the post of CEO of B2B," which startled all the colleagues but no one spoke a word...

Later, Peng Lei who just resumed her post as the CEO of the Human Resources Department of the Group went on the stage to speak. When it came to true feelings, her tears welled out. She didn't wipe them with a tissue, nor did she turn her back, she just let the tears stream down her face. In the pause of 15 seconds, the audience was still as silent as a grave, those seconds were a century long.

After the meeting, I accompanied Jack Ma to the airport. "The world" had learned about it at this moment. All the way to the airport, there were incoming calls from entrepreneurs to Jack Ma one after another. I could vaguely hear the voices at the other end of the phone. "Jack, this is a heavy stroke!" one said. "Isn't that too loud? Firing a vice president could well show your determination, why should you fire Wei Zhe?" another asked. "Jack is Jack, I hail for you!" the third one said.

"Chen Wei, if you are fighting in the battlefield and are stabbed by the enemy, you won't feel too much pain. But if you cut your own hand at home, the pain..." Jack Ma said to me after the phone calls, wearing a complex expression on his tired face.

On the same day, all Alier received an email from Jack Ma.

In the past month or more, I have felt grave pain, I've been very upset, very angry...

But this is our growing pain, a price we must pay in our development, very painful! But, we have no choice! We are not a company that will never make mistakes. We may often make mistakes in the future judgment, but never the mistakes on principle compromise.

If today we don't have the courage to face reality, to bear the consequence, and to bite the bullet, Ali will no longer be Ali. Adhering to the dream and mission of 102 years would be empty talk and a joke!

The world doesn't need one more Internet company, nor does it need one more company that makes money.

What the world needs is a more open and more transparent, more sharing, more responsible, more global company.

The world needs a company that comes from society, serves society, and dares to take responsibility for future society.

The world needs a kind of culture, a kind of spirit, a belief, a kind of undertaking. Only with these, can we go farther, better and more comfortable in the hard entrepreneurship.

Naked "Mongolian"

In January 2010, Jack Ma shipped two art sculptures from Beijing. One was made of copper, a pair of naked man and woman standing on a lotus. The sculpture showed verdigris, made to be antique-like. It was 2.2 meters high and was placed at the side of "Starbucks" on the campus. The other one called "Mongolian" was a robust naked man of 3.6 meters tall and was placed on the lawn opposite of the gate. To make him more striking, under Jack Ma's suggestion, a few small trees on the lawn were removed.

As soon as the sculptures were set up, the reaction of colleagues was so strong that it went beyond my imagination. The abuse on the Intranet was surging just like the spring tide of the Qiantang River.

"I originally felt very proud working in Alibaba. Now every day when I come to work the first thing in my sight is a tall naked man. I am blushed with shame," someone said.

"With a pair of 'rusty' naked man and woman placed at the side of 'Starbucks,' we all feel embarrassed to drink coffee, and think even the coffee is rusty," another said.

Some even dressed the "Mongolian" in pictures with all kinds of costumes by Photoshop, protesting to move away the sculpture, or dress him with clothes.

Jack Ma was aboard then and also heard all sorts of claims. He did not see the scene effect, so he send me a message, "Is it out of tune with the campus?"

I had been to Peking University and "798" with Jack Ma and had seen many more avant-garde sculptures. I visited the scene myself, and then replied to Jack Ma. "Finish touching, no good − without it!"

"After three months, you will be ashamed for what you said today," I said to my colleagues.

The only one who shared my opinion then was Wang Yongmei, a colleague responsible for B2B administration. (She docked with me for the placement of the sculptures).

Sure enough, after a period of time, everyone grew fond of it and no longer felt "embarrassed." Many took pictures with the "Mongolian" and took a walk around the "Mongolian" after lunch.

Still the colleagues from the Reception Department had a problem, because all visitors would ask what the "Mongolian" implied.

So they began to set their minds to making up a moral; "The naked body stands for Alibaba's openness and transparency. The robust figure represents Ali's 'strong and enduring' culture."

Jack Ma found this was both funny and annoying. "If I plant a tree there, will you ask me the moral of it? It is a sculpture. You like it, fine; you don't like it, no problem. If a colleague by your side is not pretty, will you not work hard?" "This is only 3.6 meters tall. After the Taobao Town completes, I will put a 6.3 meters tall naked woman with huge breasts and see what they would say," he said jokingly.

At the end of 2010, the company's most popular gift is the pony edition of the "Mongolian," just like the Oscar's trophy, with the name of "Awesome."

Intertwined "Entertainment" Complex

In April 2009, Zhou Xun, as the Environmental Protection Ambassador, was in Hangzhou. She was still with Huayi then. As we all knew, Jack Ma, a movie fan, was one of the big shareholders of Huayi. Zhou Xun planned to talk with the "boss" of promoting environmental protection using a network platform. Jack Ma had been committed to environmental protection too. He was holding a Taobao's high-level meeting at the Yongfu Temple on that day, so his meeting with Zhou Xun was arranged there.

I got to know Zhou Xun as early as 2001 when *The Legend of the Condor Heroes* was in action. Jack Ma was still in the meeting when Zhou Xun arrived, so I chatted with Zhou Xun's team over a cup of tea. Although I didn't have any idea of the cooperation, it didn't affect my enthusiasm for "bragging." Zhou Xun seemed to enjoy our conversation, although her legs were bitten all over by the "yet-to-be Buddha" mountain mosquitoes.

Jack Ma joined Zhou Xun's team at the dinner table after the Taobao meeting. They talked over the vegetarian food made in the temple which was well-cooked and won the full praise from Jack Ma and Zhou Xun.

Later, the premiere of the movie *The Message* was held in Hangzhou.

Zhou Xun invited Jack Ma to go but he did not have time and arranged me to go instead. I selected four girls from different branches. Before setting off, I raised two very excessive demands to Amei, the assistant of Zhou Xun; "At the press conference before the show, the reporter should question specifically the girls from Alibaba, and take group photos with the Alibaba girls. Zhou Xun agreed to both requests.

Once I went with Jack Ma for a meeting in Beijing. We ran into Sun Feifei in the lobby, who played "Aju" in *Sword Stained with Royal Blood* in our crew a few years ago.

Speaking of Taobao, Sun Feifei was very excited. She was more familiar with Taobao than me and had bought almost all her cosmetics and daily necessities from Taobao. She said that many actresses did so. They didn't have time to go shopping during filming. "With Taobao, the stores are always with you," she said.

Sun Feifei also drew a comic to explain her Taobao strategy and insight.

After I got back to Hangzhou, I asked the chief editor of weekly periodical Tao T to contact Sun Feifei. Soon there was an issue with an article about Sun Feifei and her comics on the front cover. That was an extremely beautiful picture, very much like Hepburn's classic photo.

In December 2009, *Vogue* magazine's annual conference was held at the National Indoor Stadium. Jack Ma and Shi Yuzhu was rated "Men of the Year."

That night many stars showed up, Zhang Ziyi, Sun Honglei... one after another, a real feast for the eyes but with little time to digest. No wonder Huang Bo, the best actor said on stage, "I climbed up and up, thought I had reached 80th floor. But when I looked up, I found myself still in the basement."

Vogue's leadership team was quite familiar with Jack Ma too. Jack Ma once did a sharing with their cadres of middle-level and above to exchange ideas. Their innovative ideas were well thought by Jack Ma. "I used to think no one would read these magazines. But after exchanging with you, I understand women are animals living in fantasy. They think that they will be as beautiful as stars if they wear what the stars wear. In fact, women are smarter than men. Reality or fantasy, to be happy is the absolute principle," Jack Ma said humorously.

Shen Guojun, President of Yintai, was one of the best friends of Jack Ma. Many people had the same view as I did that President Shen was someone from the entrepreneurs that could "mix" in with the star team just by his good looks. Shen was handsome and very modest. I used to think Shen was the "undone toff" of the "rich second generation." It was not until after I read about Shen's early history in *Vogue* did I realize it was totally different from what I had thought. That's really something!

Shen was a quiet person. His achievements in Yintai did all the talking for him. A lot of people are like me, even in a department of less than 10 people, we need to "brag" constantly to prove our existence.

At the end of 2009, Jack Ma and I flew to Changsha. Although he had always admired Chairman Mao, this was the first time for Jack Ma to visit Hunan. We first visited the Yuelu Academy, and then went to Orange Isle. The enormous Chairman Mao's head portrait sculpture was completed at the Orange Isle just then.

After seeing the "Qin Yuan Chun, Changsha" engraved at the Orange Isle, Jack Ma said, "After reading Chairman Mao's poetry, I understand what having the mind of the world is; after looking at Chairman Mao's handwriting, I know what following one's inclinations is."

In the evening, we met Ouyang, head of the Hunan Satellite TV. Ouyang is a legend in Chinese television industry. Hit shows *Super Girl* and *Supper Boy* are all his works.

Wang Han knew Jack Ma very well before. This time, he decided to take part in the planning and hosting of *HiTao*, the program cooperated by Taobao and the Hunan Satellite TV.

At dinner the next day we saw a lot of people, including a tall, thin, very dignified Hunan local. He had a pleasant talk with Jack Ma, but left in the middle. "I'll go and get ready, see you later!" He said.

After dinner, we all went to listen to "Tan Dun's New Year Concert". When the concert started, I saw a tall, thin man standing on the stage. At this time I knew he was Tan Dun, whom I only just heard the name before.

Jack Ma's Interests

As you all know, Jack Ma was a martial arts lover since childhood. He is also fond of learning English and playing Taiji. As a matter of fact, Jack Ma's interests are far more than these.

Jack Ma likes seeing all kinds of movies, especially the movies about the

Second World War. He would review some movies again after some days. "Chen Wei, please go and buy a legal copy, a movie about Eisenhower and Patton, with the word 'dawn' in the title. I have seen it before. I'd like to see it again," Jack Ma said to me one day.

Jack Ma also likes operas. Once in Beijing, he dined in the former resident of Mei Baojiu with some friends. Young men and women conducted some Beijing Opera for the guests there. Jack Ma requested one piece after another and cried out "Bravo! Bravo!" from time to time.

He bought a lot of classic Beijing Opera records after he returned to Hangzhou. "So-and-so's singing voice is excellent. I don't like so-and-so's voice. It is horrible. Chen Wei, don't you think so?" He commented while listening.

"I'm sorry, Jack Ma. It's all the same to me, one flavor," I told the truth.

Jack Ma also likes to listen to bel canto, especially, Luciano Pavarotti. He often listens at home, sometimes sings along, with his eyes closed, very intoxicated. At first I didn't like it. "Jack Ma, I thought karaoke was the only activity to build one's happiness based on others' pain, now I found there is bel canto." But as I listened more and more, I found listening to bel canto was very good.

When Jack Ma had free time in Hangzhou, he would take us to see Shaoxing Opera and the Kunqu Opera.

Once we went to Taiwan to see the stage play *The Village*. It was really good. The story was told vividly and very touching just through language in such a simple setting.

Jack Ma and his wife are good friends with Shaoxing Opera artist Mao Weitao who always informed Jack Ma when she would be performing.

I went to see Mao Weitao's *The Butterfly Lovers* with Jack Ma and President Shao. Jack Ma offered a flower basket at the end of the show to the backstage and had night snacks with Mao Weitao. He Saifei and others were there too, along with Bai Yansheng, the famous opera host of CCTV. They told us a lot of classic stories of the old artists, talking and performing vividly.

Then the artists wanted to hear stories from us. Jack Ma assigned the task to me as a representative. I told some funny stories in a letter from Tang Monk to Sun Wukong who went on a holiday at the Mountain of Flowers and Fruits: "Wukong, after you left, we have moved on. But the address has not changed, because we took the door plate... Wukong, Pigsy is more sensible after you left. Any secrets I told him, he would tell everyone in the village, he said that there is strength in numbers. Let everyone come together to keep this secret! Monk Sha is more polite than before. He always respectfully asks the ladies to go first, especially in the mined field... Kingdom of Females is really a place with beautiful girls as many as clouds. We have seen none, because it is a bright sky with no clouds..."

Bai Yansheng said in a hyperbolic tone after hearing it, "Oh, dear me! Network Circle is really a lair of dragons and tigers (a place where people of unusual ability are to be found)!" He turned to Mao Weitao, "We obviously showed earlier!"

"This pattern is really nice. Any kind of stories can be threaded in. I plan to read Sun Wukong's return letter to Tang Monk at the next annual meeting letter, ha-ha!" Jack Ma said afterwards.

During the 2008 Olympic Games, under Jack Ma's recommendation and invitation, *If You Are the One* was shot in Xixi Wetland in Hangzhou, which greatly enhanced the popularity of Xixi. During the filming, I accompanied Jack Ma several times to visit the crew and also chatted over tea with Director Feng Xiaogang. I experienced Feng's humor at close distance and met Ge You and Shu Qi, Alex Fong, Vivian Hsu, and other stars.

In November 2008, one night Jack Ma took me to Feng Xiaogang's home. Director Feng's home was full of artistic appeal. Some of the sculptures were off-beat too, close to the things in "798." Some celebrities also came to his home that night and Lu Yi was among them, as I recall.

Lu Yi is really handsome. In Director Feng's hallway, there was a long mirror. When Lu Yi and I walked by one after another, I looked at the two people in the mirror. I formerly claimed myself to be "super cool", but I suddenly lost all confidence. Except for my 1.83 meters height being a little taller than him, I was good for nothing. It was a day I felt most disappointed about me in the mirror since the founding of new China.

We saw the "raw footage" of *If You Are the One* at Feng's home. There was no music and subtitles then.

After we saw the movie Feng told us that there was another scene about Qin Fen's blind date. A stylish woman has a rare American lizard climbing on her shoulder. Qin Fen asks, "Where does the lizard come from? Not easy to get, is it?" The woman replies, "Pumpkin, nothing is 'not easy to get' nowadays. I bought it on Taobao." Feng said, "This was supposed to be a fashion trend. But if it were released, it would be taken as planting advertisement. I reluctantly had it cut."

Two days ago, I saw *If You Are the One II*. Indeed there was the trendy element: "The wheelchair you ordered from Taobao is here."

I was worried after seeing it in Feng's home the other day. I thought it was not as good as *Big Shot's Funeral* and other previous ones. But a month after the release, the box-office proved me wrong.

So I began to reflect on myself. It could be that I was not keen on the story type of *If You Are the One*, or perhaps I had heard the "cloth-wrapper (suspense)" during the shooting. Master is master. He is not at the service of a certain group, but for "the most fundamental interests of the masses".

It was very late when we got to the hotel after the movie. "If Zhang Ying doesn't ask you, don't tell her we are very late tonight or she would say I did not have a good rest," Jack Ma said.

"What if she asks tomorrow?"

"Then you add one sentence, seeing movies is a kind of rest too," Jack Ma explained.

On May 22, 2009, I accompanied Jack Ma to Shanghai to attend a meeting. After that we drove back to Hangzhou. We had dinner with Feng Xiaogang's team at "Shan wai shan (Mountains Beyond Mountains)." Director Feng decided to shoot part of the footage of *After Shock* in Hangzhou. In the play, the daughter's university was decided to be the campus of Zhejiang University near Pagoda of Six Harmonies where my university was. At my college time, a movie was also shot in the campus, called *A University in Exile*, themed with the story of Zhu Kezhen as the President of the University during the anti-Japanese war.

Director Feng was a good story-teller. He talked about the story of *After Shock*, which moved all the people on-site. We all cried out bravo again and again. It is said that Feng decided to shoot it because the story had a distinctive "highlight": A mother faced with two biological children buried under a concrete slab, a son and a daughter, but she can only save one, which one shall she choose? This is one of the most painful choices in the world, but as a story, it is also the point that strikes the hearts of people most.

Feng has a sharp eye in selecting "highlights". No wonder his movies are always so popular.

Director Feng admired Jack Ma too. On November 8, 2010, at the 10th anniversary celebration of *Yang Lan One on One*, held at Beijing Yintai Center, Jack Ma and Feng Xiaogang were both rated the "Enterprising Figures of the Decade." Feng said as he came up to the stage, "Jack Ma is a prophet. He told me five years ago that in five years, there would be a Chinese film that will earn over 500 million *yuan* at the box office, *If You Are the One* achieves this; there would be a cultural company listed in the market, and Huayi made it..."

Chapter 9:
Different Jack Ma and Different Ali

Unique Scrambled Eggs

J ack Ma was born different and making the best of his advantages be came second nature to him. Jack Ma's mother once told me a story: the family had a cooking competition between Jack Ma and his siblings. Jack Ma was the most incompetent among the three. He just scrambled eggs, but he won, because he dressed a beautiful "heart" with peanuts on the cooked egg.

Primary School and College

Despite his many recommendations on the current education system, it does not stop Jack Ma from holding a great deal of respect for teachers and teaching.

One day, Jack Ma received a letter from his primary school for their 50th anniversary celebration. They invited him, but he was very busy at that time. I assumed that he wouldn't go. "I will go! However busy!" he said. He still re-membered the names of his head teacher and English teacher from the prima-ry school. "There were no English classes in other primary schools except ours. It was a pilot base for one-year English teaching, and our English teacher majored in Russian. She did not know much English and went to training class every morning and taught us in the afternoon." And with such a teacher, Jack

Ma grew interested in English. Education is not indoctrination, but enlightening in a way.

On the day of celebration, the two teachers looked at Jack Ma with motherly-like eyes. Jack Ma was also like a kid who just returned to mother after a long separation. "Teacher, I've just had my hair cut bald. Can you see the scar on my head now? Do you still remember the incident?"

How could the teacher forget that? It was as fresh as it just happened yesterday. Students from higher grades bullied Jack Ma's classmates. To 'get even,' Jack Ma attempted the impossible and both sides ended up hurt. From the fight, he received almost 10 stitches on his head. Bleeding all over, Jack Ma was taken to the hospital by the head teacher. Jack Ma didn't cry during the suture. For this matter, the teacher never criticized Jack Ma. "Good boy, good boy," she comforted him during the suture.

But it didn't mean the teacher didn't reason with him.

Encouragement makes the best students.

God can't be in every home, so he created mother; God cannot educate every child, so he created teachers.

After the celebration, Jack Ma donated a sum of money to his alma mater, a seven-digit number.

Jack Ma also had the same feeling toward his college, Hangzhou Normal University. He not only co-founded Alibaba Business School with his alma mater, but also attended the opening ceremonies many times and delivered speeches to encourage his fellow young students. "Hangzhou Normal University is the best university in the world," Jack Ma would claim this everywhere he went.

In September 2011, Jack Ma attended another opening ceremony of the Hangzhou Normal University. When it came to social responsibility and the donations to the disaster areas, Jack Ma expressed his opinions, "Donations may not only change the disaster areas, but it will also change you!"

Magic

Jack Ma has always taken an interest in magic. At an International Conference in 2008, Jack Ma showed some of his magic tricks to foreign delegates at the dinner table. He is especially fond of Louis Liu. "Several times, I watched his magic trick close up but I couldn't see how he did the tricks. I guess he really is a psychic." Someone tried to decrypt Louis Liu's magic but Jack Ma stopped him and said, "No, please. I'd like to take it as real."

Before the 2012 Spring Festival, Louis Liu invited Jack Ma to Macau to watch his show. Jack Ma took a huge group of friends to see the show. It was excellent! After the show Louis Liu invited Jack Ma backstage where he met Louis Liu's mother and his teammates who all were fans of Jack Ma. So we swapped the "Idols" for group photos. "The magic of the three rings is amazing, is it psychic?" I asked Louis Liu. "A secret told is no more a secret," Louis Liu whispered mysteriously by putting his index finger on his lips.

Jack Ma's addiction to magic is intermittent. Some days he would carry a pack of cards in his hands from morning till night. It happened during the 2013 Yabuli meeting. As soon as they got aboard, he began to play magic to his entrepreneur friends on the plane. He enjoyed looking others' slack-jawed faces. Even when some of his magic was seen through, Jack Ma never felt discouraged. He would think of ways to improve and would never get bored with it.

Up to now, Jack Ma's best "magic," the one that stupefies everyone, is Alibaba and Taobao. More than a decade ago, everyone believed that what the best the Internet could provide was electronic media. But Jack Ma insisted that e-commerce was the most worthwhile attempt. This is by no means the last "magic trick" from Jack Ma. New magic is yet to appear.

Playing the Piano

One time in 2011, Jack Ma and I arrived back from the United States after midnight. So I stayed in Jack Ma's home. The next morning when I got up, I heard the sound of piano, an old song popular in the 1980s. I followed the sound and found it was actually Jack Ma who was playing in the hall. I am a frequent guest at Jack Ma's home. The only furniture against my taste was the piano. I never said anything about it, but I've always been thinking. Now that you are not a corny boss, why should you use a useless piano to show that you are civilized?

I had never seen Jack Ma play the piano before. I am at nowhere to judge for I don't understand anything about the piano. I think Jack Ma played equally as well as Lang Lang, except he didn't wag his head.

When I disclosed this secret to my "daughters" in the company, Li Yang who passed the 10th level in piano certification became extremely excited. "Chen Ba, in the next annual meeting, I will PK CEO Ma!"

Dogs and Their Fates

Jack Ma is known for his love for dogs, especially German shepherds. Because of his influence, many entrepreneurs began to raise dogs. In early 2011, the highly bread female gave birth to a litter of puppies and they were soon reserved by others, leaving only one for Jack Ma.

Many people know Shi Yuzhu has a German shepherd sharing the same name as a President of the United States. There is a story behind it.

In early March of 2011, Shi Yuzhu came to Jack Ma's home with his majestic team to take the German shepherd he reserved previously. Before meeting its new owner, the little dog was taken to a pet store to be spruced-up the day before. But accidentally, it got its leg broken while getting a bath. It was tied with gauze on the leg when it met its new owner.

Shi Yuzhu showed much regret while having lunch at Jack Ma's home. After going through tremendous torment in his heart, Jack Ma decided to give Shi Yuzhu his favorite German shepherd. Shi was naturally overjoyed.

The dog with a broken leg seemed to have had a heavy blow to it. Later Jack Ma gave it to Master Yuezhen at the Yongfu Temple. Jack Ma would go to see the dog whenever he went to the temple for tea.

Our destiny often takes place with great change from some minor events, so do the dogs'. The dog that has the same name of the President is enjoying a luxurious life with meat and milk every day. Its hair is combed clean and bright by beautiful girls; whereas, the dog at the Yongfu Temple has become a vegetarian and is evidently not as sturdy as the "President." Its barking sounds slightly merciful too. Amitabha! Bless it to be happy.

Jack Ma often went to Beijing on business. If he had more than two hours of free time after business, one of his paramount choices was to go and look at the dogs. At the end of 2012, an entrepreneur friend of Jack Ma brought back a 13-month-old champion dog from Germany. Jack Ma gleamed with delight. Now if you go to Jack Ma's home, that dog will be the first to come to you.

Trip to Maotai

Ji Keliang, Chairman of the Kweichow Maotai Winery (Group) Co., Ltd., an old friend of Jack Ma, had invited him to visit for two years. On the May Day holiday in 2011, Jack Ma took us and came to the legendary Maotai Town after crossing countless rivers and mountains.

Chairman Ji personally showed us around the winery and Wine Culture Museum. At the end of the tour, Jack Ma burst into laughter when he saw the rice paper placed on the desk. It was something he feared most, writing calligraphy!

It was hopeless to decline the kind offer, so Jack Ma showed his courage at the critical moment and wrote down, "Choice Wine under Heaven". I took the venture and had a glance. Not too bad! Better than imagined.

In the Conference Room, Chairman Ji took out his own collection of many years, the only bottle of Maotai Liquor left from the year 1980. I did my own math and learned that a small cup was worth my one month's salary. I drank three cups, which made me feel like I got another year-end bonus.

After three rounds of wine drinking at the dinner party, we talked more freely. Chairman Ji came to the Maotai Winery after college graduation, which was the year that Jack Ma was born. "Heroes are alike". I heard from the various staff that Chairman Ji's daughter-in-law was a staff in Alibaba for many years. None of us knew who she was. The Ji couple didn't tell us even though we requested many times because their daughter-in-law wanted to keep it from our knowledge. What an employee!

We went back to the hotel after dinner and found the Maotai Town was "loomed" in the scent of wine.

The lift of the hotel was not spacious. Another friend of Jack Ma's, who also came with us for the visit, was overweight and jammed the lift when he got on. He had to step out of the lift and carry his 200 pound plus body up the stairs. Jack Ma patted the still gasping man on the back when he arrived upstairs and joked with him. "You're the one who knows the distance. You actually wanted to squeeze in such a small lift. It would be overloaded even if you took the lift alone!"

In order to cope with the future embarrassment of writing calligraphy when occasions arise, he invented his own Ma-style calligraphy, which was to draw characters. He knew that it took a long time to practice brush work to gain the proper effect. When he gave lessons in the company's internal "Feng Qingyang" Class, he talked about *Master Sun's Art of War*. His writing of "wisdom, faithfulness, benevolence, courage and strictness" was really something.

Visiting Staff

The most relaxed and funny thing for Jack Ma was to see his staff, but because he was becoming increasingly busy, it became more and more of a luxury.

Once he met two girls from Alipay in the lift. "CEO Ma, you haven't been to our Alipay building for a long while. We have a screening room and a room for punching (set up for the employees to distress themselves) now," one girl said.

"Ah? A room for punching? I should go and check whether the room has my portrait — although it would be just fine if you put Peng Lei's," (Peng Lei was CEO of Alipay then) Jack Ma said jokingly.

When Jack Ma was out on business trips, he would first think of going to visit the local staff if there was a base there. In September 2012, Jack Ma was tied up in Guangzhou. Even so he still called older employees nearby to have a collective dinner. The older employees were all happy as if celebrating the New Year.

It was the same case in Hangzhou. He would make a tour to different departments to take group photos and sign his name when there were opportunities. If he saw someone playing table tennis, he'd join them or sometimes making jokes when playing. "I'm not very good at it. But I have a friend. I bet you can't win against him. His name is Liu Guoliang." The employees all burst into laugh.

Angel Falling from Sky

July 2011, Wu Juping of Alibaba got comminuted fracture and passed out when she caught a little girl, Niuniu, falling from the 10th floor. She and Niuniu were sent to different hospitals for treatment.

Jack Ma send a tweet on weibo.com after hearing the news. *After the Second*

World War, a child asked, "Grandpa, are you a hero in the war?" Grandpa answered, "I' m not. But I fought and worked with a group of heroes!" I am honored to have worked with you (Wu) for seven years. Wish you and the child to get well soon.

Jack Ma was a particularly careful man. He sent me on his behalf to visit Wu Juping and Niuniu's parents who were waiting outside the intensive care room.

"Many leaders went to visit Wu, why did you not..." I asked.

"Now so many reporters are at the scene. My showing up will only make trouble, right? Will they report Wu Juping's deed or interview me? I'll go when it is less crowded," Jack Ma said.

After I went to see Wu Juping on Jack Ma's behalf, later in a sparsely populated afternoon, I accompanied Jack Ma quietly to the ward.

Jack Ma had a very special way of praising people; "Wu, I guess you did a bad job on physics at school. Niuniu's falling speed was at least twice as fast as Usain Bolt's speed on hundred meters race. Chen Wei learned well in physics. He would have run if it were him."

"He'd go and catch too. Everyone would have done the same thing." Wu said with a smile.

While Jack Ma and Wu Juping were chatting, I found a pen and paper and had a physics lesson for Wu. The speed for a free fall after 30 meters is basically 25 meters per second.

"I just got back from the Hulun Buir Prairie. The environment was well protected there. I plan to take more employees to visit there in the future. Good staff will go there in summer and the bad ones will go in winter because after they experience the temperatures of 40 or 50 degrees below zero, they will work harder and be better," Jack Ma and Wu Juping chatted playfully.

Wu Juping giggled throughout the conversation, very delighted.

Niuniu's condition was critical. In addition to fracture, her internal organs were damaged. Her life was threatened.

I went to give encouragement to Niuniu's parents under the instructions of Jack Ma. "Every cell of Niuniu was given by you. She will sense it if you have faith. If you don't give up, Niuniu surely will make it. All the miracles happen when you have faith..." I said to Niuniu's parents whose eyes were filled with tears. They kept on nodding while still crying. I have conveyed Jack Ma's intention, "If there is problem of medical costs, please do let us know."

Like a miracle, Niuniu survived and she was free from any further disease or disorder which we had worried might happen. Now occasionally I would take Niuniu's family out to dinner and each time I would brag the same thing and repeat the words I had encouraged the parents then as if Niuniu's survival was all because of me. They seemed to enjoy listening to it, or so I thought.

Stepping Down

On March 10, 2013, Jack Ma announced that from May 11, 2013, he will step down from the position of CEO, but remain as the company's chairman.

On March 22, 2013, the 20th Huaxia Fellowship Meeting was held in our company. Some of the fellow students had attended classes at the Cheung Kong Graduate School of Business, some had attended classes at the China Europe International Business School (CEIBS), while some registered and studied at both. So they set up the organization through association on their own and it became today's Huaxia Fellowship Association.

Besides Jack Ma, members included Feng Lun, Chairman of the Vantone Group, Tian Suning, Chairman of the China Broadband Capital Fund, Niu Gensheng, founder of the Mengniu Dairy Group Co., Ltd., Li Dongsheng, Chairman of the TCL Group, Zhu Xinli, Chairman of the Beijing Huiyuan Beverage Food Company, Pony Ma (Ma Huateng), Chairman and CEO of Tencent, Robin Li (Li Yanhong), Chairman and CEO of Baidu Inc., and Liu Chuanzhi, former Chairman of the Legend Holdings Co., Ltd., etc.

The afternoon meeting was held in Taobao's headquarters in Chengxi. When he was asked about "stepping down," Jack Ma said, "One thing I want to make clear, we came to this world not to do things, but to be humans. Younger generations will definitely do better than we did. The thing is whether you want to find them or not. I am exploring the way for Pony Ma and Robin Li, unless you never want to retire. A few years ago, Feng Lun and I discussed running a private corporate university when we went to the so-called 'a country of sweet air' Bhutan. I think this is interesting to enlighten the young people. I will not be a CEO, but a CKO, 'Chief Knowledge Officer.' It's pretty good. When I was the CEO, I said to my employees, 'Don't love me, and listen to me.' Now I am no longer the CEO, my demand changes: Don't listen to me, please love me."

Rounds and rounds of applause sounded in the meeting.

The next morning at the Hangzhou Four Seasons Hotel, Jack Ma made summary for the Huaxia Fellowship Meeting. The following are some of the thoughts:

"Lao (Old)" is the teacher; "ban (board)" is rules. So, boss (Laoban) is the teacher of employees and the one who sets rules for them.

Suspect the people you employ and employ the people that you suspect, or it means you are not confident.

Trust has two meanings, trust people and employ them.

The "general" should have a personality but not the "commander" who needs to be all inclusive.

Experts and scholars are two different things. The latter can be acquired by learning but the former only by doing.

About the last one, here is a case to share. Terry Gou, Founder of the Foxconn Technology Group, has more than 1.4 million employees worldwide. The imports and exports of his company account for more than 4% in China. The CFO running the large and complex company's funds did not graduate from a famous university but a distant relative started the business with him at the age of 17.

"Feng Qingyang" Class

Jack Ma attaches great importance to the cultivation of the talents. Everybody knows the value of talents. If you are the president and you have a CEO like Jack Ma, you wouldn't worry about anything, right?

Everyone has a martial arts ID (nickname) on Taobao.com. Jack Ma's ID is "Feng Qingyang." Jack Ma organized several "Feng Qingyang" Classes comprised of some of the company's most reliable hardworking young staff and part of the vice presidents. He taught the classes himself and the basic content was "discussing principles", focused on the principles of how to conduct oneself.

One of the lessons was about team work. "We must distinguish between the character and moral quality. Do not suspect others' moral quality due to different characters, learn to be tolerant. Joe (Cai Chongxin, English name Joe Tsai) has sharp eyes and can grasp every detail; Professor Zeng (Zeng Ming) focuses on macro strategy, the future; Peng Lei holds steadfast to values; Lao Lu (Lu Zhaoxi) does solid work: cut it out. Show me what you've done. Everyone has his own characters and this makes up a perfect team. If all the staff talk about dreams every day as I do, then the company will go nowhere..."

In mid-March, 2013, Jack Ma held a collective class by joining in "Feng Qingyang" Class 1 and "Feng Qingyang" Class 2. When the topic came to his stepping down as CEO, Jack Ma said, "Now I am in my best state in all aspects, it is time to arrange for a replacement. This is the rule. The most powerful time is the moment of giving birth to a child...The CEO attending every morning meeting at the age of 70 or 80 is never my idol, but the tragedy of the company. Before the age of 48, work was my life, after 48, living is my work. I will give a good lead for you and wish you will give a good lead for young people in the future. I hope you can leave your work behind at the age of 45. In this way, the young talents in Ali can know their prospects. You can come to chat with me when you have nothing to do, if you have something to do, please go to the CEO..."

End of the World

It was in the afternoon on December 21, 2012, rings were granted representing "Golden-Five" (Wunian Chen). The staff members in Alibaba will be referred to as "Golden-Five" after five years of work and they would receive a ring customized by the company. Jack Ma quipped, "It is said that 3:00 p.m. today is the end of the world, because there is a time difference between Hangzhou, China and Maya of South America. But it's already past 3:00 p.m. and nothing has happened. What if doomsday doesn't come? Continue to work hard, especially those who have been working at Ali for five years."

On festival seasons, Jack Ma would receive greeting cards, many of which were from female fans. During the 2012 Spring Festival, he received a small ark which read: Jack Ma, in the year of Ark, you are the man I am bringing on board!

"Bragging" at the Press Conference

Jack Ma enjoys reading Mai Jia's spy novels. He has written book recommendations to Mai Jia, who has also made weibo promotions for my book, *Jack Ma: Founder and CEO of the Alibaba Group*. We get along well and sometimes would dine in Longjing. In 2011, Mai Jia wished to have his new creation, *Pointy Blade (Dao Jian)* first published at our company and at the same time, put the book on sale at Taobao.com.

I began to take up this matter for Jack Ma. It was when the company's network security departments were carrying on the "Searchlight Action" of cracking down on Internet piracy and protecting intellectual property rights. The press conference would be held jointly at the company's Binjiang Park.

Unexpectedly, on the day of the press conference, Jack Ma went away on business. Thus, I was pushed up to face the music. I bragged ramblingly on the stage. "Everyone has a pair of wings of dream, but only a handful of wings can fly high in the sky, most of the wings are stewed in the pot, so not many people can achieve their dreams... People before Einstein considered 'indestructibility of matter', and people after him thought 'mass-energy conservation.' Actually, the real thing that is indestructibility is information. The so-called information indestructibility is that everything happens in the world will rise into the air, hide in the cloud, this is also the reason why we are doing 'Ali Cloud.' To strengthen your faith, God will occasionally take out a small piece and display it on the sea, which is a 'mirage.' If you still do not understand, God can only say, 'I cannot help you anymore'... The ancients said, 'the article was created by nature, one only received it by chance.' In other words, stories were not created by writers, but are received by them. The so-called 'inspiration' is, in fact, when the signal is strongest. The skin is the receiver for the inspired, that is why some writers strip nude to receive inspiration for writing, which increases the area to receive the signal."

After the conference, we held a new book sale and signing activity for Mai Jia at Binjiang Park. It was very lively.

Proverbs at the Taoguang Temple

When meetings for the discussion of principles or strategies are to be held, Jack Ma still prefers to go to the Yongfu Temple or Taoguang Temple. Both temples are at the west of the Lingyin Temple, connected with each other by the mountain trails. This place is covered by tall trees, far away from the noisy and blundering cities and close to Buddha. It is unlikely to make wrong strategic decisions. If there is a wrong decision, I think Buddha will drop a twig or bodhi down as a warning.

On a warm winter day in 2011, Jack Ma and Professor Zeng and others were discussing how to cooperate with other companies in the Taoguang Temple. The terrace at the Taoguang Temple is the best place of fengshui in Hangzhou. Looking to the east, two mountains form a fan and below the fan is the West Lake and above it is the city.

I just remember three sentences spoken by Jack Ma that day:

"The so-called synergy is for you to change yourself to adapt to others.

If it is not good, no problem. The problem is you think it is very good.

All strategies are gambling, but not all gambling are strategies."

"November 11" Carnival

November 11 used to be the "Singles' Day." In recent years, it has become the Taobao shopping carnival. There is a reason for choosing this day; it is in the middle of National Day and Christmas, and in a transitional time of seasons. It is the best time for discounts and sales promotions.

The gross sales amount for Taobao was about 5 billion yuan on November 11,2011.

On the eve of November 11 in 2012, Taobao had confidence of gross sales exceeding 10 billion *yuan*, so they invited people from Yunfeng Capital to witness the expected event that day. Yunfeng Capital was launched jointly by Jack Ma and Yu Feng. That day we were joined with a lot of other entrepreneurs. The entrepreneurs present on that day included the chairmen of the famous brands of "Smith Barney", "Septwolves" and "EVE de UOMO" that took part in the November 11 promotions.

Due to the large flow of sales, all the major commercial banks encountered some difficulties with payment transmission, the records were refreshed one after another.

At noon, Jack Ma took the people from Yunfeng Capital to Longjing for lunch. At 1:00 p.m., Jack Ma announced, "Everyone, I have good news and bad news. The good news is that our 10 billion *yuan* goal has been reached in advance. Let's have a premature welcome. The bad news is that I originally expected we would exceed 10 billion yuan at dinner time and wanted to arrange a small ceremony. Now plans have to be changed."

Everybody toasted "cheers" to celebrate!

In the afternoon and evening, we visited Alibaba, Alipay, and Taobao. We also made a special tour for our guests to the "Temporary War Rooms" and they were impressed.

The gross sales by the end of November 11 were 19.1 billion *yuan*. Everyone made a prediction beforehand, and the closest figure was 18.8 billion *yuan*, which was predicted by Song Lixin, Director of the *Talents* magazine.

An Unsuccessful Sharing

On March 23, 2013, Jack Ma would make a closing speech at the Huaxia Fellowship Meeting. Before his speech, he asked me to talk about Alibaba corporate culture for ten minutes or so. The audience was all my idols. I was very nervous and even prepared an outline on a piece of paper.

"Hello, dear idols, I am Chen Wei, CEO Ma's assistant. I am a different assistant. The assistant who introduced the company's business yesterday was someone who didn't attend to his work properly because he knew the business. What is an assistant? He is like a sword scabbard whose duty is to protect the 'sharpness' of the sword and feels at ease to be 'blunt.' If the scabbard is too 'sharp,' it will hurt itself.

"I never dig into business, fortunately Alibaba has something irrelevant to the business. The first is the corporate culture. Every year on May 10 is 'Ali Day,' a day that walked out of the SARS isolation 10 years ago and a day that announced the establishment of Taobao. The centerpiece of the day is the group weddings for the employees. Over the past few years, more than 500 couples have participated every year. The company takes care of the return flight to Hangzhou and accommodations. And there is a huge party in the evening, with more than 10,000 attendees. But I regret to tell you that although each year CEO Ma is the witness of the marriage and the newlyweds promise to love each other for eternity, there were a few couples who get divorced the following year. The day is also Ali's Open Day, the staff can take their family members to visit the company and the reception standard is like that of a Prime Minister and the routes are even longer. The company also provides simple meals at noon.

"June 1 is Ali Children's Day on which the staff members can bring children to work. The administrative departments will arrange the children to play all kinds of games. On that day, the whole campus is like a children's wonderland.

"The company often holds various interesting activities, such as 'Ali Guinness' which is to select the one with the largest eyes and the longest hair and so on in Alibaba. A girl by the name of Adou participated in "the loudest voice" game with a decibel meter at her side. The game photos were published and some hostile foreign media commented, 'Chinese students are overstrained from schoolwork and can only use this way to vent their frustrations.'

"Daily activities include 'Ten Ali Sects.' In fact, it has more than 20 Sects now. In addition to all kinds of ball games, there are also the 'Music Commune' for singing fans and the 'Dance Club' for dance lovers. Food connoisseurs can join in the 'Food Sect.' Alibaba is a company that practices the AA system most, because everyone has an Alipay account. One person pays the bill and all the others 'pay' him back, which is not only convenient, but also can be accurate to the penny. The current boom for activity is in the 'Single Sect' for the singles are full of the desire to make friends, and we are striving for working couples to keep the opportunities to the insiders.

"Some people say that Taiji is one of Alibaba's corporate cultures, and I think it differently. Alibaba is a byproduct of Taiji culture in the 'Rampant Growth' of network age. Now we have six coaches, all of which are national championships. We have also trained 18 assistant coaches, including vice presidents. This year forward, in the training program for Alibaba's new employees, there is a compulsory course for Taiji, which not only aims for better health, but more importantly to learn the thoughts of Taiji.

"Now I will talk about Alibaba's public welfare undertakings. 3‰ of Alibaba Group's business turnover will be used for public welfare, which is not a small number. Employee Public Welfare Committee consists of 10 staff winners through the campaign of all members of the company to discuss, investigate, and to make decisions regarding public welfare projects.

"We also encouraged our 7 million Taobao sellers to participate in public welfare activities together. Now Taobao has a lot of public welfare goods. There will be a set of payments that goes into a designated public welfare project with every deal successfully made. The total money count now has exceeded ten million *yuan*.

"The company has also organized a variety of 'happiness groups' to help the disabled or the elderly.

"The most moving thing is that there is a virtual team from Taobao and Alipay who use their spare time to develop software to connect with the screen readers to enable the blind to go on Taobao shopping. The amazing thing is that some blind college students have opened Taobao shops. It's really unbelievable."

After talking about the corporate culture, I also introduced "Tao Girls," a platform providing non-professional models to Taobao clothing sellers. I didn't make myself understood then. So I said jokingly, "It is a professional platform other than being 'mistresses' for those beautiful young girls who don't want a regular job."

After this event, Jack Ma commented on my style of sharing in private; "Not well done. It is far from the usual talking style of yours. The biggest problem was the paper with your outline. You were nervous and relied on the paper. Besides, don't talk culture for the sake of talking culture; it is better to tell some real and vivid stories for others to feel the culture."

Jack Ma's comments were of great help to me. Later I went to Zhejiang Xiaobaihua Shaoxing Opera Troupe to talk about Taiji. I didn't bring the paper and didn't even make mental notes. I talked whatever came to my mind randomly and the result was good, or so I thought.

New Year's Address

The drips and drabs of corporate culture cast the enterprise's soul. A company with a powerful soul is a strong company in the real sense. To outsiders, Alibaba developed very smoothly in recent years. In fact, the company made a lot of mistakes in the last decade or more. "Alibaba has made all the mistakes that the 'time-honored stores' once had made. We just pulled out our legs from the mud of error a bit faster than the others and this was owing to the soul of enterprise," Jack Ma stated.

In 2012, Alibaba made a lot of changes within the group and the "seven swords" were split into 25 business groups.

Jack Ma wrote this in his New Year's Address on the *Alier* magazine:

Dear Ali relatives and friends:

Happy New Year!

2012 has come and gone, and a new era has begun!

As in all previous years, Ali experienced a lot of changes during 2012. Each change brings pains and some are heart-breaking pains. I hate frequent change as much as you do. But if we don't change today, tomorrow it would be more painful. The world is undergoing great changes, and I'm sorry to tell you that Ali's change is not just temporary but will be constant. Fortunately, Alier are strong enough to withstand these changes.

In 2012, I am very glad to see a large number of young Alier rise to their feet. Their progresses in all aspects are beyond imagination. Behind these, there was containment of trust, support, and encouragement of thousands of Ali relatives and friends. Thank you very much!

Development, innovation, and progress are the absolute truth! But I earnestly request you to remember: Progress is absolutely necessary. But above that is absolute health! Health is everything! Take care of your life and enjoy your work! Only in this way will we have the opportunity to realize the results for all the things we expect to happen!

In the new century, we'll march on shoulder to shoulder as usual.

Chapter 10:
Jack Ma and Celebrities

Unexpected Sponsorship Fee

I n June 2011, I went to Hong Kong with Jack Ma for a meeting. During that time, Jack Ma and Yu Feng had dinner together. The two are the founders of "Yunfeng Capital" and they are good friends. Yu Feng is the President of the foundation, and he is the best well-proportioned entrepreneur that I know. He is good-looking with a perfect build and is 1.85 meters tall. His usual attire is famous brand and low-key western suit, famous brand and low-key jeans, famous brand and low-key casual leather shoes.

As if he suddenly came up with something when we were eating, Jack Ma asked, "Yu Feng, did you say you'd invest money to help Chen Wei publish his book?"

It happened before the publication of *Jack Ma: Founder and CEO of the Alibaba Group*. Jack Ma had shown him part of the draft. "I did. I meant if no presses would publish it, I would pay to get it released. Now that it is already on the market and different presses have vied..." Yu Feng said.

"So you want to deny it?" Jack Ma cut in before Yu Feng finished.

"Of course not..."

"Chen Wei, Yu won't deny it. Give him your account number." Jack Ma immediately turned his head and said to me.

Yu Feng smiled. "Well then, Chen Wei, give me your account number."

It wasn't quite clear to me what was happening and I took it just as a joke and said, "OK!"

I sent my account number to Yu Feng after the meal. The second day there is an increase of money by 6 digits in my account!

Thank you, President Yu! Actually the so-called denied debt was just a fabrication. Jack Ma and Yu Feng just wanted to make me happy. Subsequently, Yu Feng issued a copy of *Jack Ma: Founder and CEO of the Alibaba Group* to each of the big investors at Yunfeng Capital. By the time of reprinting, President Yu also wrote a recommendation for me: "... to be honest, this is the only book about Jack Ma I read to the end."

From then on, I began to tease all the writers that I met. "Look at you, you have to beg here and there for your shitty book to be published, hoping a celebrity to write you a preface or recommendation. And many of you wrote it with the celebrities' consent. But people wrote recommendations and sponsored my book. Ha-ha! "

Shen Guojun

Shen Guojun, the Chairman of Yintai, is a good friend of Jack Ma. The two of them are preparing for the China Smart Logistic Network.

Shen is my idol, an approachable idol.

Once in our long flight to the United States, Chairman Shen shared his story with us.

Hardships in childhood: Helping father tie seaweed seedlings, tiny hands soaked in cold sea water, frozen and numb; on the weekends he would catch mudskipper with bamboo sticks on a muddy beach and sell them on the streets to earn tuition money; with tears in his eyes, carrying the seaweeds, that weighed far heavier than himself, up the hill to dry them again and again...

Hard life after father's death in a car accident: His mother and another widow opened a breakfast bar at the entrance of the village. Every morning she got up at 2 or 3 o'clock in the morning yet the customers were limited. And those who did come were out of sympathy for her situation. He never saw his mother receive a note more than one *yuan*...

Mother taught her children to stand on their own feet, rich or poor, always return others' favor.

The most moving thing I heard was that his mother refused to sleep on the wooden bed whenever she was seriously ill, because it was the only valuable thing in the house. Mother hated the thought of dying on that bed for fear it wouldn't sell for a good price...

After Shen Guojun's success, he took all the villagers in the town to eat and sent each family a gift. The villagers would talk about the meal for at least a year afterwards. All the villagers who needed help would go to Shen Guojun's parents' tomb on Tomb-sweeping Day because they knew that he and his brothers and sisters would definitely be there...

Every story touched me deeply and also made me think about how a person's moral quality was formed.

I personally think that a person's success, intelligence, opportunity, and persistence and so on are all dominant factors. But the deeper hidden reasons and logic chains run throughout the growth process, which are a continuous and very detailed accumulation and can't be decrypted just by choosing a few points.

Guo Guangchang

When it comes to Taiji, we have to mention Jack Ma's other good friend Guo Guangchang, Chairman of the Fosun Group.

Jack Ma was the head of the Students Federation of Hangzhou during college and Guo Guangchang was the student leader while studying at Fudan University in Shanghai. Both of them sacrificed a lot of time from studies to organize activities, including carrying a broken recorder and organizing a weekend ball, arranging grade basketball games, and so on. Superficially, doing these things didn't demand much skill, but in fact, the experience of solving problems during the whole process unknowingly honed their forces and skills and made them winners as the university's "second starting line."

Three years ago Jack Ma recommended that Guo Guangchang practice Taiji, which he gladly accepted and fell in love with it, leaving his once favorite golf clubs behind. He said, Taiji is not subject to conditions, and he can practice at anytime and anywhere and that was really nice!

As a man of great executive ability, coupled with the fitness companies he owned, Guo soon spread his "i-Taiching" in Beijing, Shanghai and other places. He also "roped in" some entrepreneurs and celebrities to join his "Guo-style" Taiji. Over the past two years, as long as he took part in large-scale events, he would personally lead his team to perform Taiji.

Jack Ma and Guo Guangchang are consistent with the basic concepts of Taiji, yet their Taijiquan belonged to different "sects". Entrepreneurs are now divided into the "Ma-style" and "Guo-style." Needless to say, the "Ma-style" represented by Jack Ma and Jet Li had more people and I believe over time there will be more and more. Jack Ma would often joke to the Guo-style entrepreneurs, "None of the mistakes matter except for standing in the wrong line."

The bickering between the two sides has been unceasing. Many of the people in the Ma-style are national champions and some of them are martial arts champions and can fight with the Shaolin masters.

The Guo-style claimed, "We play Taiji to keep fit, not to fight."

The Ma-style argued, "We also keep fit, but Taijiquan is embodied in Taiji thoughts in the martial arts. The art of attack and defense may not necessarily have a philosophy, but it definitely won't have philosophy without it. It is not 'boxing,' that is 'drilling'."

The bickering will continue and the journey of promoting Taiji is still a long way ahead. Just wait and see.

Jet Li

Jack Ma and Jet Li have jointly initiated The Taiji Zen International Cultural Development Co., Ltd. The goal is to promote 'Taiji,' the strong Chinese symbol and Chinese traditional thoughts.

Jet Li said that Taiji is about Yin and Yang, heaven and earth, Taiji Zen is someone thinking between heaven and earth. It teaches you to be healthy and happy.

Jet Li is not only good at Kung Fu, but also very eloquent. He shared many stories with us when we were together.

When *Shaolin Temple* was projected in the rural areas, village children had no money, could not even afford two cents for a movie ticket. The head of village asked each child to bring a brick to cover the ticket. Guess what, on the next day they saw half of the toilets in the village were taken apart.

Zhou Xun said when she first met Jet Li, "One summer holiday, for two months, I watched *Shaolin Temple*, every single day."

Jet Li was touched by hearing this. "My father was in charge of the projector and I had no place to go in the summer. I really got sick of it," Zhou Xun went on.

Once Jet Li went to South Korea; 50 policemen couldn't stop thousands of crazy fans. One of the policemen had to run about wildly with Jet Li. They caught up with a wedding car. The police pulled out the bride and groom and put Jet Li into the car so he could "flee the scene".

Jet Li likes to study Buddhism. A lot of people thought Jet Li was enlightened by the 2004 tsunami and began to learn Buddhism. As a matter of fact, Jet Li's tie with Buddha was far deeper than people had imagined. Li Liansheng, Jet Li's elder brother, is my good friend. For a time in Beijing, we had dinner together every day. He told me his grandma was a lifelong believer of Buddhism and every night would sleep in meditation. One day 50 years ago, she felt flustered and fidgeting at home in the northeast. She sensed something was about to happen. So she took the train overnight to her daughter's home in Beijing. The next day when she was going to her daughter's home, she met up with her daughter and son-in-law, who were on their way to the hospital to have an abortion; the baby was Jet Li...

Still, I shared many different opinions on Taoism and the ideas of Taiji with my idol Jet Li. For instance, in Chapter 42 of *Tao Teh Ching, "The Tao produced One; One produced Two; Two produced Three; Three produced All things. All things leave behind them the Obscurity (out of which they have come), and go forward to embrace the Brightness (into which they have emerged), while they are harmonized by the Breath of Vacancy."* Jet Li thinks that "Three" refers to human, otherwise 'All Things' do not make sense. I think this is somewhat biased to idealism. There is no right or wrong about philosophy except for ways of thinking about it. I tend to agree more that "Three" refers to "Breath (qi)," "harmonized by the Breath of Vacancy" is to say Yin and Yang exist in all things, with the intervention of "Breath" there can be harmony and stability. "Breath (qi)" is generalized in sense. In the Yin and Yang of the pair of heaven and earth, it refers to the physical air, while in the Yin and Yang of the pair of male and female, it is the ideological "love." And the "qi" in Taiji's "to push qi by form" and the "energy, qi, spirit (jing, qi, shen)" is the mixture of energy and idea.

Jack Ma's point of view is most common to understand, "Taiji Zen" is a kind of attitude about life.

To live better, move more; to live long, move less; to live longer and better, move slowly − Taiji.

Deng Yapping

In 2011, Deng Yaping was invited to a Women's Forum at the Alifest of our company. She just took over "Goso" and came a day earlier to talk to Jack Ma. Deng Yaping was very talkative and we could still see the vigor of a world champion. She was concerned about things of the Internet, while Jack Ma was more interested in table tennis. The two people had a very nice talk.

Jack Ma asked her, in playing table tennis, what do you do if you can't tell what kind of spin ball you are served? Deng Yaping said, "Sometimes you can decide by the spinning direction of the ball, sometimes by the trademark of the ball. If neither, then smash. Overcome the spinning with speed."

The idea of "overcoming the spinning with speed" inspired me a lot. We often do not know how to make decisions in a complex environment. In fact, belief is important at this time. Let the belief be strong. Let it become a "smash" moment and things will turn in the "smash" direction. This echoes to the "bearing it in mind constantly and eventually there will be a response" in Buddhism, right?

The next day before Deng Yaping made her presentation on stage, she met Jack Ma again. When asked how she had prepared, she answered, "I am still a little nervous. I knew too little of Alibaba's culture; I especially read the book written by your assistant."

Zhou Libo

Jack Ma and Zhou Libo met at an event. The two best speech-endowed in the region south of the Yangtze River regretted they hadn't met sooner and finally became good friends. One day in Shanghai, Zhou Libo invited Jack Ma to his home for lunch to discuss doing public welfare. Jack Ma's meeting was already over-timed, plus there was the traffic jam, so when he arrived at Zhou's home, we were exactly an hour late. Zhou came to the door. Although he was in his own house, his hair was shiny and his pants well-ironed. At the door, he put on a very dramatic expression, spreading his hands, said jokingly to Jack Ma, "I've been waiting too long. I've nearly become a whining and annoying woman."

"I've become a whining and annoying woman too for the traffic jam. Bobo, can't you do something about Shanghai's traffic?" Jack Ma attacked in his defense.

"It is not the first day for the traffic to be like this. Don't tell me you don't know."

"The most punctual ones are the retired workers. You inform them to assemble in the park at 7 o'clock, but by 5:30, most of them will be there. I will come to your home two days in advance if you invite me after my retirement."

Before the public welfare discussion, the two had begun to sharpen their tongues.

Fan Zeng

Fan Zeng is an excellent calligrapher and painter. Wang Lifen invited him to Hangzhou to visit our company and to exchange ideas with Jack Ma. Fan Zeng's assistant showed me Fan Zeng's paintings on the computer, which were really remarkable. Fan Zeng was not only an accomplished painter, but also had high attainment in Chinese ancient civilization. I think he is the one who knows best about Chinese culture among all the painters and the best painter among the people who study Chinese culture. I benefit a lot from some of his views, such as: "The leaders should be conservative to advocate something beyond their field of businesses, otherwise it will be overdone." Just think, the emperors in history taught us a good lesson by being addicted to deer raising, corals collection, crickets fighting, and so on.

During that time, he saw a small muscle man sculpture on Jack Ma's desk. "Who is it?" he asked.

"Me, of course!" Jack Ma said in jest.

"You? The muscle..."

"That's the future me. I'm still young. In a few years I'll grow to be like that."

Later Jack Ma found that Fan Zeng really liked the sculpture, so he gave it to him as a gift.

Terry Gou

Terry Gou and Jack Ma were kind of decreed by destiny. The first time he came to stage in Guangdong, mainland China, he had a dialogue with Jack Ma. Later, he came to Hangzhou. Jack Ma invited him to go boating on the West Lake. When he got on shore, a little girl chased him to sell flowers, 10 *yuan* for a rose. He fumbled all his pockets and didn't find a penny. Huang, from our company, produced 10 *yuan* and was about to hand it to the little girl. Terry Gou, grabbed the money, like a little child, saying, "Gimme the money. I'll pay her. Then I can say I bought this flower for my wife. I'll return the money when I go back." It has been six or seven years since it happened. But the 10 *yuan* was never returned. Next time if you see Terry Gou, please remind him that he still owes Huang 10 *yuan*.

In 2012, Terry Gou increasingly learned more about the power of the Internet. Many times, he brought his team to our company for panel discussions. Every time he would speak of himself as "a little white rabbit that just broke into the Internet".

His recent visit was in the evening. Jack Ma was late because he went to witness the wedding of a senior executive. He arrived half an hour later in the middle of the meeting. "Welcome Jack Ma to give guidance to our 'Tmall'," Terry Gou said as soon as Jack Ma stepped in the door. Everyone laughed. "Sorry, I went to witness a marriage for a guy. He finally got married. Man is iron and woman is water. Only married men are steel, because they have been soaked in water," said Jack Ma.

Two days before the 2013 Spring Festival, Terry Gou invited Jack Ma to the headquarters of his company located in Taiwan for communication. It was the only time that all his leadership from global factories would gather at the headquarters. Jack Ma's two and a half hours speech was marvelous. Everyone gave a standing ovation at the end of the speech. "What you talked about is not commercial but philosophy. You are not an entrepreneur but a philosopher. Others were all happy to listen to it except me. Formerly I was the No. 1 in the company, now I have become No. 2," Terry Gou said while seeing Jack Ma off.

Stephen Chow

Stephen Chow is my idol too. Many years ago, I saw him in Zhejiang TV. The mainland marketing of Stephen Chow's movie *Journey to the West: Conquering the Demons* shot in 2012 was in the hands of Huayi and Jack Ma is one of the big shareholders. Wang Zhongjun ,the President of Huayi, arranged a dialogue between Jack Ma and Stephen Chow prior to the release, also as a way of doing propaganda for the film.

The dialogue was carried out at the Communication University of China (CUC). Jack Ma and Stephen Chow had never met before, so the two had dinner in the dining hall of the university to "break the ice" prior to the event.

The two started teasing each other as soon as they met. "I grew up watching your movies," Jack Ma said.

"I grew up watching your TV speeches. I think it is unreal to see you standing in front of me," Stephen Chow teased back.

Stephen Chow could not speak mandarin very well, so he talked slow, but still one could sense his typical Chow-style humor from time to time.

When the activity started, a sea of students packed the site even though the final exam was coming soon.

The atmosphere of the dialogue was ardent. Stephen Chow even learned a couple of strokes of Taiji from Jack Ma at the scene.

Huang Bo and Chai Jing were also present that day.

Haircut

Jack Ma has a quick brain, so his hair grows faster too. During the 2012 National Day, Jack Ma went to inspect the primeval forest in Scotland while having environmental friendly topics along with the Nature Conservancy. For convenience, Jack Ma had his head shaved before departure. Shi Yuzhu did not go, but he received a photo from a friend who went and he posted the photo on weibo.

Jack Ma's head shave caused all kinds of speculations from the media. One of the consistent opinions that two small e-commerce sites were fighting fiercely for prices. Jack Ma and Shi Yuzhu made a bet which side would win.

Jack Ma lost the bet and had to have his head shaved. Some friends came to Jack Ma to verify. "I never bet with anyone when the answer is not in my pocket," said Jack Ma.

It was not possible for Jack Ma and Shi Yuzhu to bet for small websites. I also send a tweet, "Have you ever heard senior students bet for lower grades?"

George is Jack Ma's "imperial" hairdresser and a friend to us too. He often participates in the hair style grand prix held in places such as Russia, Germany, and Japan, as the only one or only two judges from China. George's native home is Xuyi, Jiangsu. We often praised him, saying "Xuyi had only three things in its history, Zhu Yuanzhang, crayfish, and George."

Having his haircut is a good leisure activity for Jack Ma. In the one and a half hours, from washing hair to cutting hair, he can neither make a phone call nor watch the news. Many of the interesting stories and classic statements of Jack Ma were told to us during this time, such as "A deaf heard a mute say a blind saw a ghost" and so on. Feeling relaxed, Jack Ma often laughed very loudly. Sometimes it would startle three or four people outside the haircut box. "Jack Ma, do you still know me?" Someone would come up and ask.

Usually such scenes would appear. "Familiar. If you remind me with three characters in your name I'll know who you are," Jack Ma would say.

"I am Liu Yufeng. I participated in the second annual Alifest eight years ago. You even shook hands with me." They evidently overestimated Jack Ma's memory.

But in recent months, Jack Ma was extremely busy to stop and get a haircut. Once when he was booked to be on Sally Wu's telecast, Zhejiang TV's "Sally's Charrette". Jack Ma's hair was so horrible to bear that they gave him a haircut on site. The second time was for the annual meeting of the China Entrepreneurs Club. Jack Ma had his hair cut on site. The third time was at the award ceremony of China's Economic Persons of the Year. At the scene of Big Shorts of CCTV, he had another haircut. "I've saved a lot of money on haircuts these few months," Jack Ma joked while having his haircut again.

Too Late to Regret for the Investment

On March 22, 2013, the 20th Huaxia Fellowship Meeting was held at our company. Pony Ma, Robin Li, Feng Lun, Shen Guojun, Chen Dongsheng, Li

Dongsheng, and my other idols were all here.

The morning meeting was held in Binjiang Park. "This is the first time for me to come here. But I came to Alibaba once. I also took part in the 'West Lake Summit' 10 years ago. Back then, our companies were all very small. I remember Jack Ma was driving a broken car," said Pony Ma.

"It was not a fancy car indeed. But it was a new white Honda, ha-ha!" Jack Ma corrected him in laughter.

"When Taobao was being launched, Jack Ma offered the opportunity for a 15% investment. On the one hand, it did not look promising to me and I thought my share was too small. It should be at least 50%. It is too late for me to regret," Pony Ma continued.

"Same thing for me. I had 500 million *yuan* in hand then. Someone suggested that I should invest in Tencent. I often saw Pony Ma, but never once did he tell me what Tencent was, or that I would be to help any charity I want now," another entrepreneur cut in.

The greater the business thrives, the more and greater the chances one will miss along the way. This is dialectical.

Although the bosses looked relaxed at the sharing, and the audience laughed away, in fact, some of their mistakes have become the pain in their hearts forever, or so I thought.

Revitalization of Shaoxing Opera

Shengzhou of Zhejiang is the hometown of Shaoxing Opera. Song Weiping, the President of the Greentown Group, is from Shengzhou. Jack Ma is Shengzhou's son-in-law. Mao Weitao is the leading figure of Shaoxing Opera; so the three often get together for the development of Shaoxing Opera.

Jack Ma and Song Weiping had jointly set up a project for Shaoxing Opera, but people thought it was not enough and the investment was not big enough in entertainment spirit. So, in a recent party, they invented a new idea: Jack Ma and Song Weiping would play cards ten times in 2013. Each side would have five people at a time to join in the game. Every time the losing party would donate a sum of money to the project. Everyone thought it was a great idea. But before the game, the trash talk started.

"Although I've only played this kind of card game for only three years, I am already a world winner," Jack Ma said.

"Those who have played for two or three years all have this kind of illusion. We will let you know how great the gap is between the people who have played this card game for 50 years and those who played for only three years," Song Weiping responded.

"The age for card playing and the age of a man is the same. It is never the older the better. A boy could piss sky-high in windward but an old man can only wet his shoes downwind," said Jack Ma.

In the end, in addition to donating money to the Shaoxing Opera project by the losing party each time, people proposed a new idea that depended on the total score at the end of the year. If Jack Ma loses, he will have to go to Greentown to be a security guard for a week; if Song Weiping loses, he will go to Alibaba to be a security guard for a week. And they must wear the uniform. If someone comes around to watch, they will have to hold up their heads and speak "I'm proud" in Henan dialect just like the sketch performed in the Spring Festival Gala.

Jack Ma was thrilled by this idea, clenching his hands and beating the table on and on.

Let's wait and see and find out who would be on guard at the end of 2013, "Security Song" or "Security Ma."

Chapter 11:
Travelling with Jack Ma

Face

With the expansion of the company's business in the United States and the need of capital operation, from 2011, Jack Ma went to the United States more often.

We usually made our entry from Alaska. Jack Ma liked the sparsely populated place. "Next time we'll stay in Alaska for a couple of days and go fishing at the seaside," he would say this each time. I have gone through a number of "next time", but there has been no time to go fishing at the seaside. I'm still waiting for the next "next time."

Alaska is near the Arctic Circle, so it is still bright at 9 or 10 o'clock in the summer evenings. Each time when we passed through the airport customs, the hall was very clean and tidy. There were only two or three security staff members at work, armed with guns as a deterrent, but always wearing a smile. There was a conspicuous writing on the wall; "We are the face of America." Jack Ma appreciated their work and expressed this complex in a Taobao "Tolling Meeting" later. "... We need to have theory discussion meetings ... the goal is to be pragmatic. What we operate is not electronic commerce, but trust and experience. Of course, we're nothing without electronic commerce. What Starbucks sells is not coffee, but experience. Taobao should be the second life space of modern people. Taobao started from insecure to confident, then to self-conceit. Some of the Xiao'ers (shop assistants) are even arrogant. We are not urban management; we are armed police with a smile. We are the face of Taobao."

California Burgers

At the end of May 2011, we went to Los Angeles and stayed at the seaside.

The second day we met Jerry Yang. He was darker, thinner, longer-haired than he was in Hangzhou in 2009, but more handsome. He was still as nice as usual. Maybe it was related to his life status these last years: breeding horses, growing grapes, and brewing wine. Obviously, Jack Ma wanted to see him as an old friend, but this time he also wanted to talk about buying Yahoo. I can't reveal to you the specific content of their discussion. Not because it is a secret, but because I don't know. When they held the negotiation meetings, I was walking on the beach.

The sunshine in California really deserves its name. The beach is even more beautiful. Next door to me was a Japanese couple who made special trips to the beach to take wedding photos here.

The next day we visited the headquarters of Walt Disney and Hollywood Hills. A white-haired old staff member introduced the company to us with familiarity; starting from the initial establishment to the present. We could tell his infinite love for the company, which Jack Ma admired very much.

At noon, a foreigner colleague John, who went with us, took us to a very famous burger restaurant at Hollywood Street for lunch. The line was very long and the price for a burger was double the price at any other place. We got our burger after half an hour of waiting, but after eating, Jack Ma and I didn't feel anything special about the hamburgers. John told us that he heard this place was very famous. "There is indeed something special, more people and expensive hamburgers, ha-ha," I joked.

At the D9 Conference

The consultant of our company in the United States came to see Jack Ma that night. He was a very handsome American but looked very nervous, because Jack Ma would take part in the D9 conference sponsored by the *Wall Street Journal*. This was a conference being conducted to question CEOs of famous enterprises. The participants were leaders and the heads of major investment institutions from around the globe. Previously many of the world famous company CEOs didn't know how to answer some questions and were very embarrassed. Jack Ma was the first Chinese to attend this meeting. Our consultant did very careful work and cited all the possibilities. But Jack Ma was very easy. Apparently he was more prepared for skillful maneuvering.

On the venue of the meeting the next day, there hung a picture of the CEOs to be questioned on the wall, and Jack Ma's portrait was the largest. CEO of Nokia was questioned before Jack Ma. When he passed by, I noticed that sweat was on his forehead.

Jack Ma came on the stage. He answered the questions without any hitch and there were rounds and rounds of applause.

After the meeting, a well-known investor stopped Jack Ma and they chatted for a little while. He then invited Jack Ma to tea at his home in the evening. It seemed as if they were good friends long ago.

In the evening we honored his invitation. His house was the only one on the hillside, a big white villa inlaid within the green mountain side. The rain was drizzling when we arrived at the security gate. The man who opened the gate for us with a smile was a black man in a black uniform, with a height of over 2 meters and presumably weighing over 300 pounds! He was holding a huge black umbrella. It seemed like a scene in a movie.

That night, the investor said he had decided to invest in a company in China. "Since you've made your decision, I wish you good luck!" Jack Ma said.

A year later the investor called Jack Ma, "Why didn't you stop me that night?" Obviously, the company he invested in didn't do well. "There is a price to pay for any lessons," Jack Ma answered with a smile.

After that, we went to the eastern part of the United States. The rivers looked like golden dragons under the reflection of the sun from a bird's eye view on the plane.

Quick Glance of the People

The former President of GE, Jack Welch, was an old friend of Jack Ma.

He had invited Jack Ma to attend the G100 annual meeting presided over by him a year ago.

It was the first time I met Jack Welch, although I had seen his photographs before. He looked obviously older and his voice was trembling.

Not many people were present at the meeting, about 30 or 40 or so, but all of them were the presidents of major American enterprises. Everyone was wearing a dark suit and only Jack Ma was in his sweater, very easy to spot. Jack Welch arranged for Jack Ma, "the Chinese Jack" to give a speech at the meeting. I can't remember what he talked about, but I remember him being interrupted several times by applause.

In the afternoon, we met Rupert Murdoch at the headquarters in Wall Street. The vice president welcomed us downstairs. After we got upstairs, Murdoch smiled and ushered Jack Ma into the room. Although Mr. Murdoch had visible wrinkles on his face, he was hale and hearty. I watched TV in the outer room while waiting for Jack Ma. Coincidently, the TV was broadcasting about a woman with the surname Qian from Jiangsu of China who was doing export business through Alibaba. The voice over was very funny, "Her family name means dollar."

In September 2011, Jack Ma took us to Washington, DC. When we passed the gate of the White House, we saw several groups of people at the rally. Some were making speeches, all against the government, but all in an orderly fashion. Just then a booming sound came from high above. A military helicopter landed at the lawn. We assumed that Obama was back.

Chinatown

We had lunch at Chinatown in Washington. The Chinatown in Washington was not very large but cleaner and tidier than those of New York and San Francisco. We went into a busy restaurant. Unexpectedly, all the Chinese there recognized Jack Ma. Before we could sit down, the place was packed with people. We hurried out and found a less crowded restaurant.

After lunch, the service staff asked to take group photos with Jack Ma, to which he gladly agreed. A very beautiful young lady gave Jack Ma a piece of paper, stating that she was a student and would go back to China after two years of school. She said that her boyfriend, who was already in China now, was outstanding and she hoped that Jack Ma would recruit him into Alibaba. From her eyes, we could see that she was in passionate love with her boyfriend. On the way back, Jack Ma said: "See, if you are looking for a wife, she is a good example."

There is common characteristic in Chinese restaurants abroad. They would give each one a "fortune cookie" after a meal, a hollow fried wonton, which has a little short note with written words inside. The things written on the notes were just for fun, but many times I found it came true. This time I got a note with these word: "This weekend will bring you a surprise." I thought since I was a stranger in the strange land of the United States, how could there be any surprises? Guess what? On the weekend, the foreign colleague John went shopping and found a pair of shoes at a mall that he felt was just right for me. And he bought them for me as a present.

Zhu Min's View on Child Raising

One day, Jack Ma invited Zhu Min, vice president of the International Monetary Fund, to have dinner with us. He talked about the importance of finance to modern enterprises and also said, "More than half of the market value of a company is credibility." Zhu's views on raising children were also unique. "The world doesn't lack a successful man. But the child is your irreplaceable family! This is very important. I learned many things during the growth of my child and my child taught me many things too."

He also told us about his work experience when he was young: he had to review and proof-read each word, each page of files that were a few meters thick.

Behind all success and fame there is the arduous sweat.

Joseph Tsai, the Noble

Jack Ma's views on talents are different from the rest. He believes that the diplomas of masters and doctors of famous universities are just a receipt. The one suitable for enterprises and bringing value to the enterprise is absolute right. Jack Ma said, "Those who pay more personal income tax are talented. No boss is so silly to pay you 3 million *yuan* by just looking at your doctoral degree (large amount receipt)." Even so, Jack Ma did not "discriminate" those highly talented people like Joseph Tsai (Cai Congxin) who "happened to" graduate from famous universities.

One morning in early October, 2011, Jack Ma and Masayoshi Son as well as investment banks had a meeting in the Silicon Valley, Joseph Tsai was among them. There is the old saying, "Three generations of officials, proper dress and proper meal." There is another saying, "Three generations of Yale, real noble." Three generations of Joseph Tsai's family graduated from Yale University. He is the noble of our company. He is a very approachable and humorous person. Once, while sitting behind him, I glanced at his computer screen displaying numbers and curves. "I just saw the top secret of the company," I said jokingly to him. "Wonderful," he said, "tell me if you understand it. My brain is racked!"

Once, Joseph Tsai and I took the same flight to the United States. When speaking about the topic of "starting point" and "result," I said, "It's like a woman having breast implants. The starting point is good, but there are four kinds of results: big difference, no big difference, still not big, one big and one small." He rocked with laughter. "Please repeat it. I want to make a note of it."

Jobs' Rainbow

The sun was shining again after some rain in the morning. When our car reached the Four Seasons Hotel for a meeting, long and short concentric circles of rainbows appeared in the sky. The short one slowly faded. The long one became longer and longer, clearer and clearer, and finally became a semicircle. Half an hour later, I heard the news. Steve Jobs passed away. Did the rainbow come to fetch him? I hope so!

The Governor of California

A few days later, Jack Ma was invited for dinner at the home of the Governor of California, Jerry Brown. He was once America's youngest governor of the state, but now the oldest one. When our car arrived at the gate, a tall old man in a white suit of graceful bearings was walking a dog. He led Jack Ma into the house with a smile. It was said that the previous Governor stayed in office for six or seven years without pay and even used more than USD 20 million from his own pocket, but California's deficit continued to increase by more than USD 10 billion. It seemed that it was not enough just to be honest as government officials. Perhaps such evaluation of the previous Governor was not fair. There might have been more deficits if others were in his shoes for those seven years. Maybe he was not lucky.

Jack Ma introduced Chinese history and China's current progress to the new Governor, with a mention to his hometown Hangzhou. Previously, Governor Brown didn't know anything about Hangzhou and the West Lake. And that day the seed of the West Lake was sowed in the Governor's heart. In April 2013, the Governor came to China and squeezed-in some time for a quiet trip to Hangzhou. Jack Ma took the Governor and his wife on a gaily-painted pleasure-boat on the West Lake and they had Hangzhou cuisine on the boat. The governor couple was full of praise for the scenery and food in Hangzhou.

Making up Martial Arts Stories

While in the United States, Jack Ma often told us the martial arts stories made up by him at night. He would slowly put the firewood in the fireplace and begin his stories in a relaxed and leisurely mood. One story goes like this:

A prince, who was good at playing the lyre, chess, writing calligraphy, and painting since childhood, has recruited various martial arts masters for a deep-rooted love. He finally gets on a road of no return of overthrowing the dynasty. He is known as "Lord Seven" of the rivers and lakes, not because he is the seventh child of the family, but because he is said to have seven fingers on his left hand which is always covered by a glove. No one has ever seen it and all those who have are dead. The story has its ups and downs and is full of unexpected suspense. Jack Ma told it in a way as if it was his experience in a previous life. Even if there were some alternate plots at the following night, you would think that the previous night was wrong. During the period of our stay in the United States, every day in the morning we wished the day would go quickly so that we could catch up with the stories.

Someone asked me what Jack Ma would do after he resigned as CEO. "He would want to finish this story," I guess.

The Hulun Buir Prairie

In July 2011, the Nature Conservancy organized a trip to investigate the Hulun Buir Prairie and to discuss the protection and development of the grasslands.

Other entrepreneurs and their wives shared our trip. Some of them had their children studying overseas, so "kids" became the center of their topic. "The school is very beautiful, even the dormitory corridor is very neat. But the dorm is another world, an utter mess. You can't even find a place to stand. Every time I go there, I will tidy up and conduct a thorough cleaning." One mother said.

A few of the entrepreneurs were long time good friends of Jack Ma and would occasionally ask about something confidential regarding the company's business. Instead of answering them, Jack Ma would say, "A person's weight is determined by the weight of his coffin and the weight of the coffin is decided by the secrets he takes away. If a person hasn't taken any secrets with him after death, then his life is in vain."

The host, Niu Gensheng, received us with great hospitality after we reached Hulun Buir. He told us that Hulun Buir covered an area equal to seven United Kingdoms and a Switzerland combined.

We first visited a grassy wetland reserve and then went to a small town at the Russian border with grassland songs being played all the way. In addition to the grassland, there were different woods and different breeds of horses along the way. It was in July, large tracts of rapeseed flowers were in full bloom.

I felt we passed Genghis Khan's tomb although I couldn't tell exactly where the place was. The legend has it that the funeral procession of Genghis Khan trekked through the grasslands for seven days and seven nights without leaving any marks on the road except for bringing two camels, a mother and her son. In the vast grasslands, only camels could find their way. So the son of the camel was buried with Genghis Khan. In this case, when people visited the grave next time, the mother overwhelmed with grief, would know where her son was buried. Humans were so cruel!

It was already dark when we arrived at the border town. At the dinner table, I raised some questions to the entrepreneurs, which I had consulted some locals on the way. One of the questions was: How many nipples does a cow have? No one got the right answer. "A milk bag, four nipples," Niu Gensheng unveiled the riddle. You think that the cow is also like a sow and a bitch with double-breasts, right?

I didn't sit at the same table with Jack Ma at dinner. After three rounds of drinks, I felt my shoulder was touched. I turned and found it was Jack Ma who was slightly drunk. "They invited me to sing songs after a while. You prepare the program of imitating Hitler too," he said. Suddenly, I was all nerves! It'd been years since I put on the show. I had forgotten the lines, so I ran to the restroom to rehearse several times.

Later entrepreneurs and workers went to the stage one after another. After Jack Ma sang a grassland song, Niu Gensheng came to the stage with his granddaughter. "I announce that the first place goes to Jack Ma. The judge is my granddaughter. When Zhang Youcai sang, she ran outside, and when Jack Ma sang, she wanted to climb up to the stage."

After a burst of applause, Jack Ma had completely forgotten all about my performance. Actually, that was what I hoped for.

Grassland Games

The next day we went back to the central grassland. We watched some performances before eating roasted whole lamb. There was the archery (piercing a willow leaf with an arrow from the distance of a hundred paces) and the wrestling. The eight wrestlers were all had stocky and imposing bodies. It was single knock-out matches and the winner would be the one last standing on the stage. Just then, the wrestlers invited the audience to compete with them and said that it could be three against one of them. So bully! Huang Nubo and others put on wrestling wardrobes and went on one-on-one with them and were knocked out by them in a second. But they would never dream Jack Ma would be prepared this time. He brought Taiji pushing hands champions along. He sneaked away and chose the most powerful one of the eight wrestlers to meet the challenge. In a few rounds, the opponent was 'turned turtle.' They wouldn't yield, and asked for another game but was 'turned turtle' again! The entrepreneurs issued thunderous whoops and cheers.

There was the tug of war in four groups in the afternoon. At the finals, both sides had outsiders to help. So there was another tug of war. Then some-one complained that the winning party had "foreign aid". "I am an impartial judge, as long as one party is not convinced, I will let you tug on," said the chief referee, Niu Gensheng. We tugged four times and finally everyone was "convinced" and tied for the title. I felt my arms obviously longer than before after all the tugging.

There was a bonfire party after dinner. Jack Ma organized and requested that everyone tell ghost stories under the starlight. Although the ghost stories were the same that had been told during childhood, Jack Ma's story still made us feel creepy.

Snoring

That night, half of the entrepreneurs slept in the Mongolian yurts. It was in July, the grasslands was still very cold and wet at night. Jack Ma, Shen Guo-jun, our Taiji champion, and I slept in the same yurt. The whole night was very quiet; I didn't even hear the sound of bugs.

Early the next morning, Wen Jia, who was five yurts away from us, came to us. "Someone snored from your direction last night."

"Really? I didn't hear anything at all," I said.

"Of course you didn't," Jack Ma said, "It was you who snored!"

I felt very guilty. The snoring could be heard across five yurts. You could imagine what a cruel living condition it was that night1 for Jack Ma and Shen Guojun!

Postscript:
An "Alier" with the Least Pursuit

Those who have worked in Alibaba for three years are addressed as "Aliren (Alier)" and those five years are called "Golden-Five (Wunian Chen)." Jack Ma said he "knew his fate" at the age of 45, five years earlier. I finally can say I am Wunian Chen now.

I have the chance to attend various high-level meetings inside the group, which others are most looking forward to and it is the best way to understand the company's business as well as to improve oneself. But I often sneak out of the meeting room after a few minutes. It is the same case in various national entrepreneurs meetings. Sometimes Jack Ma would text me, "Come and listen."

Jack Ma said I was the one who had the least pursuit in Alibaba. Sometimes he would add, "Luckily for you, your work doesn't demand pursuing too much."

I agree. Business department and innovation department need to pursue more. I think the scabbard's duty is to protect the "sharpness" of the sword and I feel at ease to be 'blunt.' Besides, having listened to Jack Ma's speeches so many times, to listen to others' talks would be tormenting; they would have to tie me down to a chair.

Jack Ma once said these similar words on different occasions, "...I had a dream when I first started my business, that one day I could drink morning tea in Rome, to have lunch in Paris and dinner in New York. Now I realized that is a disaster..."

"Daughters" and Love Poems

At the end of the 2010 Yabuli meeting, Jack Ma and Shen Guojun of the Yintai Group returned to Beijing by a Business Liner of a young entrepreneur. On the plane, the entrepreneur said excitedly, "After my cultivation, I have already asked so and so to be in charge and so and so to be in management. Now I basically have a day off every week." He went on, "If so and so can catch up quickly and manage for me, then I can have two days off a week, just like ordinary people." His eyes were full of endless longing when he said this. I thought, Buddy, just work hard! The life you desire I will help you experience. (From 2010 the departments of the company grew, I was allowed to accompany Jack Ma to participate in various activities of my own "choice.")

People often say that one should behave just the same in the presence or absence of leadership. Jack Ma expressed a different opinion.

"If it is the same when you are present or absent, why should the company spend money to hire you? The company wishes to make a great difference by having you," Jack Ma often said this to executives.

After careful thinking, I totally agree with Jack Ma's words! Because most of the time presence even is more important than doing. Throughout history, many major events happened when the emperors were absent. With the presence of the old emperor, even if he did nothing every day but drool with saliva, or call Zhang as Wang, others wouldn't dare to rebel.

To prove that Jack Ma was right, when he went abroad without me, I would be very slack. Every noon I would take different young people from the company for lunch, most of them were girls. The company is not far from Lingyin's and Longjing's picturesque scenery and fresh air. We would eat farmhouse meals in the open air, talking about movie stars or Jack Ma's stories. I do not know since when they began to call me "Chen Ba (daddy)."

"You mustn't be taken in by Chen Wei. To distinguish seniority is to keep you off guard. He learned this trick from a famous scientist," Jack Ma reminded them several times jokingly.

Although I often would treat, I still owed more and more "debt." Because I often said "I'll take you to lunch" as a hello. Later I made an announcement, "If the speaker is serious, it is a pledge; if the listeners are serious, it is a promise; if neither side takes it seriously, then it is a joke. Everything about going for lunch is a 'joke'."

Bragging is a Healthy Life Attitude

Alibaba Business School was established. I would go there to give lessones during my free time when I was invited.

Alibaba Business School was established through the joint efforts of Jack Ma's alma mater, Hangzhou Normal University, and our company. In October 2009, the school invited me to present a hall lecture, "Behind Stars".

When I arrived at the school, I saw a big poster of me near the school gate guest starring Yuan Chonghuan along with an overstated introduction. I began to become very nervous.

After the dinner with the school leadership, I went into the lecture hall with trembling fear. The hall was fully packed with audience. I stepped up to the podium to face the music.

I then started, "This summer holiday, a restaurant received two tables of customers. All came to celebrate their children being admitted to the universities. The owner of the restaurant came to propose a toast. At the first table, he asked, 'Young lady, which university are you to go?' The girl said, 'Hangzhou Normal University.' With his eyes wide open, he said with full admiration, 'Congratulations! Soon you will become the fellow schoolmate of my idol Jack Ma!' After that, the owner went to the other table and asked, 'Young man, which university are you to go?' The boy said, 'Tsinghua University.' The owner silently walked behind the boy and tapped him on his shoulder, saying, 'Don't be sad, it is also a university!' The hall burst into laughter. After that I became relaxed. I talked about the funny things that happened before Jack Ma started his business. I mentioned Zhang Jizhong, Tsui Hark (Xu Ke), etc., also the anecdotes of the crew. In between, there were Questions and Answers periods and the prizes were Jack Ma's books with his autograph. Questions included: "A producer should take everything in consideration. Sometimes a very minor thing can have a negative affect for the whole shooting. There is a scene in *The Deer and the Cauldron* in which Wei Xiaobao and his seven wives playing their part in the water. The performers are all there, the weather is warm, water very clean. But a few days passed, and the scene could not be shot. Why?"

Students could not give the answer. "The probability for all the seven women to enter the water on the same day is very low," I said.

The students broke out in a riot of laughter. The lecture was like a comedy show.

"Last night went well?" Jack Ma asked me when I met him the following day.

From his tone, I knew someone from the school had reported to him.

"Just so-so. I talked an hour and half. But it took me two hours to get out the hall," I mentioned lightly.

"Does it take so long to trample you down and drag you out?" Jack Ma made fun of me. I should have expected that no good will come from bragging to Jack Ma.

On March 3, 2010, the big department I was in held an annual meeting in Hangzhou. I had been informed to make a speech, but when I came back with Jack Ma from Beijing, it was already afternoon. Jack Ma would have to take part in a tree-planting activity. Constant calls urged me to the meeting after we landed. So I entrusted other colleagues to accompany Jack Ma and I rushed to the venue. Had I got to the meeting half an hour later, I would have missed the opportunity to "brag".

My speech didn't come up with a topic. "... I recently heard an explanation of a noun, 'kiss' is two souls meeting in the lips. My dear Alier, please ask yourself, have you ever really 'kissed'? There is another saying, 'Every man dies, not every man really lives.' We need to think about it. How can we really live to the fullest... These two years, I followed CEO Ma and travelled extensively. I got to know some outstanding entrepreneurs. I once heard Feng Lun say in his speech, 'Greatness comes from endurance.' I was immediately amazed. Later I read the same thing from a book by Emperor Yongzheng: 'An emperor becomes an emperor by endurance.' So I think, actually 'endurance' itself is a 'great' accumulation. For instance, the 5-*yuan* glass on the desk, it doesn't need to do anything. If it can endure for 800 years, it will be worth 5 million *yuan*... Guo Guangchang once said, 'Good life is always wasteful.' With this he gained my admiration instantly. After that, I began pondering about 'virtual' and 'real.' Sometimes 'virtual' is more important than the 'real'. As for the glass, we bought it for the price of glass. But glass is not what we want. What we need is the middle part. We spent all our savings to buy a house, what we paid are for the rebars, cement, bricks, but we never use them. What we use is just the space in between them. I also discovered that the company executives are all very interesting people. The President of Ali Cloud Computing, Dr. Wang Jian, is a man of great versatility. You'll find chatting with him very rewarding. For example, he will tell you the helicopter isn't an airplane, but a conveyor that can fly. That is why no country has put the helicopter in the air force. Every technical person within the company admires Dr. Wang, although they don't quite understand what he says most of the time. I said that is right; for the 20% that you understand, you know how things work out; while the 80% that you don't understand, you believe that the company will have an unexpected future... 'Chief of Staff' Professor Zeng Ming said, 'we are doing something that has never been done. Don't fantasize our original idea will be definitely right, we must not fear trial and error.' Very philosophical! Later I figured it out and that is, 'Failure is the mother of success'. The remarkable thing about Professor Zeng is that he can turn a cliché into beautiful sentences, to impress you... Taobao President, Mr. Lu Zhaoxi's name is very interesting. 'Lu' is '6.' 'Zhao' in Chinese vocabulary can mean million; also can mean millions of millions, which is trillions. 'Lu Zhaoxi': if the annual turnover is 6 trillion, I will be happy. Apparently, the name aimed at Wal-Mart at the very beginning..."

The Uncultured "Imperial Envoy"

Generally Jack Ma will instruct me before he goes abroad: "Go and take a look at each subsidiary. Try to understand our operation. If you find anything wrong, let me know."

What is this? My dear friends, this is "verbal instructions"! It means for the next couple of days I will be the "imperial envoy."

So, in addition to checking mail and receiving visitors and other "required courses," I will go to the subsidiaries to sniff around. There are a few friends I will have to see, such as Wu Wei, the CFO of B2B under Alibaba, (Now the CFO of the Alibaba Group), etc. I will go to spend my "least pursuit" time with the people of "most pursuit".

Wu Wei is the most clear-minded woman I've ever met. Because she is in charge of finances, she knows best the running state of the whole company.

And she can make me understand the things I completely don't understand before in just a few words.

She is my "Wechat friend." We send each other funny jokes. She often teases me, "It is really a miracle for people like you to survive in Alibaba."

"CEO Ma said, Alibaba is not a farm, but a zoo. The more animal 'species,' the more ecological it is," I responded.

Wu Wei's office faces the east. There is a huge bookshelf behind her seat, but I can't read any of the books; but for those in her drawers, they're just pieces of cake for they are all comic books. One day I went to her office at lunch time and she happily opened a comic book which made her laugh unstoppably. She insisted on reading it to me, although I knew those words too. At last she gave me a book *Blush (Da Hong Lian)*, with an infinite generous and reluctant look.

The other day I send a message to her, "I'm going to compile these years of assistant work into a book."

She replied mockingly, "Writing a book needs to be cultured, right?"

"Wrong. Reading a book needs to be cultured, not writing one," I replied.

After thinking about it, I proved this seemingly 'unreasonable theory' and went to Wu Wei, "The knowledge needed to write a book is all learned in primary school. For example, in Chapter 64 of *Dao De Jing*:

The tree which fills the arms grew from the tiniest sprout;

the tower of nine storeys rose from a (small) heap of earth;

the journey of a thousand li commenced with a single step.

The three sentences mean the same thing, but the third one is the best. You must have learnt that in primary school and it will be enough for you to write a book. The first two sentences are just so-so, but others may write them out to fool you. So in order to read a book, finishing primary school is not enough, you still need to have further education."

Jack Ma knows that I have always held this attitude toward life, love bragging, content with mediocrity and have no desire to make progress, but still he sometimes asks me why I "have no pursuit."

Once in Beijing, we were not as busy as usual. Jack Ma took "Bigfoot" (Jin Jianhang, one of 18 founders) and me to dinner. The two took turns to question me to learn if there were deeper causes or events that made me like this. "When a man climbs from the ground floor to the ninth floor, what he experiences is the ninth floor instead of nine floors. As a matter of fact, each floor has its own unique scenery," I answered at that time. In fact, I didn't have the answer to this question either. It just came out of my mouth.

"If there are no problems on finance and personal ability, how would you like to live the most?" Jack Ma asked again.

I forgot how I answered then. But now I want to say, in June 2013, the Hangzhou Taobao Town would be built and a new era would begin. I wish I could be an "inspector" in the Taobao Town, go to any department I am interested in and brag with anyone I like.

Appendix

Appendix I Adam Hesitated

After 15 years of Alibaba history, everyone has drawn different interpretations about the company. I think, the company is in a kind of "initial success" of thought at present. What is this thought? Where does it come from? And where will it go?

As you may know, Jack Ma, Bill Gates, Warren Buffett, Bill Clinton, and George Soros are good friends. They will have in-depth exchanges, brain storming when the opportunity presents itself.

Jack Ma has a very tight schedule, but he still attempts by all means to squeeze some time in to see Buddhist monks, Taoist priests, philosophers, and so on.

Sometimes I had the honor to sit in. Sometimes I could only stay in the outer room as a "Protective Dharma." Sometimes I could get some inspirations. Here is one of the excerpts I will share with you.

Adam Hesitated

Human history, in a certain sense, is the history of exploring the ultimate meaning of the universe.

Philosophers of all ages went through their inner journey and formed different philosophies. But in terms of the ultimate meaning, they either leaned toward theology or became pessimistic; thinking the universe was aimless and meaningless.

Actually the universe has the ultimate meaning, but it is not yet to be revealed. There is only one reason, allow me to borrow a religious story, I think that's "Adam hesitated".

In the Garden of Eden with beasts of prey and poisonous serpents, the survival of the blind Adam and Eve merely relied on the blessings of God. Due to the temptation by the serpent, Eve convinced Adam to eat the apple and he had his vision. Adam had ears, nose, tongue, body, and mind that God gave him before Adam had the "six roots." But the "six roots" could only sustain his life, but not enough to help him know the whole universe.

At that time, if Adam ate all the fruits in the Garden of Eden bravely, unhesitatingly before God came, he and his offspring – human beings, would have "A sense," and "B sense," in addition to visual sense. We conclude these increased "senses" as "apperception (*ming jue*)." In that case, we might be like God and have the ability to understand the ultimate meaning of the universe.

Human's confidence, however, far exceeds human's wisdom. They think wisdom can make up for the shortage of the senses, actually otherwise. For example, can you express clearly the red color to a man born blind? If humanity has the common deletion of one or more common senses in perceiving the world – "apperception," will they still have a correct understanding of the world?

Mahatma Gandhi said that simplicity is the essence of universality. If humans have "apperception," perhaps the ultimate meaning will be like a fly on a bald head – obvious!

The Defect of Materialism

One of the cornerstones of materialism: Consciousness is the product of the brain and the brain is physical, so the material determines consciousness. This reasoning is obviously unsound. If the brain comes first, and the consciousness second, material decides the "birth" of consciousness, but it can't decide the activities of consciousness. It is like the relationship between parents and children. Parents can't decide the development of their children. Materialism also believes that all deep thoughts and strong feelings are only the transformation and combination of human brain particles, and the movement of any particle follows a certain law. If it was true, humans would have no sense of freedom. Our thoughts would just be like the movement of human brain particles according to the law, which is fundamentally different from what we experience. We believe that humans have consciousness of freedom.

The Trap of Science

Before Bacon, science and theology, in many cases, were mixed together. Bacon said, "Knowledge is power," and "Knowledge comes from practice." Science has made considerable development since then. More and more people believe that knowledge is science, and science is the truth. Now science has been able to detect electromagnetic waves in the brain, and some scientists think that human consciousness is electromagnetic waves. It's not. The electromagnetic waves measured by scientific means are not consciousness itself, but the splash "waves" when consciousness "swims" across the brain. Consciousness cannot be detected by material instruments. Not only are physical instruments ineffective, even using consciousness to explore consciousness is unworkable. The future is still uncertain.

So we doubt: could science be a trap, a kind of "inducement" set by God? And we lack the "apperception." Human beings may walk into a scientific dead end and feel hopeless about the world.

Religions' Gambling

Human is the most embarrassing species. Other species do not demand to know and understand the universe while they may also have a rebirth, or eventually reach the new world in other ways. Humans have a need to know the ultimate meaning of the universe but without the ability. Humans never willingly accept their incomprehensibility of the world, although each deep exploration of the universe shows deeper incredibility.

Human beings have realized the limitations of the "five roots" of eyes, ears, nose, tongue, and body, so they gamble on the sixth root: the "mind." All religions have similar enlightenment, hoping that the "consciousness" will "leap" to understanding the ultimate meaning.

God exists, but it is not the god in Christianity. God may be a kind of power to be perceived by "apperception" or may be "apperception" itself.

Because humans have a common deletion of "apperception," we may not be able to reach the ultimate truth. Well, at least we can know why we don't know, because Adam hesitated.

Appendix II The Model of Acquired Metamorphosis – Eagle

When I published this article, CEO Ma was still in his 72 hours of retreat. In his last retreat CEO Ma meditated to open the new commercial civilization for the next decade.

This retreat was to supplement the vigor consumed in this half year, and at the same time to think about Alibaba's layout and direction in 2010. CEO Ma wants to be an artist and to carve the art of Alibaba to the height of perfection.

In CEO Ma's retreat clearance, we could see each other, but he could not speak. At break time I wrote the story of the eagle for CEO Ma:

Most animals' survival ability is inborn, but the eagle's is quite different. If we domesticate a baby eagle, it will grow up to be like a chicken!

The eagle can live to be 70 years old. Each eagle can hatch three or four eaglets. The adult eagle often keeps the eaglets starving to the extent that they can barely stand. If the eaglets can still look up at the sky and cry in anger, the adult eagle will feed them immediately, thinking they have the potential to be real eagles.

The wings of the eagle are not innately strong. The adult eagle will break the eaglet's wings with its mouth, challenging it to live or die! After a period of time, the newly grown wing bones are much stronger than before. But before it heals, the adult eagle will push the terrified eaglet off a cliff. Some fall and die, and some endure the terrible pain and fly into the blue sky. Due to the flapping of their wings in severe pain, the wing bones grow stronger.

In the subsequent 40 years, the eagle overlooks the earth, turns its nose to the strong, and almost has no natural enemy.

But after the age of 40, the eagle appears to have aging symptoms: its mouth is too long and too curved, affecting hunting and eating; feathers are in disorder, affecting the flying; claws grow web, affecting its successful hunt for prey.

The eagle makes an incredible decision through meditation: It perks its head up, slams into a cliff and cracks up the aging mouth. It doesn't eat or drink until the new mouth grows. And then it uses the new mouth to pull the aging feathers out and let new feathers grow. At the same time it removes the web between its claws with its mouth.

The rebirth wins the eagle 30 more years of life, 30 years of dignity!

CEO Ma has heard this story before, and maybe you too. This goes well with Ali's culture — ordinary people do extraordinary things.

Maybe you are not an eagle yet, but if you can stand the metamorphosis, sooner or later you will become an eagle! If you are an eagle, and there is no sky that you want to be in, here is a Russian proverb for you: Eagles can fly as low as the chicken, but not always so!

Khalil Gibran said:

Life is indeed darkness save when there is urge;

And all urge is blind save when there is knowledge;

And all knowledge is vain save when there is work!

Alier have the urge, the knowledge and the work, so life is meaningful!

Appendix III Jack Ma's Internal Articles

In July 2008, Jack Ma, from Alibaba's data, had clearly perceived that the global economy was approaching a serious problem. Our order data showed this kind of problem three to six months before any official economic data. Jack Ma hoped that we could realize the seriousness of the problem and be prepared for the "winter" ahead of schedule. So he wrote the "Mission of the Winter." But the Beijing Olympic Games were to begin in just 10 days or so. Some corporate executives had concerns — would this be a good time to voice this? Ma thought that the truth could not be covered up. The sooner we talk about this, the sooner we can be prepared. It is good for everyone.

Mission of the Winter

Dear Alier,

I'm sure your mood is very complicated on Alibaba's B2B trend of stock! Today I want to share with you my views on the current overall situation and the future. Maybe it will be a little helpful for you.

You may still remember, in the staff meetings held in February, I said winter is coming. We need to prepare for the winter! Many people took it for granted. Actually when our stock soared nearly three times from the listed price, amidst cheers, the dark clouds and thunder behind had already been fast approaching. Because any swift and violent passion and enthusiasm would fade equally and surprisingly fast! I hope you would have a reasonable thought about stock prices. In the listing ceremony last year, I said that we would keep our sense of mission as always and would not change it because of the listing. In the face of the stock market in the future, I hope you forget about the fluctuation of the share price and always remember "customer first"! Remember our long-term commitment to customers, to society, to our colleagues, to our shareholders and our families. When these commitments are fulfilled, the stock will naturally reflect the value you create for the company.

Our basic judgment for the global economy is that it will have a major problem and the economy may usher in a very difficult period for the next few years. My view is that the whole economic situation is not optimistic. The coming winter will be longer, colder, and more complicated than we thought! Let's prepare for the winter!

What should we do in the face of winter?

First, we must have confidence and preparation for the winter.

We're not afraid of the winter, but we're afraid that we are not prepared for it. We're afraid that we don't know how long and how cold it will be! Everyone is equal before opportunity and disaster! Those who are fully prepared have a better chance to survive. Strong desire to survive and confidence for the future as well as overall ideas and material preparations are the important guarantees for winter survival. After the last round of severe winters with Internet and "SARS" and other series of blows, the Alibaba Group already has a certain amount of anti-strike capabilities. Last year we seized the opportunity of the listed financing, from which we're blessed with over USD 2 billion cash reserves for the winter. The Group's strategy, "dig tunnels deep, store grain everywhere, be better, stronger but not bigger," at the beginning of the year has already been firmly implemented in each subsidiary. I think, in the face of the approaching winter, Alier should bring out the lofty sentiments in those years: If not now, when?! If not me, who?! In 2001, we said to ourselves, be the last man standing! Even if we are on our knees, we'll be the last to fall! With Alibaba's strength today, we may not fall ourselves, but today we shoulder greater responsibility than in the past. We ourselves should not only stand. We have a responsibility to protect our clients − not to let the tens of millions of small and medium-sized enterprises worldwide, that trust and rely on Alibaba services, fall! In today's economy, many enterprises will face great challenges for survival. To help them survive is our mission — let "There is no such thing as a difficult business" have the most perfect interpretation. We must bear in mind: If all our clients fall, we can't see the sun next spring either!

Second, do what needs to be done in the winter.

A company is great not just because it can seize the opportunity many times, but because it can sustain catastrophes again and again! In 2002-2003, in the cold winter of the Internet, we vigorously carried out the construction of Alibaba's corporate culture, organization structure, and personnel training. Today, while we are thankful for the opportunity brought to us by the listing last year, we shall also learn to be grateful for the huge opportunities brought to us by today's world economic adjustment. Alibaba began the venture with 18 people and today we have more than 10,000 people. Our culture, organization and personnel construction also faced challenges under rapid growth, but opportunities were presented as well, which allowed us to have a vigorous experience during the five years: establishment of Taobao, Alipay, acquisition of Yahoo China, creation of Ali software, Alimama and the investment in Koubei and eventually to last year's listing. We hope to have a few years of rehab. Thanks to this age, this period gives us another great opportunity!

We have thought about this deeply, and based on our principles of "customers first, employees second and shareholders third" our goals for the next decade are:

1. For Alibaba to become the world's largest ecommerce service provider.

2. For Alibaba to become the world's best employer.

In order to achieve these goals, we must grasp the opportunities this harsh winter presents us! Let us now return to our ecommerce roots and our founding principles! The power of a great army is not shown when it is advancing; it shows when it is in an organized retreat. The power of a great company is shown when it can survive in a harsh environment with a positive attitude while continuing to adjust, learn, and grow.

In this new globalizing world, the Chinese economy will play an ever greater role. We are pleased to see that world leaders are learning to communicate and coordinate their activities better on major issues like the Asian tsunami, earthquakes, fighting diseases, and fighting global warming. These are all good signs of a brighter future for humanity. This will change the world from the one that is solely reliant on the US dollar to something more multilateral! The Internet powered by ecommerce will play a revolutionary role in this change! "Push for consumer spending and creating jobs" will be our major mission and opportunity in the next stage of our Internet development! The future of ecommerce is bright, and we will help our small and medium sized customers to survive this crisis, and when we emerge in 10 years, it will be a whole new world!

Dear Alier, let's be the messengers and witnesses to this whole new world!

Jack Ma

July 26, 2008

Jack Ma was inspired from the many talks of the staff on the intranet concerning the system and corporate culture. He wrote down the article of "System, Culture, and KPI." Although Ma said he was not good at typing, this article was the longest one typed by him so far.

System, Culture, and KPI

The discussion involves many problems. They are very interesting and worth exploring. Because I'm not good at typing, and I'm especially not good at writing articles, I can only choose a few issues to discuss with you.Purely academic discussions at a philosophical level, but I am not a good scholar either, just take it as my personal opinions! Please excuse me for the poor logic and many typos. (My Chinese is poor since childhood and my composition skill is poorer.)

Two topics today: 1. Rule of man and rule of law; 2.KPI.

I spend most of my personal time learning about our customers. I can't say I know what customers are complaining about one hundred percent, but almost every day I spend time on our own sites "listening to" the users. Of course, I also pay attention and listen to the voices of colleagues. I like to go on the intranet most, to listen to your discussion, to watch you write programs, answer calls... I also like to see your smiling faces in the lift most. Of course, I often feel depressed, weak, and wanting to be understood as you do. I believe the best way is to put myself in the position of the customers and the staff because when I do that I find it easy to understand a lot of things.

These two years I am busier and have a tight schedule, the opportunities for me to see you are fewer. But I never forget that I am an entrepreneur and the least to say I am an Alier! The difference between the vast majority of entrepreneurs and me is that my journey is longer and my experience relatively unique. The difference between the vast majority of Alier and me is that Alibaba has given me more opportunities, more resources, more responsibility. I believe that our colleagues have greater pressure than me, either in life or work!

You are much stronger than me in micro aspects, but I think I spend more time on comprehensive and macro development, because it is my duty as a CEO. Every day I think about what problems will lead to cancer (if not well dealt with); what problems are like a cold and will be recovered without much treatment.

Currently, many people in China believe that the uneven development of China is because of the "rule of man" rather than the rule of law. It seems that with a better system, China will become better. Personally, I think the "rule of man" is not a bad thing. The correct "rule of man" is the management of "people-oriented." It should be higher than the rule of law, but it must be established on the basis of the rule of law. "Rule of man" is not necessarily bad governance. Li Shimin of the Tang dynasty and Qianlong of the Qing dynasty were rulers of the "rule of man" in Chinese history, but they made the country thrive and the people prosperous! Of course, the construction of rule of law was the most powerful at the same time. So in my opinion, it is not the matter of "rule of man" or "rule of law," but we need to set up all the basis of the rule of law and rule of man – the cultural values system we can truly identify with!

I've travelled to many countries and regions, and I found a problem. In the west, most people first think of how to obey a law when it is established. They will abide by it even if they don't agree with it; whereas, in China, after laws are issued, most people will first think how to bypass them, the so-called "counter-measures". There is no such thing as a perfect system. The system is to give guarantees to the majority of the people. But most of the time, for the future benefit of the majority of people (our later generations), we have to offend the interests of the majority of people today. A good system must have a close relationship with the handling of the executors. The system is cold and dead, but people are not. The system needs to be performed. And most of the time a good system is performed thoroughly wrong. Stipulating the system is not the most difficult thing. Most of the time, what we lack is not the system, but the process. What we lack is real execution, the psychological identity of the system and the wisdom and experience of the system design. For example, Alibaba doesn't lack the customer security system, even the first article we write in the assessment of values is "customer first"! Then what is the result?

I am not blaming the management or the employees. Because with "customer first" we are no different between staff and management. I don't think we (including myself) make "customer first" as the conditioned reflex on ideology, on the system design process, on wisdom, on the concrete judgment or on the dribs and drabs of operations! We can develop countless systems and have countless meetings, but if we don't recognize it completely deep in the heart, it is all in vain! We have established a good system. But do we respect users? Have we taken the following steps to pass on the system? 1. Enlighten them (users) with reasons (We understand our real starting point); 2. Motivate them with emotions (Moving others by moving yourselves first); 3. Convince them with courtesy (It is painful to understand others' change); 4. Bring them to justice (The ones who do not obey the system must be dealt with according to the rules of the system).

Many of my former colleagues are working in state-owned enterprises. They have almost the same complaints: SOE system is too bad! Shit! But under the same system, why do we have "China Mobile", "Industrial and Commercial Bank of China" and "CNOOC"... Complaining is the easiest thing in the world. But few people blame themselves. And I found within the circle of my friends, those who blame others and who blame the system are all losers, but most of the ones who blame themselves are very successful.

For an organization, the most terrible thing is the complaint of system from management (They don't know they can be builders and participants of the system), the complaint of managers from employees (They don't know one day they will also be managers). A good organization would rely on its staff if the system is not perfect! Rely on the system if staff members are not perfect! Sometimes I hear people say that xyz company has a perfect system, powerful culture, I just want to laugh. Alibaba can never have a perfect system and we can never have perfect employees, but we will always walk the way that leads the company to perfecting the system! Culture should not pursue the strong. Culture is definitely not to seek the similar, but the goal is for mutual longing. Good culture is definitely not to exclude all others, but to have recognition from the hearts. That will draw us closer to goodness, progress, and the realness of human nature.

By now, I really want to say, we need to constantly improve the system and the regime today. And this work absolutely is not only the management work, but also the work of all Alier. I see our colleagues work overtime, our sales and supply staff work through severe winters and mid-summers; I listen to our "TrustPass" colleagues talk with hoarse throats... (Take one day to listen to the telephone service of Taobao customer service and see how hard they work and how helpless they are. And I suggest that we all listen to them when we are free) every time I do, I am moved to tears. I think we should be able to use more wisdom; more innovative ways to do our work better and make our customers more satisfied and we should let our colleagues go home earlier so that their families will be worry-free from working overtime every day. We should be able to have a better way to make our work more efficient, people grow better, take more income home. But today we are still just a small company with nine years of history! Our company is too young; our industry is too young; our cadres are also too young. But I believe that as long as we don't give up faith and hold on to our dreams, as long as we keep improving and growing, the next nine years we will be much closer to our goals!

That's a lot. I really feel like I am talking about philosophy. Now let's get to the Key Performance Indicator, or KPI. I hate the KPI as you do! It kills our ideals, our goals, and it keeps us constantly on the run through various unnecessary means! It also kills our fun at work. It kills our innovation and passion! We hate it but we can't move forward without it! After some rational thoughts, I think KPI is not the problem, but the problem is with our design and execution people. What is the KPI? I think the KPI is performance indicators of some work goals. If there is no KPI, we won't have specific indicators to assess our work performance. But with only KPI, it never means that our work is done very well! I think the KPI is doing a doctor's job in some way. When you go to the hospital, the doctor will check your temperature, blood pressure and blood test index which can only prove you are not sick, but can't prove that you are absolutely healthy! Healthy or not, you are the one to know. KPI is a must, that is the foundation, but besides the KPI, there are too many other things we need to pay attention to. Most of the fatal diseases are not shown in KPI. When it does, it is dying. KPI designing involves making judgments of customers, the business, competition, and future! It requires courage, wisdom, and accumulation of the experience of success and of failure! Doing it right may not necessarily be right, but doing it wrong will certainly be wrong. It is not an easy job for anyone!

This year, the presidents of each company have two indicators: the first is the KPI set by the Group; the second is "satisfied" or "not satisfied" by me which is called "rule of man". That is to say, even if you've done well in KPI, but I am not satisfied with the results, it still won't do! If you haven't done well in KPI, but I think you've done well, you still can get the points. But if the KPI is not complete, I usually won't be satisfied!

Well. It's the first time for me to write so much in one breath. I'll take a break and drink some water. Comments are welcome! But do not affect the job!

Jack Ma

September 12, 2008

Jack Ma would post messages before each Spring Festival to wish everyone a happy New Year.

Toasts on Spring Festival Eve

Dear Alier,

This year on the Eve of the Spring Festival, at 8:18, if you are with your family and friends, please remember to propose a toast on my behalf to your parents, wife ,husband and children, brothers and sisters, lovers, and family friends! At 8:19, the second toast is to all our colleagues on the job at work during the Spring Festival! At 8:20, the third toast is to thank ourselves, thanks to 2008, and bless 2009! By that time I will propose the toasts to the sky to extend by gratitude. Please remember!

Jack Ma

January 1, 2009

Jack Ma is strongly against employees working overtime endlessly. He hopes everyone can have fun after work or on weekends. "Occupying the various places of entertainment in Hangzhou" is Jack Ma's slogan. But to complete or exceed the task, especially those whose income is directly related with their work performance, there are situations of working overtime, which is either required by the departments or out of their own will by the staff.

One of our staff's families sent an email to Jack Ma. And the following is his post regarding this matter.

Work Happily and Live Seriously

I've received an anonymous letter from a staff member's family. I feel very sad and I want to share something with you.

I think the best works of Alibaba should be our youthful Alier, as a group of people who can bring a smile back home after work every day, and bring happiness and wisdom of life back to work the next day!

I hope Alier is a group of people who have dreams and passion and who can do solid work, but also can lead a better life! Those who ignore life for work are not true Alier; at least they are not "Ali" enough! I dislike people who have no ideal and no passion all day long (like chickens, ducks at the farm). I also dislike those who only work hard but have no life's interests (like a running machine). A person who does not work hard is unlikely to have a better life, but a person who doesn't understand the meaning of life can't work well either!

Dear colleagues, we'll have to struggle for 102 good years, we are not a company that aims for only 12 months. Excessive consumption of our physical strength consumes our personal lives and will not sustain us for long! I sincerely hope all of you: for ourselves and for our families, for the healthy development of Alibaba, please "work happily and live seriously"! Those who contradict life and work must seriously reflect on this!

Jack Ma

February 11, 2009

On the morning of Valentine's Day, Jack Ma found the company was filled with roses. He said humorously, "I thought I came to the wrong place and ran into the flower market!" So he posted the following message.

Season's Greetings

Every year on Valentine's Day, I always see "flowers all over the mountains and plains" and on the tables of many colleagues in the company. I hope and believe next year there will be more flowers.

Bless those who love you, loved you, you love, you loved, you miss and missed! Sow your love, harvest your love, and enjoy your love. Those who haven't harvest love, today is the best time to sow your love! Go ahead! Bless you!

Jack Ma

February 14, 2009

Tong Wenhong is the vice president of the Group who takes care of the Real Estate Department of the Group. She majored in electronics and is my fellow schoolmate from the same department at Zhejiang University. In 2000, after giving birth to her baby, she came to apply for a job with the company, which at that time the only vacancy was at the front desk. She didn't feel being a receptionist lowered herself esteem. Through her own efforts, she worked all the way from the front desk, administrative, and then to vice president, also from a laywoman of building construction to the "construction contractor" of the company. If I had her vision, the founders of Alibaba would not be only 18 people, but 19!

In August 2009, the Group's first own campus — 100,000 square meters of Binjiang Campus was built after 700 days of infighting (The Company had rented office buildings before that). Jack Ma posted a message on the Intranet, more or less like Chairman Mao's "Million Mighty Armies Crossing the Yangtze River" written in April 1949.

Successful Completion of Binjiang Park

Salute and applaud to the contractors of the new building, the Administration Department, and the IT Department!

Recently, I am deeply moved by the builders of Alibaba's new buildings in Binjiang. Our people are not experienced in construction. Since breaking the ground two years ago, many colleagues transferred here from their beloved posts. Every day they ran across the city, in cold winter and hot summer. To complete the building on time, they paid an amazing price! Let's leave the others aside. The complex "relationship" of this project was incredible. Even the renovation of our small homes may frustrate us immensely, not to mention the huge living and working project for thousands of people. Every time I see their gaunt faces, I felt heart-broke. Thank you, Tong Wenhong and your team!

I also want to extend my deep respect to the administration and IT team responsible for the moving task! You might find it hard to imagine the complexity of the matter. The moving of your own house alone is already hard enough. But they were responsible for moving thousands of people, drilling for the move took them more than half a year while at the same time attending their daily work. Such large-scale relocations and server migration was actually carried out very well. I'm really proud of you!

I witnessed many people who fell sick, had fevers from fatigue because of moving the company ensuring that everyone had the feeling of having a home, the colleagues of the relocation headquarters almost worked day and night, with bubbles on their mouths! Words fail me. I see another team that beat over the "SARS"!

Dear Alier, perhaps not everything will be smooth after we move here. You may not be satisfied with this or that kind of things, but I still want to ask you to applaud with respect to the builders and devotees of the new building! With their efforts, we have a new home. With their efforts and sweat, we stride from the West Lake times to the Qianjiang era!

Complaining is the easiest thing. The perfection of the new buildings may need at least two years. Even if we are not willing to spend time to participate in the construction, at least we should learn to be grateful, to respect and to applaud!

Alier are the luckier generation, because we are grateful!

Two days before the 10th anniversary celebration of the Company, friends from all over the world came to Hangzhou. After finishing the day's work and reception, Jack Ma posted this message that night.

A Promise a Decade Ago

Dear Alier,

A few days before the 10th anniversary of Alibaba, at the time when Alibaba's B2B had a sound development and clear future strategy, at the time when Alibaba's first stage was coming to an end and another exciting new era was about to start, I decided to sell some shares of listed companies of Alibaba to bring some sense of periodical achievements for myself and my family members!

10 years ago, when I decided to borrow money, to sell our apartment for business, I depicted a future "large cake" to my wife; "10 years later we will have the money, we'll have a good house, a car, more capacity and strength to help others... we'll have our own disposable wealth and freedom!"

Today I am very happy. After 10 years of efforts, many of our dreams have gradually come true, but some ideals have just begun... I am more pleased that I finally have a chance to prove many of my views and ideas of wealth I held to as a young man. Thank you for all your efforts, for giving me the chance to practice. I also want to take this opportunity to share with you views about wealth and happiness.

Through the ten years of hard work, I roughly understand the meaning of money and wealth. If you have millions, you are rich; if you have hundreds of millions, you can be counted as having capital; but if you have hundreds of millions or even billions, in fact, the money is not your own money, but the resources belong to the whole society. You have the right and more responsibility to make the best use of these resources for society! Money and wealth are two different concepts. Having money is not the same as having wealth. In my opinion, wealth is an undergoing, an experience. If you can't turn the money into experience to improve your sense of happiness as well as others,' what you have is probably just a lot of symbols and a pile of colorful paper.

We often say that "Money makes the devil go around," but in fact many people in the world go around for the devil! Money is used to solve our problems, to serve us, to create more joy and happiness and opportunities for people! Money is not for showing off, not for worshiping, and more so, not to waste. Neither no spending nor excessive spending will show respect for money. Maybe many of you will think, what you say is great truth, all lectures, is just the rich talking to the poor. When I get rich, I will say so too (I used to think so). Of course, the talk will go nowhere if you don't have any money at all. But I find that many of my rich friends actually are not living a happy life. And many of the people from ordinary households have far more sense of happiness than many rich people! The reason is that happy people have a pursuit outside wealth. I always believed that only people with money who spend it wisely can hopefully create more money, more wealth, and more happiness! Now that I am still young, I have a lot of things to learn, to do, a lot of people to thank, a lot of things to be grateful for. And I will do it now!

Alibaba has experienced 10 years of ups and downs, especially the baptism in the financial storm. I have never been as full of confidence about the future of the company as I am today! When B2B went to market, the board of directors passed the resolution to let all employees hold 20% to 50% of the shares, and to convert their length of service and other elements into the shares of listed companies so that everyone could have money to use when in need. Joseph Tsai and I, as the company's deputy chairman and chairman, based on the confidence for the future of B2B and the support for other business of the Group, selected very few shares of the listed companies. Today, as we envisioned, B2B has begun to enter the best state in 10 years. I believe it will be more and more successful. You will have more and more wealth! I don't want to wait to get old and the only thing I can do is donate money! I need to learn how to spend money to do things from now on, to experience the meaning and responsibility of being wealthy. We should not wait to do things after we get old. Let's learn to respect the wealth we created with diligence and wisdom, learn to spend money, for ourselves, for our families, for society, for all our relatives and friends who care for us and love us!

P.S.

Selling stocks now or at any time will attract a lot of criticism and even affect Alibaba's stock price. A year ago, an executive of our company sold some of his own stocks for urgent matters. It so happened that the stock market declined, so many people voiced criticism to the executive...

That kind of criticism was unfair. Stock share options are the rights of each employee given to you by the company. Every Alier has the right to deal with their assets, including me. And we must learn to adapt to the ups and downs of the stock market for any reason possible! For short-term, the high and low of stock price may be affected by some business behaviors or market trend, but look to the future. I firmly believe that the share prices will be proportional to the efforts we invest, proportional to our confidence for the company!

Jack Ma

September 8, 2009

On April 16, 2010, Jack Ma and Yu Feng established a fund company in partnership. After the establishment of the fund company, the first investment of the cultural industry was funding Zhang Yimou's "impression series" of the "iron triangle. Actually, Jack Ma had contacts and cooperation with the "iron triangle" before. A program of Private Enterprises Pavilion in Shanghai World Expo was created and produced by their team.

Report to Alier

Dear Alier,

This afternoon, I will announce in Beijing that the former Chairman of Target Media Yu Feng and I are to set up an investment fund company with the mission of focusing on the future. We will concentrate on investing in the outstanding young entrepreneurs, with a focus on environmental protection and the cultural industry.

The participants of the fund are China's leading entrepreneurs. We hope that with a joint establishment we can make some contribution to the future of our planet, for China's future, and for young people.

Because the fund company may have cooperative relations with the Alibaba Group in the future, and because I'm involved in strategic decision-making in the fund company, there are possibilities of doing business with Alibaba in the future. Here I report this matter to the group's colleagues. In addition, I promise I will do my best to make the company become the excellent funds towards a new commercial civilization.

Jack Ma

April 16, 2010

In 2010, to defend the interests of consumers and further support the integrity of sellers who offer quality products and services, Taobao adjusted the search results. This move offended the interests of Internet 'black industry chain.' Hence, there were distorted accusations by the network coverage. They even instigated some sellers to protest at the gate of Taobao. Jack Ma posted the following message.

To Live for Ideal

Dear Alier,

A few days ago, a friend asked me what I believe most in this life. I said,

"I believe in faith!" Recently I found many Alier are very depressed and sad. Massive network reports blamed Taobao for adjusting search results, and even instigated some sellers to protest at the gate of Taobao. I found so many colleagues feeling wronged and even shed tears. I also found that many young Taobao people constantly asked themselves. "What did we do wrong? In order to encourage people to start business on Taobao, for seven years, we insisted on not forcibly charging members for business opening fees and transaction fees; we insisted on supporting and developing entrepreneurs and small and medium-sized sellers. After more than seven years of struggle, day and night, what we got were all sorts of blame. Was it worthwhile for us to do so? Was the road we took right for us? Shall we give up our own mission on promoting new commercial civilization and return to running just an ordinary company to make money?"

I should have communicated with you much earlier to show my opinions, but the series of problems lately...Ha-ha, I think Alier need to have such an experience. Alier have to meet all kinds of challenges. "A man's mind is broadened by grievance." I think Alier need to learn the abilities of thinking and judging on our own in the chaos of the external environment.

I chose today to exchange ideas with you because soon it will be the 11th anniversary of Alibaba. It is time for us to review the new commercial civilization we proposed last year: Alibaba will promote the brand new, open, transparent, sharing and responsible commercial civilization; provide a platform for the survival and development of 10 million small and medium-sized enterprises worldwide; offer job to 100 million people in the world and provide a platform of consumption for 1 billion people globally. From the moment we raised such a great mission and goals, I knew we must be prepared to take a difficult path on which we will meet all kinds of different types of resistance and difficulties. Today's trouble is just the beginning; we will meet more and more frustration in the future...

There is a great price to pay to insist on doing the right thing to hold on to one's ideals and mission, which is the same in all ages. Especially in today's business environment of China, promoting open, transparent, sharing, and responsible commercial civilization will destroy a large number of vested interests. What we need to fight is not only the vested interest groups, but the business practices from the 20th century as well.

Recently, Taobao made a search adjustment decision based on defending the interests of the consumer, and at the same time supporting sellers who provide quality services with integrity, I think it was the right decision! The thing I am most proud of is that our colleagues could give up today's interests to seek and create a fair method more conducive to the users' sustainability and sound development. Unfortunately, our kindness was distorted. Supporting the sellers with integrity was said to be giving up small and medium-sized sellers. The measures to protect the interests of the consumers were reported as being strictly for our own business interests. We are not living in a vacuum world. The Internet is a big world after all, Taobao is also a big society... We also have to face the fraud, counterfeit goods, and other social phenomena in the e-commerce world. Today there are many negative, blundering moods in society. Many people doubt everything, attack everything, deny everything, and always want to impose their one-sided view of the world to others... many media excessively use "punishing the evil" as a means rather than "supporting the good and removing the evil," which damages people's belief that someone in the world would want to do good things and want to work for ideals and principles...

Carry on or give up? To give up, then we'll become a mediocre company living only for self-interests. We may be very relaxed and make a lot of money over a period of time; but if we carry on our ideals, maybe we will get into the same situation every day. We'll have to fight against all kinds of powers, including huge evil forces of the black industrial chain. But carrying it on, our life and work will be more meaningful, and our company will be a company truly contributing to human society in the 21st century, making all our efforts today have unique rewards. I think Alier should, also have to choose to adhere to the principle, the ideal, and the mission of development! For those friends from all walks of society who believe in a new commercial civilization and support Alibaba to become an idealistic company, we'll say we have but only one god — users. We will continue to perfect our services and functions in the usual work. We will strengthen the principle of listening to the customers, adhering to protect consumers' rights and interests, maintaining the interests of the sellers with integrity. We firmly believe that in the future commercial society, there will be no difference between large and small enterprises; no difference between foreign and domestic ventures; and no difference between SOEs and private companies. The difference will be honesty and dishonesty; the difference between open and not open; and the difference between assuming responsibilities and not assuming responsibilities. We will fully support the enterprises with integrity, transparency, and responsibility! We apologize for our improperness, our immaturity, and our imperfection in our daily work. We promise to make continuous effort to improve and to welcome constant innovation. We do not pursue the title of being most influential; we pursue the best contribution to human beings, to society, to family, and to ourselves!

For those laborious entrepreneurs, I want to say today is the best time to start a business. The success of all dreams must be related to tears, sweat, and persistence and effort! Competition is the nature of doing business. Do it and be fearless ; don't do it if you have a great fear. But what we are fear of is the non-transparent competition, dishonest competition, and unfair competition! Those people who will embrace change and change oneself will always win over the people who always blame others and the rest of the world!

To Alier, I want to say that it is not easy for us to carry on our ideal for 11 years, but we will adhere to the ideal for 91 more years! Since the first day we made it clear that "making money is not our end," but merely our results. Our company is composed of post-80s and post-90s and must be different from yesterday's enterprises. We are grateful that our company was born in this society. We will grow because of today's social environment. We should also exist for the perfection of this commercial society! This is the meaning of our earnest work every day.

Alier, our future is determined by the positive attitude and hard work today! To the black industry chain hiding behind the network and those people hoping that we give up our principles, I want to say, we'll never change because of outside interests. We will not give up our principles because of the pressure. We will be in the face of any challenge and would rather close our own company than give up our principles!

From today on, we hope the whole society will be inspecting our adjustments over business policies, and if our adjustments were against the principle of openness, transparency, sharing and responsibility, we would listen closely and right the wrongs. Attention, you who wanted to benefit by creating disturbances and spreading lies, your actions not only hurt more than 20,000 outstanding young people's ideals, but also damaged and affected the tens of millions of small businesses who make a living through the network as well as the interests of hundreds of millions of consumers. Alier welcome sincere advice and criticism, but we won't accept the opinions of people with ulterior motives and unreasonable one-sided thinking. Even if you conduct demonstrations or even more drastic means and try to make us concede and yield, hundreds of millions of consumers will not agree. We firmly believe in, and will actively participate in the positive progress power of society!

Alier, fight for our ideal! If not now, when? If not me, who?

Jack Ma

September 5, 2010

Although every year the Spring Festival falls on a different date on the Gregorian calendar, (coincidentally, Jack Ma said he never intended to) for three years Jack has been posting articles about year-end bonuses and raises on the Intranet on January 19. Because every year there are many new employees joining the company, some content of Jack Ma's posts is repeated for emphasis.

About Year-end Bonuses and Raises

Dear Alier,

Yesterday an old Alier came to me. He heard that his salary in 2009 would have a big increase and his year-end bonus in 2008 was higher than expected. He insisted that he should not have a raise in salary. A few days ago, an Ali executive requested to cut his salary but to raise the employees'. Each time when the Ali Group decided to raise salary and issue year-end bonuses, someone would insist on not having a pay raise. I am touched and want to talk to you about my views on pay increases and bonuses.

The year 2008 was an extraordinary year. Through the unremitting efforts of all Alier, Alibaba overcame many difficulties and challenges and achieved the most rare progress and performance in its nine years! Despite the unprecedented difficulties of macro economic environment, the company still made plans on raises in 2009 and generous year-end bonus of the year 2008. According to the principle of 2-7-1, the vast majority of employees will get a raise and handsome year-end bonus. This is not only because our cash is sufficient, but because of the hard working Alier with outstanding achievements deserve praise and reward.

This year's raise is a little bit different from other years, all the top management including the vice presidents will not receive a raise. We think that the more difficult the period, the company's resources should tilt more to ordinary employees. Sense of urgency and crisis should first come from senior managers of the company.

Despite the unfavorable economic environment, as long as the company achieved the strategic target, we will reward good employees and we will not be affected by the outside world and other companies' approaches. This also means that if the economic environment is good, but our performance is poor, even if all companies raise salary, issue bonus, we will choose the opposite approach!

Salary is paid to the post. A raise means we put forward higher and newer requirements on this job. (You can refuse a pay rise, but cannot refuse our requirements for your progress on the job). In 2009, the Group will have a great new training budget. We hope to greatly enhance the post responsibilities and requirements.

The bonus is to affirm and encourage the people who show outstanding performance in their posts according to the results of the performance of the company as a whole. Bonuses are not welfare and not everyone can take it for granted. You have to earn it on your own! On the distribution, we will never go for egalitarianism. Egalitarianism is unfair to the colleagues who work hard with outstanding performance! If not so, it is impossible for Alibaba to realize "today's best performance is tomorrow's lowest requirement." It is also impossible to challenge the higher goal.

Dear Alier, 2009 marked the 10th anniversary of Alibaba. And the global economic crisis is Alibaba's initiation rite. Today everything is a cycle that any enterprise that wishes to live long must go through. Everything we experienced will become the pride of our life!

Thank you for your hard work this year. Please take your family to spend money, to consume, to enjoy the harvest after year's hard working!

2009 is calling on us. Tens of thousands of users are looking forward to our efforts.

Enjoy a good New Year!

Do remember to give my regards to your parents, children, your family, and friends! Alibaba wouldn't be so successful without their support!

Thank you, Alier!

Jack Ma

January 19, 2009

On Bonuses of 2009 and Raises in 2010

Dear Alier,

For the Alibaba Group, the past year has been a fascinating, complicated, regretful, and exciting year. Fortunately in 2008, we perceived the economic crisis situation ahead of time and adopted a series of measures. Due to our continuous hard work, our courage in meeting the challenges time and time again, and embracing changes at the same time, the Group has made great achievements. Although we are faced with a lot of problems and more and more challenges, I am satisfied with our overall performance. Today I give the Group a 75 out of 100 for this year (the highest in 10 years). Now, I want to talk about what I think about salary adjustment schemes and the principles of bonus distributions in 2010 and the KPI (the plan of each department at the beginning of the year).

This time last year we were in the midst of a severe winter of a financial storm, but we still paid bonuses and increased salaries to affirm all Alier's hard work and remarkable achievements. This year's annual performance assessment, through the discussion of Group management, we made the following decisions:

1. 2009's year-end bonuses

The keywords of this year are "rewards and punishment". We'll abolish egalitarianism. The bonus is the affirmation to yesterday's work and the stimulus and expectations to future work. This year's bonus scheme has been introduced. I believe you will find this year's bonus distribution being significantly different from those of other years. This year, we will strictly implement the system of 2-7-1, unequivocally reward the good and punish the bad. Compared with the past, we will highlight "clear rewards and punishment," "admitting defeat for bet," and "abolishing egalitarianism." We will reward the Top 20 with raises and strengthen accountability to Bottom 10, inclusively at all company levels. This is the fairest treatment to the hard working colleagues and will also inspire all Alier to challenge higher goals.

Bonus is not welfare, but earned by efforts. Not everybody can take it for granted and it is impossible for everyone to have the same. It is not a part of the salary. You get it because your performance exceeded the expectations of the company (please pay special attention to this point).This year's bonus distribution will further be open and transparent. We will publish the distribution principles of each department on the Intranet. We hope that every employee can get a clear message from his supervisor and be aware of how much his bonus is and why. In addition, the previous year-end bonuses were linked with the basic salary, but starting this year, year-end bonus will no longer be pegged to the salary, but distributed according to the employees' contribution to the company. It is decided by the performance of the employees, their department, and subsidiary companies.

2. 2010's raises

We don't think that there is a so-called best payment. Alibaba will never give a pay raise because of competitors and industry practices. This will only cause vicious competition and unhealthy industry structure. Alibaba's overall pay is reasonable and competitive. In addition to the reasonable basic income, we hope that all Alier will share the wealth of the growth of the company. We still adopt the policy of incentive options, and at the same time, the subsidiary companies have also started to develop their own equity incentive plans.

In today's economic situation, we estimated that inflation next year would be inevitable. We worry that Alibaba's ordinary staff's life will be affected. 2010 is the first year for our Group to carry out coordinated development. We will put forward higher request and expectations to everybody. Based on the principle of "employees second," we decided to continue a raise this year! The pay increase this year won't be small, but we still must strictly implement the system of 2-7-1. Our salary policy will continue to tilt to the ordinary employees. Company executives will leave the pay raise opportunities to ordinary employees. Company's vice president, P11, and levels above will not be listed in the pay increases. M4, M5, P9, P10 will see a raise in pay for special situations, such as promotion, or from problems left over from the past.

3. 2010's KPI

Alibaba must adhere to a high performance culture, to fully embody the principles of fairness and justice. Most of the work we do must be quantified. Like the indicators of our medical checkup, KPI should not be the goal of our pursuit, but should be the symbols and results of our healthy company. Completing the KPI is not all. Just because you have some normal indicators doesn't mean you are healthy. Of course, we must have some indexes to check our work. The key point is that the indicators are what and who established them. For the past two years, our KPI evaluation became somewhat mechanical and rigid; there is a very serious phenomenon of "egalitarianism" which is very unfavorable to the development of the company and must be resolutely abolished. KPI is not the result of a bargain between leadership and employees, but the most reasonable index and the resources matching put forward by company's strategy of understanding and mastery of business from the bottom up. These indicators should be the consensus after communicating with the superior levels. The KPI index also is likely to change in accordance with the dynamics of internal and external conditions. What we need at the year-end is our customers' satisfaction, growth above the industry average, and a good foundation for future development. Dream Target is our common goal and is a guide for resource deployment. Dream Target must be achieved by innovative methods, rather than simply continue to use the existing method, to "squeeze" with effort. The developments of electronic commerce are enjoying a blowout. We must grow with ultra-high-speed to continue to maintain the leading position in the industry. We will strive for our mission, vision and dream, not just complete the KPI task, least to say for bonuses.

Dear Alier, I believe most of the colleagues will support the above principles. But the enforcement is a core as well as a hard nut. I believe we will have excitement, depression, pain, struggle, and even anger in the process of execution, but perhaps this is the feeling each of us will experience in growing up. To create a new commercial civilization, there must be an appropriate culture and organizational capabilities. We must constantly change and improve ourselves!

A New Year has begun. In a decade, Alibaba will achieve the goal of "helping 10 million small businesses develop, providing 100 million people with jobs, offering service for 1 billion consumers." Almost every year is very difficult and vital. On their first day to Alibaba, I have told many new colleagues that Alibaba won't promise you to be rich and win promotion, but it certainly will promise you that you'll be wronged and suffer from injustice. Today I will speak the same thing to the 6,480 new colleagues who joined in 2009. Welcome to Alibaba! This is not a simple job, it is a dream. We all have to make huge efforts and pay price for it!

The Spring Festival is coming. Take your family to have fun, to spend money... Live seriously and work happily! Say hello to Ali's families and relatives for me!

Jack Ma

January 19, 2010

Register your Alipay Account

Dear Alier,

All Alier, please register an Alipay account by the end of the year. Please do. Be sure to! Don't regret if you haven't by then! Please tell each other!

Jack Ma

January, 2011

In 2011, Jack Ma first began by suspense. He told us except for year-end bonuses this year, he would also hand out red envelopes to employee's Alipay accounts, but the amount of money remained a mystery. All the staff started guessing. Some people said the red envelope would be a thousand or two symbolically. Some staff came to ask me. Of course I didn't know. But I joked with them, "CEO Ma asked me yesterday, 'How much does the company need if each one gets 10,000 yuan?' and I said more than 200 million. Jack Ma said so be it then." They said, "We'll take it as 10,000 yuan. You gotta make up the rest if it is not enough." No one thought it would be that much. But as a result, many people had more than that number.

In the next few days, Jack Ma posted three articles.

Year-end Bonuses, Pay Raises and Red Envelopes

Dear Alier,

This year's external environment is more complicated than usual, but our overall development is pretty good. Of course, the complex changes in the ex-

ternal situations are not supposed to be an excuse for our good or bad performances. Personally I'm basically satisfied with the development of the Group
over the past year. Here I want to give thanks to the efforts of all colleagues of
the Group. We also specially appreciate the progress of Alipay and Taobao. In
2010, we adhered to the "openness, transparency, sharing and responsibility"
and "globalization" principles and played a positive role in promoting the development of China's e-commerce. It is time for the annual summary again. I'
ll talk about this year's bonuses and raises. For year-end bonuses and salary
raises, please review the relevant principles on raises and bonuses I wrote on
January 19, 2009.

1. Due to the good full-year results in 2010, we will grant 2010 annual bonuses. The bonus this year will be more generous than normal. But definitely
bonuses are not welfare and are not given to everyone and won't be the same
for everyone either. We will strictly implement the principle of 2-7-1. Anyone
who has doubts about your bonus can settle with management. If you think it
is too much, you can return it to me or donate it to the Group's Public Welfare Fund. If it is too little, you can talk to your leadership to find out the reason.

2. Due to the rise in the CPI and the pressure of future commodity prices to the life of employees, we decided to give the employees a raise. We continue to implement the principle of giving priority to ordinary employees on pay
raises. This year we'll continue the policy of no raises to M5 and above cadres.
This year's bonuses will be paid to your salary card just like in the past. We also have some special arrangement, the red envelopes. Every employee will get
a red envelope in addition to the bonus and pay increase according to your performance and commodity price. Reasons for distribution are as follows:

(1) You worked very hard this year and the performance is good.

(2) We firmly believe that the favorable development of China's e-commerce may have nothing to do with us, but the unfavorable development must
have something to do with Alibaba. In the next few years, the Group should
strengthen the e-commerce infrastructure investment, strengthen the logistics,
data flow, provide financial support to small businesses and entrepreneurs and
other construction in order to perfect China's e-commerce ecosystem, and to
allow more enterprises to use the lowest cost to carry out e-commerce to complete the transformation and upgrading of enterprises. We decided to post-

pone indefinitely the plans to list the Group's subsidiaries.

3. We hope, as long as the Group's performance is good, even if it is not listed, our staff members will receive a red envelope from the company. The principles for handing out red envelopes are:

(1) Based on the Group's performance.

(2) Based on the employees' fixed number of years of service and responsibilities in the company. In principle, everyone has a share. Special red envelopes will be issued to your Alipay account!

For this year's special red envelopes, I have some suggestions:

1. Buy a gift for your parents, spouses, and children.

2. Give priority to consume it on Taobao and give more opportunities to the hard working Taobao sellers. If you have any complaint regarding business dealings and are not satisfied with the Taobao Alipay business, please tell the related department to improve as soon as possible.

3. Please donate 10 to 100 yuan from your red envelopes to the Group's Love Giving Fund's Alipay account (lovegiving @ Alibaba-inc.com). Here, I will thank you first for the recipient children!

It is time to celebrate the New Year. Take it easy. Go spend money, to consume. Have a good time at Chinese New Year! Work hard after the festival, for customers, for colleagues, for shareholders, and of course, for our next year's year-end bonus and the big red envelope! Live seriously and work happily!

Say hello to your family for me. Remember to make a toast to the sky on Spring Festival Eve at 8 p.m. together with me. Don't forget!

Jack Ma

January 19, 2011

Who Should We Thank for Year-end Bonuses?

I am really embarrassed to hear so many colleagues thank me for their year-end bonuses. This is not to my credit. I'm just a CEO. I firmly believe in the principles of openness and transparency, clear reward and punishment, hehe...There will be a year we do not do well and there will be no reward, no bonus. Please don't hate me and call me names then.

Who should we thank? Many people! But we need to give thanks to the age of the Internet and e-commerce. Thanks to the trust from our customers. Thanks to each of the colleagues who work hard and who have the results at your side. Thanks to our families who support our work. Thanks to...

In 2011, anyone who undermines the Internet e-commerce, who undermines customers' trust for us, who doesn't work hard and can't produce good results, who doesn't show gratitude for the support of our family... is the one that undermines our year-end bonuses and our future! If it is good, it has nothing to do with Jack Ma, but if it is not good, it must have something to do with Jack Ma! The same to you. If not now, when?! If not me, who?! Thank you for 2010. Fear 2011...

Jack Ma

January, 2011

Intern Students, Listen to Me Please

We have thought, discussed, hesitated as to whether or not to hand out red envelopes to interns. The final decision is no. Ha-ha, don't be angry. Don't despair. You'll have many days to make money. But interns, I'm glad to be witness to your efforts. Hope you make real gains at Alibaba. I also hope Alier can lend a hand to our interns, to promote their growth. For interns who have just opened their eyes, it is a great honor for Alier to have the opportunity to help them. Thanks to others who had helped us when we were young... To do something a senior fellow should do...Interns are not inexpensive helpers; they are young people with dreams... He-he... Alier, you know that!

Intern students, Alibaba is lucky to have you... we are lucky to be with you, to learn together with you for a few months... Maybe many of you can't stay with the company for all kinds of reason, but I hope you can think and advance while you are at Alibaba. I hope Alier's culture can help add enlightenment to your life and for your future. Keep in mind one thing — what you have, what you want, and what you're willing to give up... I'm glad we have you here. Happy New Year!

Jack Ma

Appendix IV　The Yabuli Speech

Recent years, Jack Ma paid special attention to environmental protection. Since he mentioned environmental protection three years ago at the Yabuli Meeting, his speech at the 2013 Yabuli Meeting was also related to environmental protection.

The following was Jack Ma's speech:

Good evening, ladies and gentlemen. I am very happy to come to Yabuli. Actually I have been here several times. Every time I find it rewarding. Before I came in here today, the rotating chairman told me at the door that I would give my speech soon. I really don't know what to say today. After listening to your speeches first, I want to express my recent thoughts and views.

I don't think Yabuli is in any way inferior to Davos. Yabuli has more flavors. The issues talked in Davos were too far, too big, and nearly had nothing to do with us. The problems talked about here all have something to do with us. Anyway, entrepreneurs speak in entrepreneurs' perspectives, and economists speak things related to economists. Each speaks on their own. I always think that most things talked by economists are not reliable and what we talk here is more reliable. For many issues, Zhang Weiying shared different opinions with me, but it doesn't hinder us to work together in Yabuli to promote China's economic development. This is to put different ideas together, which we can call harmonious development.

I want to share three things with you; first, revolution; second, crisis; third, action.

Revolution

Recently we've received a lot of comments. Some people like us, because Taobao has brought a lot of fun into their lives; many others hate us and believe we've ruined their business. The losers in China always blame others, saying that others have screwed up their 'bread and butter.' Today, electronic commerce is not a technology, not a business model. It is a revolution, changing our lifestyles, and it has just begun. I believe that the vast majority of people here haven't realized what the revolution will bring to you.

Some time ago I had the honor of going to Zhongnanhai. I said to the

Prime Minister, a lot of people hate me, because we destroyed many business-es that were very successful yesterday. Some vested interests were very angry at me, but I definitely won't give up doing the things that need to be done just because they were angry. We do not take the Internet as a business. We treat the Internet as a revolution which can change a lot of things. E-commerce has more than 600 million users. If we take the technology composed with so many talents to purely make money for ourselves, then we'll be no different from many companies in the 20th century. We'll be nothing but another com-pany. Today, in the 21st century, we think it is a commercial ecosystem, a busi-ness organization. It must play a role to perfect society.

As for damage to the vested interests, it is happening because we want to cultivate the future vested interests that are truly open, transparent, and respon-sible. So I call on you here, not to ballyhoo. I urge you to think carefully and at-tach great importance to the revolution; to become involved in the spring tide of the Internet. Actually ballyhooing you doesn't make much sense, because I don't lack your businesses.

Crisis

For Beijing's haze, I am very happy, because in the past when we ap-pealed to air, water, food safety, not many people believed it. We need to con-sider what kind of action we should take. I assume in 10 years China's three largest cancers will be plagued in every family: liver cancer, lung cancer, and gastric cancer. Liver cancer is most likely to be caused by poor water condi-tions; lung cancer from air pollution; and gastric cancer from poorly processed foods. 30 years ago, how many people know about cancer? "Cancer" was a rare disease at that time, but now it has become the new normal.

A lot of people asked me, what made you sleepless? Well, Alibaba or Tao-bao never bothered my sleep. The things that keep me awake at night are: the water is undrinkable and the food inedible. Our children can't drink milk. This really keeps me from sleeping. I was very diligent in the past. Ten years of busi-ness turned me into this. But this doesn't worry me. What worries me is that after our hardships for so many years, the money we made will all be spent on medical bills. On the plane I said that Chinese medical expenses were too high. There is nothing to applaud if Chinese medicine has good sales growth. I hope the Chinese medicine sales decrease, because it would be a sign that the Chinese people have become healthier.

The Wenchuan Earthquake killed 84,000 people, causing national devastation and shocking the world. Has it ever occurred to you how many people die from cancer every day? None of us have thought of that. I was asked what my ideal was. I hope that after 20 years, China's sky is blue, the water clean, and the air breathable. Recently people asked, what is your happiness? Have you ever felt happy? What is the most basic happiness? It is to bath under the sunshine, which is to have water, trees, food, and sunshine! No matter how much money you earn, if you can't even bath under the sunshine, it will be a great tragedy.

Pan Shiyi and Ren Zhiqiang sometimes tweet, Alas, what a fine day today in Beijing! As if they've got their year-end bonuses. It is our given right, but now it has become a surprise. This is something that worries us the most, also something we hope to change in the future.

This problem is not only caused by rapid development and not just because of government's dereliction of duty. It is because our entire society lacks an antibody, a faith. What is faith? Faith is being grateful and reverent. Lacking faith will affect our mentality. If our mentality is changed, our form will be changed, and in turn our ecological nature will be changed too. So, I think this is a crisis, a crisis of all humanity and a great crisis in China. Previously, we were proud of being the "world factory," today I believe you are aware that the disaster that comes along with the title is tremendous.

Action

The world really is in no shortage of complaints, kickers, and critics. Good men in this world must be more than the bad guys. The good people and good deeds in this world must be more than bad people and evildoings. Everyone in the world is talking about lack of trust. We don't trust the government and the government doesn't trust us; we don't believe the media and the media doesn't believe us; there is no trust between people. But in my industry, I found trust everywhere.

20 years ago, did you ever think of this − on the Internet, before receiving any money, you would give your goods to a total stranger to deliver your goods with all his efforts through the difficulties to another complete stranger? Such trust transactions happen more than 24 million times a day. There must

be trust; we just need to find it. I believe that we do not need to wait for the government. Waiting for the government is very tiring. China is very contradictory. On the one hand, we hope to have the market economy; on the other hand, we hope that the government can come up with more favorable policies.

We believe these problems can be solved. The haze of smog in China today, once also happened in Europe, in the United States, and in Japan. But they have all gone through the journey. Americans do not eat freshwater fish from some lakes. The main reason is that pollution in the past caused chemicals in the ground which causes some freshwater fish not eatable. During the Olympic Games, Beijing had a month of blue sky. If the Americans can do it, I believe we can do it too, and we must do it. If we can't do it, then 30 years later, there will not be the Yabuli talks. We'll prematurely meet in the other world. This is no alarmist talking.

I don't want the government to take any measures, because the government is also in difficulty. The measures taken by the government are often done through thorough cleaning and every time the consequences would be even worse. During the Olympics, all the factories stopped production but resumed running after the Olympic Games. Today the pollution outside the city is more terrible. When I was a kid, the polluting enterprises were moved out of Hangzhou City. We were happy with joy that the refinery had finally moved out. Where did they go? They went to Hangzhou's uptake, the water source of Hangzhou. Now the industry is moving westward to the upstream of the Yellow River, the Yangtze River. Generation after generation will suffer from this. It's a real crisis.

30 years ago, it was nothing strange for me to see people wash vegetables and clothes in the West Lake in Hangzhou. Today you may try and see. If you throw something into the West Lake, people will stop you. This is a kind of consciousness. Today we shall not only awaken everyone's consciousness, we also need to really care about every native tree which is most important compared to the hundreds of non-natural planted trees. The natural lung is the best. We forgot about our rivers. Our cities exist because of the rivers. But today we've buried a lot of ecological rivers for the city. We need to protect each ecological river; each original small animal derivative from it in exchange of the environment we desire. This is a kind of real consciousness. It is an action that involves everyone; don't wait for the action of a certain organization.

Not all our anger came from evildoings. We are angry because people are indifferent to bad behaviors. There's a well said phrase in a movie recently: "Our life does not belong to us, our life is closely linked with all the lives throughout the world." Any good or bad deeds yesterday and now will determine our future. So this is what I want to talk about. This is a real crisis. We must take actions ourselves. We must not wait for others to act.

Thank you all!